IMAGES
*of America*

# MOUNT HOLLY

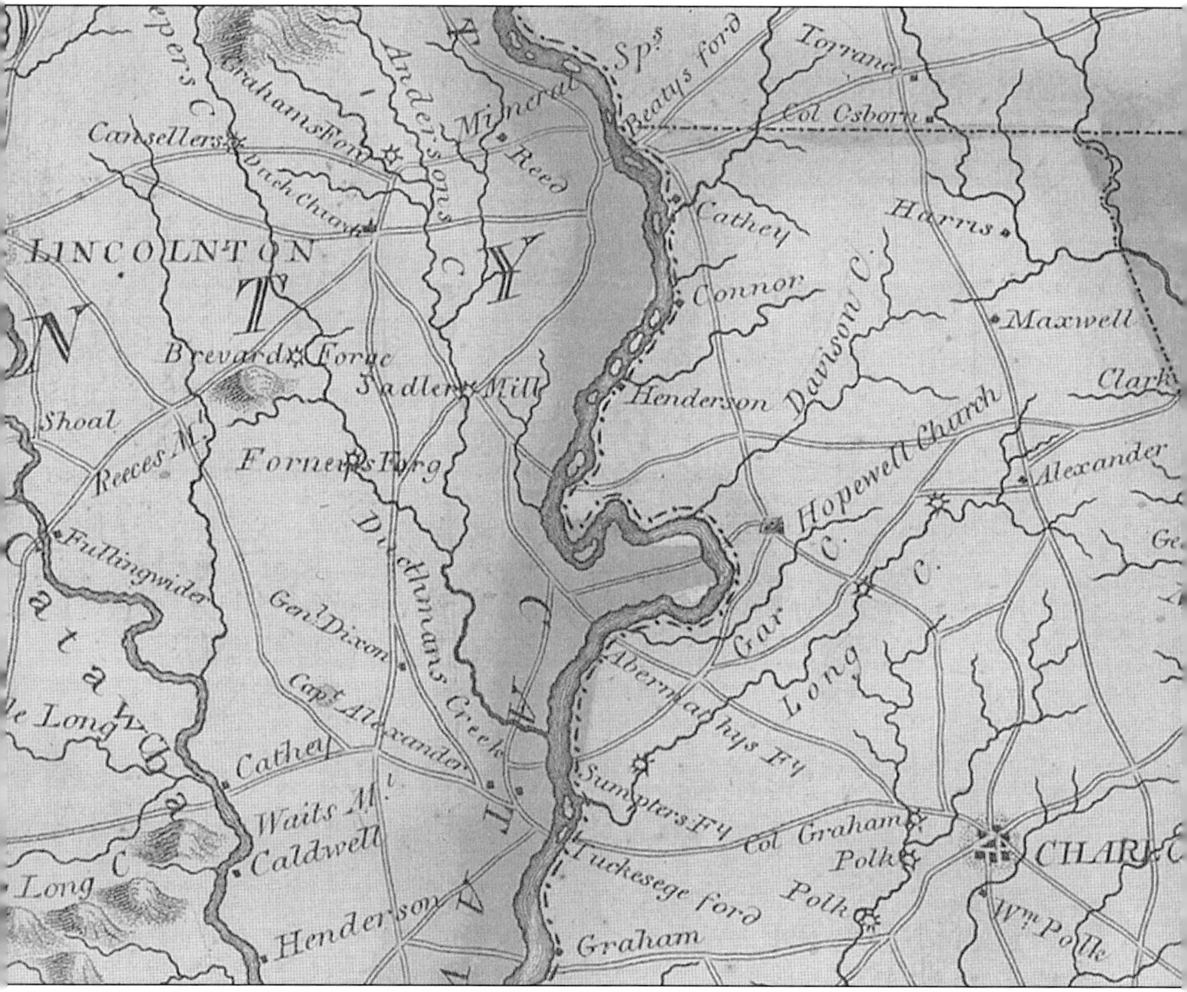


**Price-Strother Map of 1808.** Jonathon Price and John Strother completed the first survey of North Carolina in 1808. The area in Lincoln County, now Gaston County, shows the Tuckaseege Ford and Trail coming from Charlotte to Lincolnton. The Tuckaseege Ford was the major Catawba crossing for both the native Catawba tribe and the European settlers advancing west. The house site of Capt. Robert Alexander can be seen on the map. Alexander called his farm Woodlawn, and this remained the name of the pioneer community until 1879, when it became Mount Holly. (Courtesy of the Wilson Library, University of North Carolina–Chapel Hill.)

**On the Cover:** In this photograph from 1909, the Tucker-Springs general store was located on the west side of South Main Street. Note the advertisements for Old Dutch Cleanser and the sign reading "Cold Drinks Inside, Come In." Garden tools and horse bridles are also on display. The sidewalk is raised high above the unpaved street. (Courtesy of Millican Pictorial History Museum.)

IMAGES
*of America*

# MOUNT HOLLY

Lee Beatty, Jim Love,
and Charles A. Rhyne Jr.

ARCADIA
PUBLISHING

ISBN 978-0-7385-8763-9

Published by Arcadia Publishing
Charleston, South Carolina

Printed in the United States of America

Library of Congress Control Number: 2011920850

For all general information, please contact Arcadia Publishing:
Telephone 843-853-2070
Fax 843-853-0044
E-mail sales@arcadiapublishing.com
For customer service and orders:
Toll-Free 1-888-313-2665

Visit us on the Internet at www.arcadiapublishing.com

*To the children of Mount Holly*

# Contents

# ACKNOWLEDGMENTS

First, we thank Sarah Park Rankin for her digital media expertise, her prodigious effort, and her genial patience, which allowed us to immortalize these precious photographs and documents. We thank Allen Millican of Millican Pictorial History Museum for sharing his extraordinary collection of photographs. We thank Mayor Bryan Hough, City Manager Danny Jackson, and the city council for allowing us to use the excellent resources of the City of Mount Holly Archives. As a well-published historian and respected teacher, Dr. Richard Rankin gave us indispensable advice and welcome encouragement. And we thank Rick N. Hauser for his superlative photography.

The limitation of space does not allow us to express the gratitude we owe to so many people for sharing photographs, documents, and information to help us in this project. We could not have completed this effort without the assistance of Linda Thompson Sherrill, Leigh Brinkley, Carlton and Cecelia Broome, Robert A. Ragan, Essie McGill, Bobby Black, Gene Thompson, Ann K. Brinkley, Missy Cloninger, Clarence and Jessie Thompson, Bobby John Rhyne, Emily Massey, J. Frank Love Jr., Charles S. Sawyer, Rick Haithcox, Sheila Wallace, Wrene Benfield, Nancy D. McIntosh, and Woodrow Wilson "Woody" Kendall. We celebrate the establishment of a new civic organization, the Mount Holly Historical Society, which is dedicated to documenting and teaching our beloved city's heritage. We applaud your efforts and appreciate your assistance.

Last, and with great affection, we thank Kristen Wiles Beatty, Donna S. Love, and Linda H. Rhyne for their loving support.

The authors will donate their royalties from the sale of this book to the Mount Holly Historical Society, a nonprofit volunteer organization.

# INTRODUCTION

Long before there was a town, long before there were European settlers, there was the river. Native Americans who lived along its fertile banks called the river Eswa Taroah, "the Great One." The original inhabitants were called the Catawba, "the People of the River."

The earliest European settlers who crossed the Catawba River into the Mount Holly area were Scots-Irish, German, and English, trekking down the Great Wagon Trail from Pennsylvania and the Chesapeake. In the 1750s, James Kuykendall settled on a royal land grant on Fishing Creek, now known as Dutchman's Creek, the stream's name hinting at his Deutsche (Germanic) background. Relations between European settlers and the Catawba tribe had been mostly amiable. However, by 1763, decimated by two smallpox epidemics and increasingly crowded out by the new arrivals, the tribe consolidated their remaining small villages farther south to present-day South Carolina. Thus, by the dawn of the American Revolution, the Catawba people were no longer living in this part of the valley. Yet their legacy lives on in the name of the river and the local river crossing, the Tuckaseege Ford.

The historic Tuckaseege Ford linked Charlotte, via the Tuckaseege Trail, to the lands in the west. In his *Pictorial Field Book of the Revolution*, Benton Lossing described Tuckaseege Ford as a half-mile across, thigh-deep to a man, with firm bottom underfoot. The Tuckaseege Trail was the route taken from Charlotte by Gen. Griffith Rutherford on his way to the Battle of Ramsour's Mill near Lincolnton in June 1780. His patriots assembled on Gen. Joseph Dickson's farm in the Westland Farm area of Mount Holly. The Price-Strother map of 1808 shows the location of General Dickson's (Dixon) house and Capt. Robert Alexander's house, as well as the Tuckaseege Ford and Trail at the Catawba River.

Soon after crossing the Catawba, the Tuckaseege Trail led pioneers past the farm of Robert Alexander. His substantial home, the Red House, was located at the corner of Hawthorne Street and Central Avenue. His farm, known as Woodlawn, became the early name of the community springing up around his estate. Robert Alexander served in the North Carolina Legislature for many years. In 1796, he hosted Andre Michaux, famed French botanist and explorer. Michaux went on to discover many rare local plant species, including the big leaf magnolia, which still grows along the banks of nearby creeks.

Especially after 1800, Alexander and other prosperous farmers began to purchase slaves, adding African Americans to the local population. Because the area west of the Catawba near the Tuckaseege Ford was covered with small to middling farms, not plantations, slaves lived in small groups and worked alongside their farming masters. Slaves not only contributed their skill and labor to the local economy, they also enriched cooking, music, and all facets of everyday life. Their descendants would become permanent and important contributors to local history and culture.

As Robert Alexander and his neighbors were transforming a wilderness into a settled landscape, they started a pioneer church south of Woodlawn. The Goshen Presbyterian Church, established around 1764, was one of the first churches west of the Catawba River. In March 1796, Goshen Church called Rev. Humphrey Hunter to lead the congregation. Reverend Hunter lived on what is now the Thomas Springs property, just west of the present Mount Holly Middle School. In 1801, Hunter was named postmaster in the Woodlawn area, and the local post office was called Huntersville for several decades.

Led by dynamic pastors like Hunter, Goshen Church was the mother church of several local Presbyterian congregations. By 1891, Goshen Church members living in Mount Holly formed the First Presbyterian Church, whose first sanctuary was built in 1894, delayed by an epidemic of typhoid fever. The current brick facility was built in 1927 on the same site.

Although the Presbyterians had the earliest church in the area, Mount Holly Lutherans made it possible for several Protestant denominations to get started in the fledgling community. In 1881, with the help of Abel "A.P." Peterson Rhyne and Ambrose Costner, local mill owners, the Lutherans built a church facility that was shared with local Baptists, Methodists, and Presbyterians. By 1903, after their brethren had erected their own places of worship, the Lutherans built a new brick structure, which was dedicated in 1907 as the Church of the Good Shepherd.

Holding their first meetings in the old Lutheran church, the 68 charter members of First Baptist Church officially organized in January 1890 and dedicated their first building two months later. Their frame sanctuary was on the west side of South Main Street, between Central Avenue and Catawba Avenue. In 1924, the church built the large brick sanctuary building that stands one block south, beside the parsonage.

Meanwhile, the Methodists also organized a new church in 1890. They built a frame structure on a town lot next to the Presbyterians, at the corner of South Main Street and Catawba Avenue. In 1896 and again in 1912, storms destroyed the frame sanctuary. The congregation built a new brick church in the summer of 1912. The congregation moved in June 1960 to North Main Street.

African American residents established several formative churches through the years. Two notable churches established around the time of the Civil War were Mount Sinai Baptist in the Freedom community of Hawthorne Street and Shiloh African Methodist Episcopal Zion in the West Creek community. Both these churches still hold services today.

Protestant churches were the dominant institutions of religious life in Mount Holly's early history, but the Catholic Church was also an early influence. A generation before the Benedictine monks began Belmont Abbey, St. Joseph's Church near Mountain Island was built in 1843. The church served several Irish Catholic families who were part of Gaston County's gold rush in the 1830s. The church was financed with gifts from North Carolina Catholics, including the well-respected state judge William Gaston. Judge Gaston died in 1844, but his name lives on. The county that bears his name was conceived by local leaders who met in a Mount Holly general store.

Until 1846, the Woodlawn community was in Lincoln County, a large jurisdiction that stretched from the South Carolina line to the South Mountains. At an 1842 meeting at the Hoffman-Rhyne Store in Woodlawn, participants selected a committee to support the formation of a new county carved from the southern reaches of Lincoln.

Merchants were essential to the growth of industry and commerce in early Mount Holly. The Hoffman-Rhyne Store, also known as the Woodlawn General Store, was established near the present-day corner of Main Street and Tuckaseege Road, near the old Tuckaseege Trail. The commercial center of the Woodlawn community later moved a half-mile north, close to Dutchman's Creek, when the railroad came to town. Richard Kelly Davenport and his partner Charles Lafayette Hutchison started a merchandise store near the railroad. Two stores owned by John Tucker, Walter Tucker, and Junius Springs operated on Main Street in the early 1900s, while Mrs. Walter Tucker (Mamie) managed the Central Hotel nearby.

The railroad spurred this rapid growth in commerce. In 1860, the Wilmington, Charlotte, and Rutherford Railroad was the first rail line to enter Gaston County, crossing the Catawba just south of Dutchman's Creek. Thus, by the mid-19th century, water resources, a solid mercantile base, and transportation were all in place, ready to spark the development of industry at this strategic junction of creek, river, and rail. But before this growth could flourish, the Civil War began.

After the Civil War, Confederate general and scholar Daniel H. Hill briefly lived in Woodlawn. Hill was the editor and owner of two periodicals published in Charlotte, and in 1877, he became president of the University of Arkansas. Local historians assert that before he left, Hill had intended to establish a model farm in Woodlawn. Yet very soon, events in the region would transform the prevailing economy from agriculture to mass production industry.

The foundations of Mount Holly's economy had started with pioneer farms and then evolved to an influential mercantile base. Later, as these merchants expanded their entrepreneurial ambitions, they joined forces to forge the power of the mighty Southern industrial revolution—textiles.

Thomas Tate of Greensboro built the first textile mill in Gaston County, north of the Woodlawn community at Mountain Island, in 1848. The second county mill was called Woodlawn Factory, after the Woodlawn community. Located on the South Fork River and completed in 1852, it was also known as the Pinhook Mill. Moses H. Rhyne, a resident of Woodlawn, was an original investor.

The county's fourth mill, built in 1874 and still standing on the banks of Dutchman's Creek, was called the Mount Holly Cotton Mill, in the anticipation that its product would compete with the high-quality cotton yarn then produced in Mount Holly, New Jersey. A.P. Rhyne and Daniel Rhyne, sons of textile pioneer Moses H. Rhyne, and A.P. Rhyne's father-in-law, Ambrose Costner, started the Mount Holly mill. Following the hardship of war and reconstruction, this humble mill ignited Gaston County's industrial explosion.

In January 1879, A.P. Rhyne and others petitioned the state legislature to incorporate the area around the Mount Holly Cotton Mill as the new town of Mount Holly. The incorporation became official on March 14, 1879. Finally, after 125 years of settlement, the land once called Woodlawn and Huntersville had an official name and a bright future.

Soon other Mount Holly mills began to spring up along the flowing waters of Dutchman's Creek and the Catawba. The Rhynes established Gaston County's seventh mill, the Tuckaseege Manufacturing Company, in 1883, near the western landing of the ancient Tuckaseege Ford. The mill was damaged in the disastrous flood of 1916, when the water rose to the second floor. The mill was rebuilt and was Superior Yarns until razed in 1997.

Charles L. Hutchison's son, the merchant Charles Egbert (C.E.) Hutchison, joined forces in 1890 with the Rhynes, Dewstoe, Costner, and others to invest in the Rhynes' 1888 Mount Holly Knitting Company, which was renamed Albion Manufacturing. Today, the original roof beams and brick of this mill form the Grand Hall of the Mount Holly Municipal Complex. In 1891, C.E Hutchison and his partners Ike Lowe, Luther Nims, R.K. Davenport, Dewstoe, and several others built the Nims Manufacturing Company on an oxbow section of Dutchman's Creek a half-mile from Robert Alexander's Red House. In 1905, the Woodlawn Manufacturing Company, situated between the Mount Holly and Nims mills, was the first electrified mill in town. Stuart Cramer, a textile pioneer, designed it as well as 25 village houses.

Charles E. Hutchison was the first Gaston County mill owner to consolidate all of his independent holdings into one controlling corporation. American Yarn and Processing Company was thus chartered on July 31, 1920. The company then owned seven mills with a capacity of 53,000 spindles and employed 1,000 people. The Hutchison group of mill companies consisted of Armon Manufacturing (Old Mountain Island Mill), Nims Manufacturing (1891), Woodlawn Manufacturing (1905), Adrian Mill (1916), American Processing (1918), Alsace Manufacturing (old Mount Holly Cotton Mill), Union Cotton Mills in Maiden, North Carolina, and Madora Mill (beside the Adrian), added in 1922. Hutchison operated the company successfully until just before his death in 1942, when it was sold to R.S. Dickson and Company. The company operates today as American and Efird, Inc., subsidiary of Ruddick Corporation. American and Efird has become one of the world's foremost manufacturers of sewing threads and industrial yarns, and its world headquarters is on a large campus near downtown Mount Holly.

Complementary industries enhanced the expansion of textiles in Mount Holly. In June 1905, the Duke brothers, James and Benjamin, incorporated Southern Power Company. The new company, later named Duke Power, initially provided hydroelectric power, as the free-flowing Catawba was tamed with dams like the Mountain Island. Among Southern Power's first ventures into coal-fired steam power were the Mount Holly Steam Station on the river near the American Plant and later Riverbend Steam Station.

Another Duke brothers' enterprise was the Piedmont and Northern Railway (P&N), which began in 1910–1911 as an electric interurban line for passengers and freight. The Mount Holly P&N station was built in 1911. The P&N in North Carolina had about 50 miles of track between Charlotte and Gastonia. This connector to the Southern Railway allowed shipments of manufactured goods from the textile mills of Mount Holly and Gaston County to the consumers of the nation.

And so, by the 1920s, the industrial economy in Mount Holly and the region was at full throttle. Many of the iconic landmarks that form Mount Holly's sense of place and purpose were built during this era. As industry blossomed, so too did the institutions that make a community livable and memorable. No community institution is more memorable and influential than its school system, and Mount Holly has had a proud school history.

The first mention of schools in Mount Holly is the one-teacher school of Robert Beatty, located on the west bank of Tuckaseege Ford in 1781. More formal schools in the Mount Holly area started in the pioneer community of Woodlawn during the 1870s. The Wells School was first, led by schoolmaster Abram Wells. Next came the Hunter School, another one-room schoolhouse, followed by Woodlawn Academy, a two-story building on Piedmont Street. Like many schools of that period, the Green School, located on the Richard K. Davenport property, was supported by the state for four months a year.

Around 1902, plans were made for a two-story graded school in Mount Holly on North Main Street. The first class graduated in 1906. By 1910, the enrollment had outgrown the building, and the first brick building was completed on the Central Avenue campus. The second brick building was constructed around 1916, and the third quickly followed in 1923. All three of these buildings were aligned together and faced east, toward downtown and the river. A new high school was built in 1927 on Hawthorne Street and moved again in 1960 to a site behind the old high school.

The Rollins School was the African American community school until the schools were integrated in the 1960s. From Rollins, African American children went on to Reid High School in Belmont. In 2009, a monument was erected on South Hawthorne Street commemorating the Rollins School. It was dedicated by members of the Mount Holly Black History Forum.

The Mount Holly schools have a proud tradition of athletic accomplishment. The 1930 and 1941 high school football teams were undefeated. Mount Holly High School won two state football championships in the 1960s. The 1963 team won their championship on the night that President Kennedy was assassinated. The 1967 team, now integrated with the young men who went to Rollins School, won the state championship over Glen Alpine in a thrilling come-from-behind game. These teams were led by coach Delmer Wiles. Coach Wiles and his fellow teacher, Mount Holly High School band director Robert Black, were the first inductees of the Mount Holly Sports Hall of Fame in 2007.

This book is a brief pictorial compilation designed to provide readers with a sense of the evolution of Mount Holly from the early beginnings of Woodlawn and its textile heritage to the early 1970s. The images reflect the hardships, the spirit, the industry, the places, and the proud people of a Piedmont town tied closely to its river heritage. It is the authors' hope that readers will use this book to explore and embrace the institutions, families, historical sites, and enterprises that together weave the rich and enduring fabric of Mount Holly.

## *One*

# To Ford the Stream
## Early History

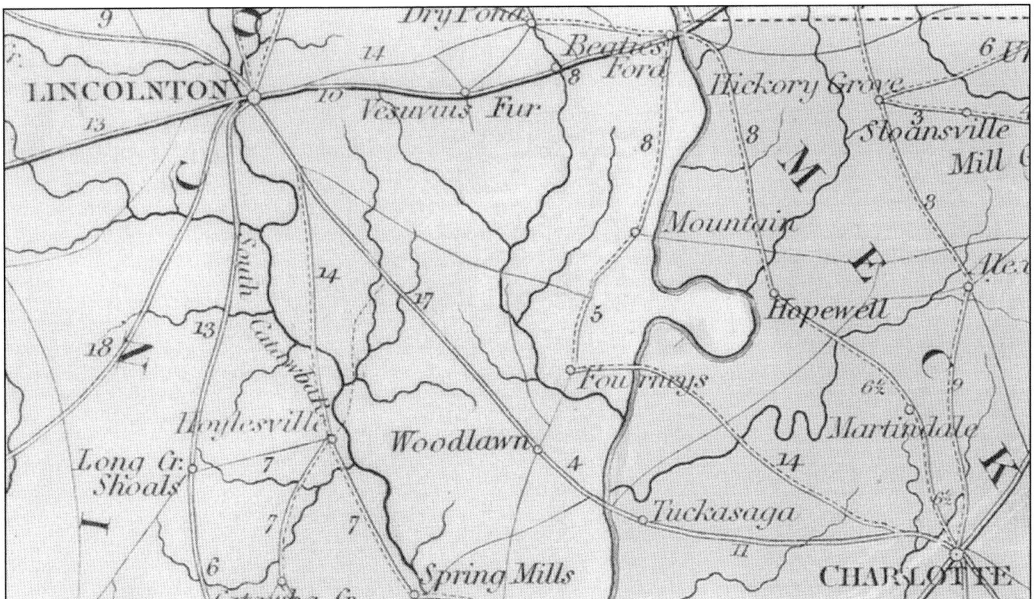


**The River and the Ford.** This 1839 post office map by David Burr shows the early landscape of the area that became Mount Holly. Woodlawn was the post office on the Tuckaseege Trail, the main route from Charlotte to Lincolnton. This road into Lincoln County crossed the Catawba River at Tuckaseege (Tuckesege) Ford. Even in 1839, the pioneer community was well established. (Courtesy of the Wilson Library, University of North Carolina–Chapel Hill.)

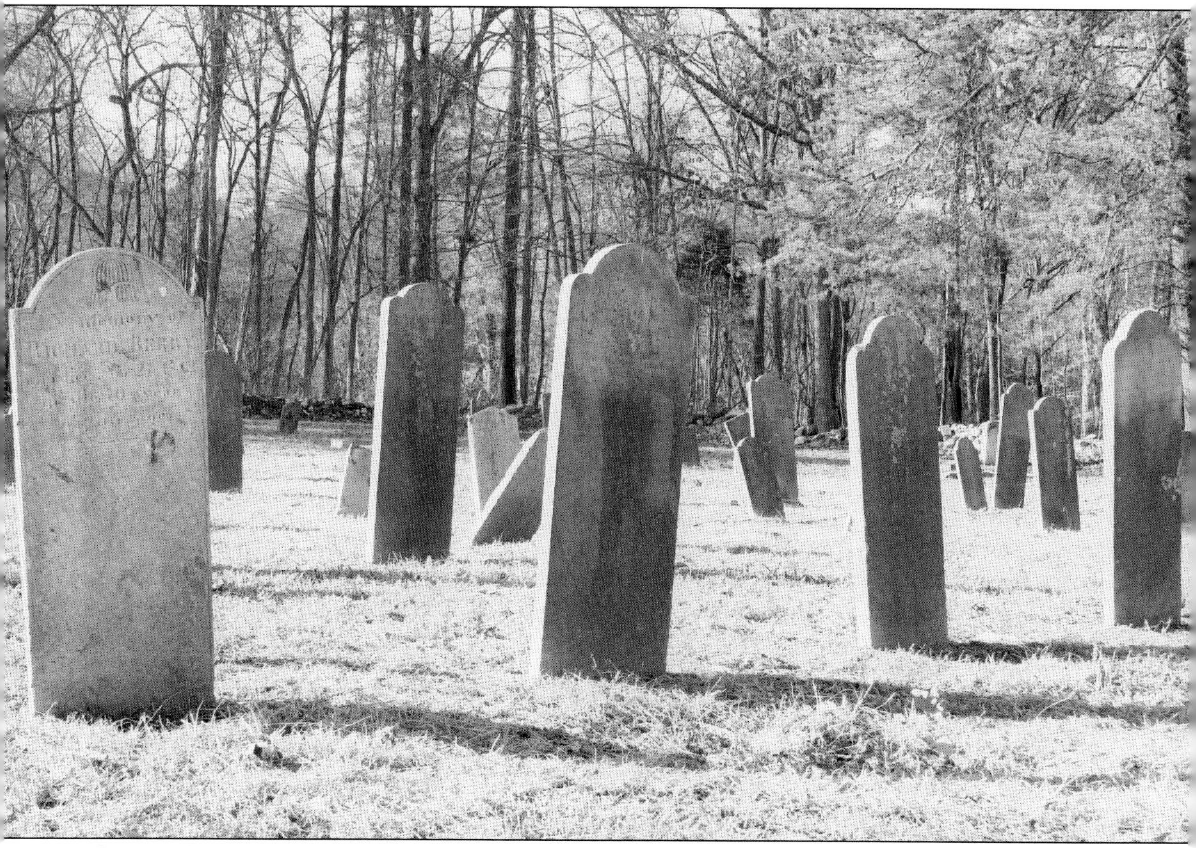

**Goshen Burying Ground.** In 1935, a bronze plaque was placed at the historic Goshen Cemetery to honor the Revolutionary patriots who are buried there. From what is now the Mount Holly area are Capt. Robert Alexander, George Cathy, Peter Fite, William Rankin, Samuel Rankin, James Rutledge, and Samuel Martin, along with 15 comrades from the nearby South Fork area. These liberty-loving men made their greatest contribution at the triumphant Battle of Kings Mountain on October 7, 1780, a turning point of the American Revolution. Eight of the 29 Patriots killed in that battle were from this section of the county. The battle pitted Patriot militia, including the South Fork Boys, against Loyalists led by British major Patrick Ferguson. The leader of the South Fork Boys was Maj. William Chronicle, who also died at Kings Mountain. His brokenhearted fiancée, Margaret Alexander, was the daughter of Capt. Robert Alexander, the owner of Woodlawn farm. (Photograph by C. Alexander.)

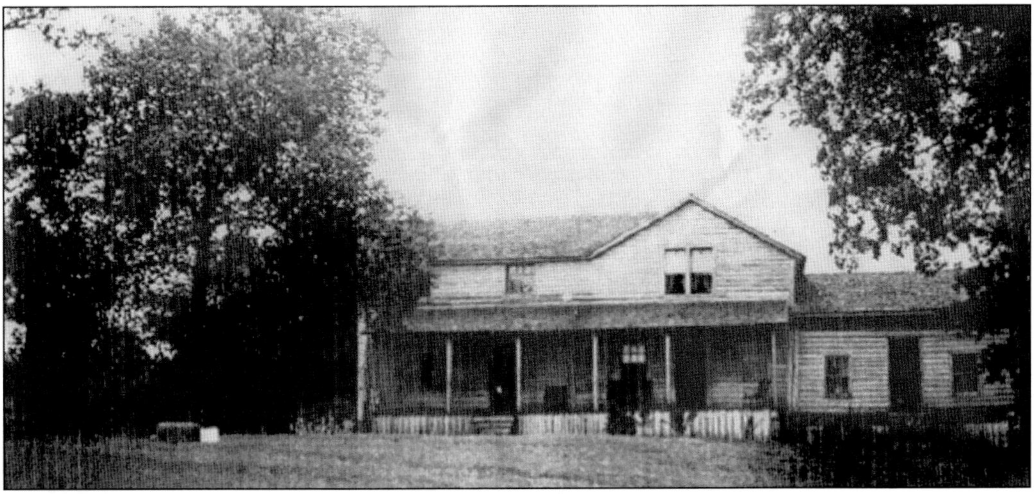

**The Red House at Woodlawn.** Capt. Robert and Mary Jack Alexander's farm was called Woodlawn, and his home was known as the Red House. It was a log structure on the corner of South Hawthorne Street and West Central Avenue. Alexander was living there before 1760. The village around Alexander's farm was named for his farm. Mary Jack Alexander was the sister of Capt. James Jack, who carried the Mecklenburg Declaration of Independence to Philadelphia in 1775. In the late 1800s, Charles Lafayette Hutchison, father of textile pioneer Charles Egbert Hutchison, acquired the Alexander house and a large portion of his land. A mulberry tree, reportedly planted by Alexander, still stands on the site, diminished by poor health but sprouting new leaves each spring. (Photograph courtesy of the City of Mount Holly Archives; painting courtesy of C. Alexander.)

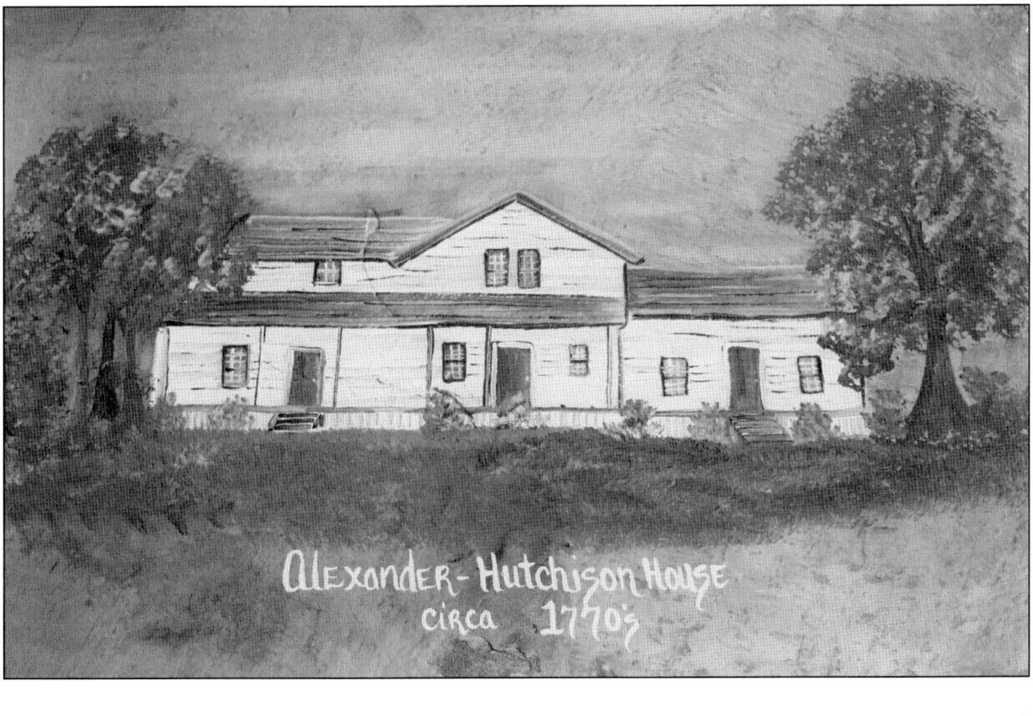

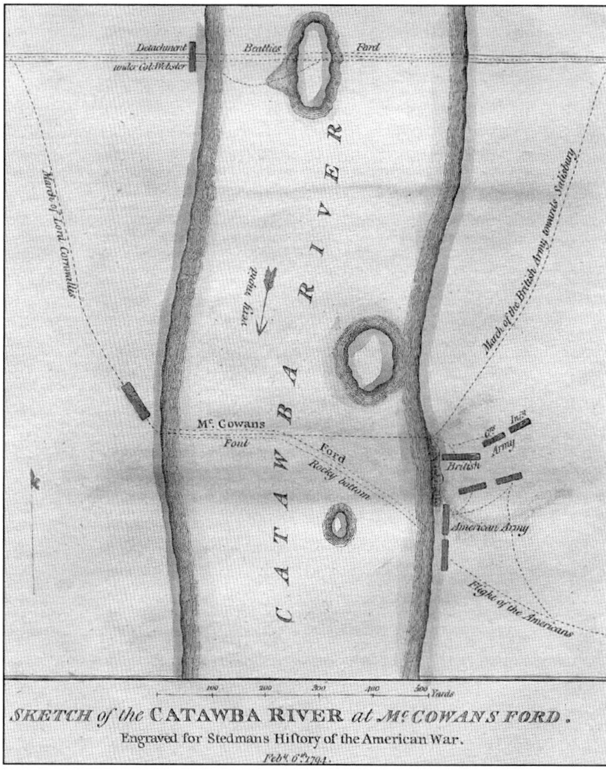


**BATTLE OF COWAN'S FORD.** The Patriots, led by Gen. Daniel Morgan, had won a glorious victory in the Battle at Cowpens. Immediately after the battle, General Morgan and his warriors started their march to Virginia, pursued by General Cornwallis and 3,000 British troops. Gen. William Davidson and a small group of local militia were charged with slowing down the British army at Cowan's Ford. Several men from the Mount Holly area were involved in the battle, including Robert Henry, a teenager, and Robert Beatty, a lame schoolmaster from Tuckaseege. During the battle, Beatty, an excellent marksman, fired twice, killing two British. After firing the second shot, Beatty yelled to Henry, "It's time to run, Bob!," but he was then felled by a British musket. (Map courtesy of James F. Love III; photograph by C. Alexander.)

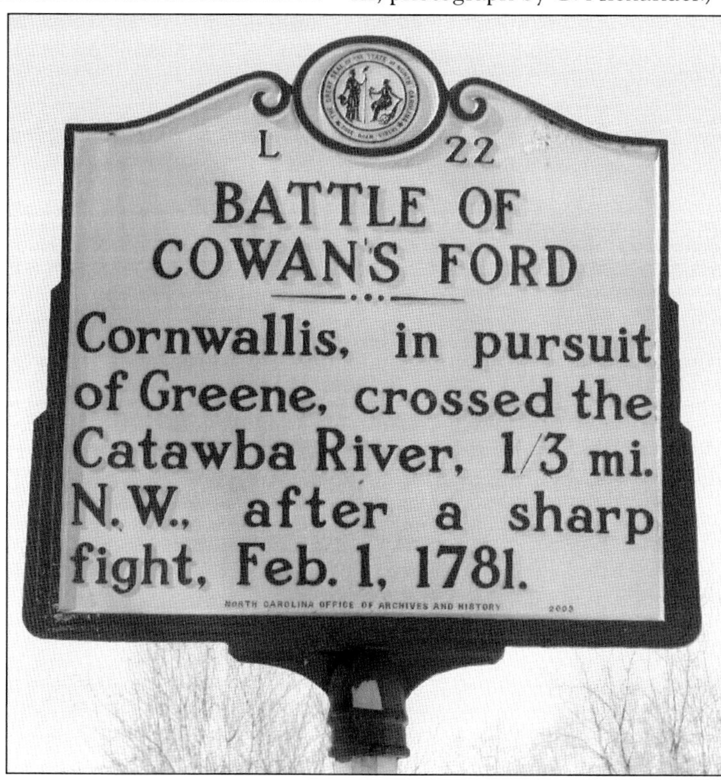

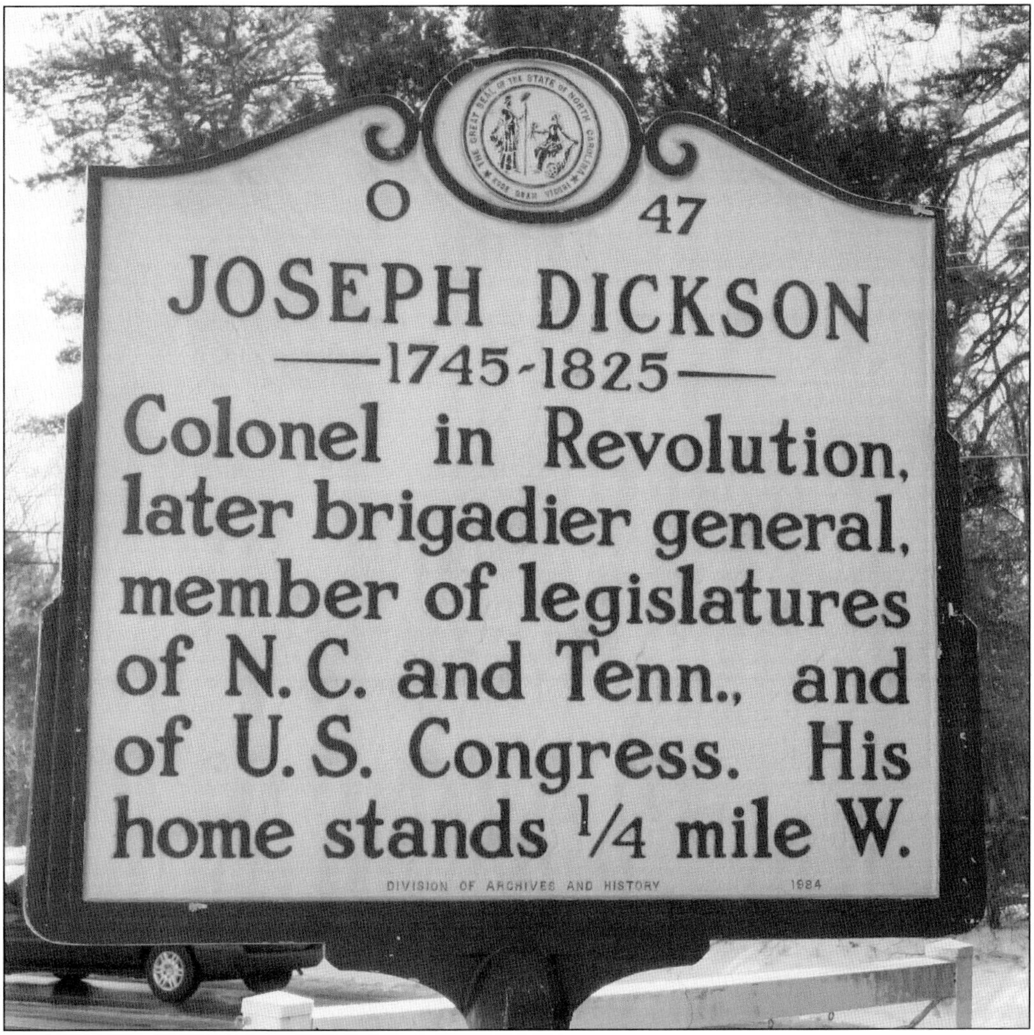


**GEN. JOSEPH DICKSON, 1745–1825.** General Dickson lived in the Westland Farm area of Mount Holly. His historic marker is on North Carolina Route 27 northwest of Mount Holly. At the outbreak of the Revolutionary War, he was commissioned as a captain, and he fought at the Battle of Kings Mountain. In June 1780, General Rutherford and his patriot troops assembled at Dickson's farm before traveling to the Battle of Ramsour's Mill in present-day Lincoln County. Dickson was made general in the militia in 1799. After the war, he was clerk of Lincoln County Court, a member of the state senate, and on the commission to establish the University of North Carolina. In 1799, he was elected as a Federalist to the Sixth Congress, serving until 1801. Like many early pioneers, the restless Scots-Irishman moved westward to Tennessee in 1803 and was a member of the state house of representatives. He and his wife are interred on the Dickerson Plantation in Murfreesboro, Tennessee. (Photograph by C. Alexander.)

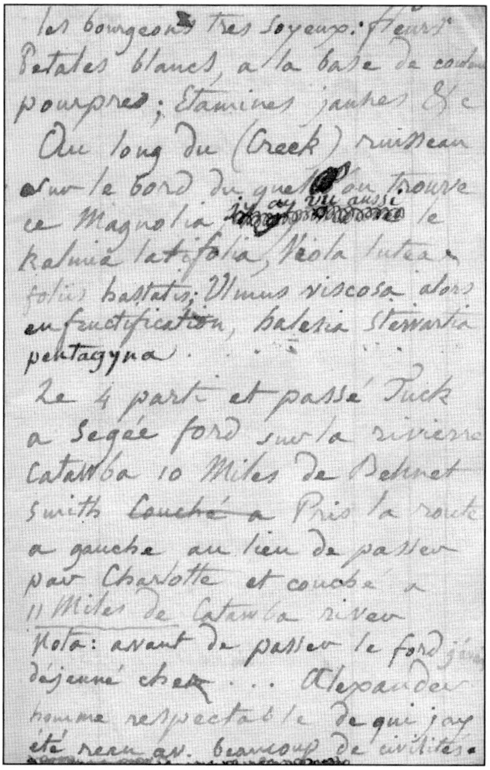

les bourgeons tres soyeux: fleurs
Petales blancs, a la base de couleur
pourpres; Etamines jaunes &c
Au long du (Creek) ruisseau
sur le bord du quel on trouve
ce Magnolia il y a vu aussi le
Kalmia latifolia, Viola lutea
foliis hastatis; Ulmus viscosa alors
en fructification, halesia Stewartia
pentagyna.
Le 4 parti et passé Tuck
a Segée ford sur la riviere
Catawba 10 Miles de Bennet
Smith Couché a Pris la route
a gauche au lieu de passer
par Charlotte et couché a
11 Miles de Catawba river
Nota: avant de passer le ford j'ai
déjeuné chez . . . Alexander
homme respectable de qui jay
été recu av. beaucoup de civilités.

**ANDRE MICHAUX'S JOURNAL, 1796.** Andre Michaux's visits to the United States in the 18th and 19th centuries are well documented in his extensive journals. The document (left) shows his April 4, 1796, visit to Woodlawn. Robert Alexander invited Michaux to Woodlawn and assisted in transport of his plant specimens, including the big leaf magnolia (below), across the Catawba River. According to the English translation by Elaine N. Norman, PhD, Michaux recorded the following: "April 4, I left and crossed Tuck-a-segee Ford on the Catawba River, 10 miles from Bennet Smith [near Stanley]. I took the left road instead of going through Charlotte and slept 11 miles from the Catawba River. Note: Before crossing the ford, I had breakfasted at [Robert] Alexander['s], a very respectable gentleman who received me with much courtesy." (Left, courtesy of the American Philosophical Society; below, courtesy of Charlie Williams.)

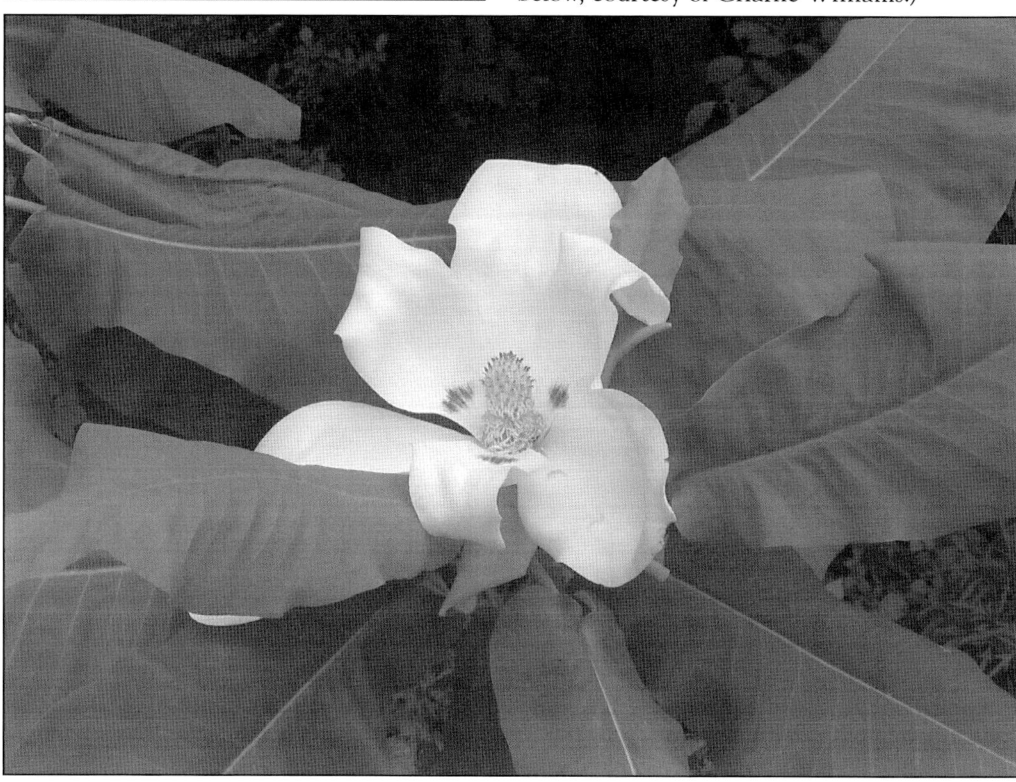

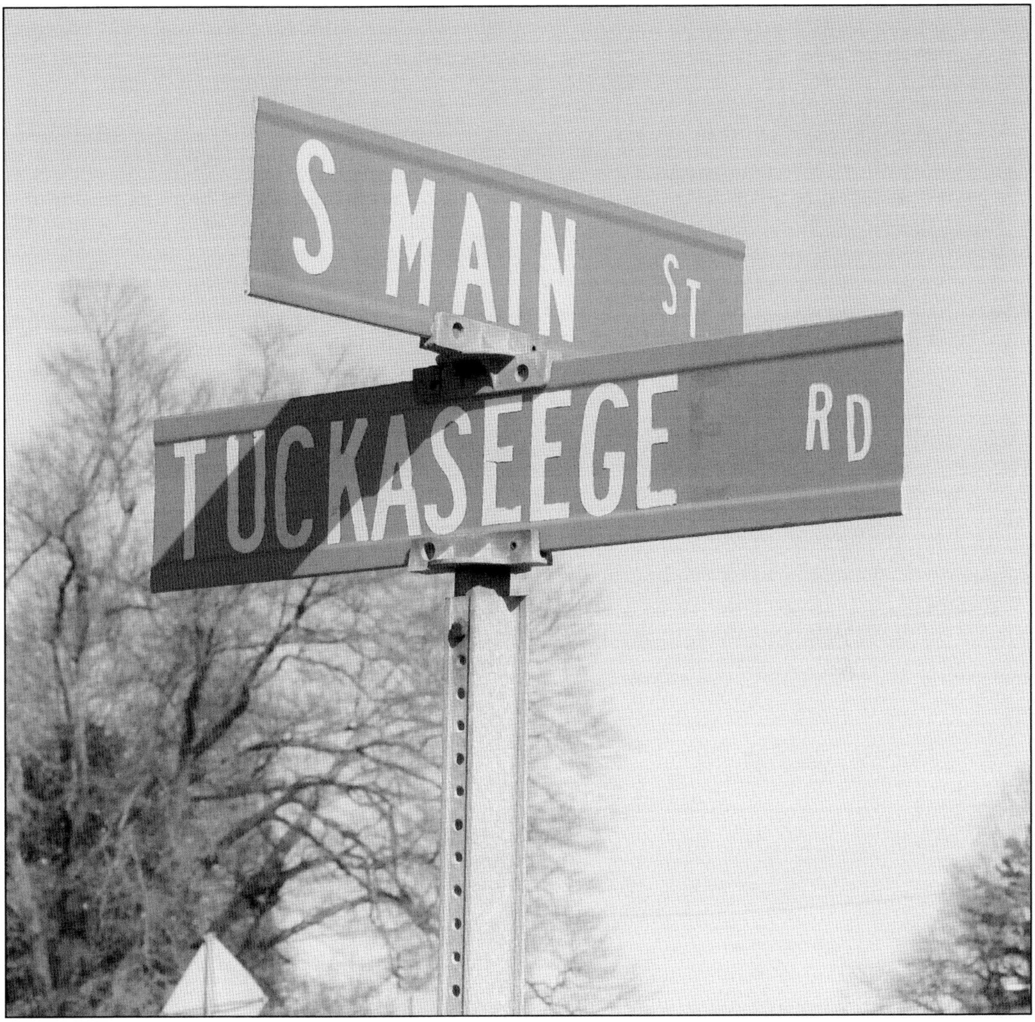


**A County Is Formed.** The Hoffman-Rhyne Store was the post office, trading center, and social headquarters for Woodlawn. The store was located on the corner of what are now Tuckaseege Road and South Main Street. It was here that the first meeting to create Gaston County took place. Cope and Wellman's *The County of Gaston* describes the event as follows: "On June 4, 1842, a group of [the area's] foremost residents met at the store owned by Fred D. Hoffman and Moses H Rhyne, a mile west of the Tuckaseege Ford. [James H.] White was there, to preside and speak. So were Richard and J.D. Rankin, Daniel Rhyne, William Hanks, Leroy and Whiten Stowe, Henry Fulenwider, Samuel Johnston, and others whose names echoed the days of the frontier's settlement and the battles at Ramsour's Mill, King's Mountain, and Cowan's Ford. White spoke earnestly, and the meeting voted not to support any candidate for the legislature who was not outspokenly in favor of dividing Lincoln County." (Photograph by Rick Hauser.)

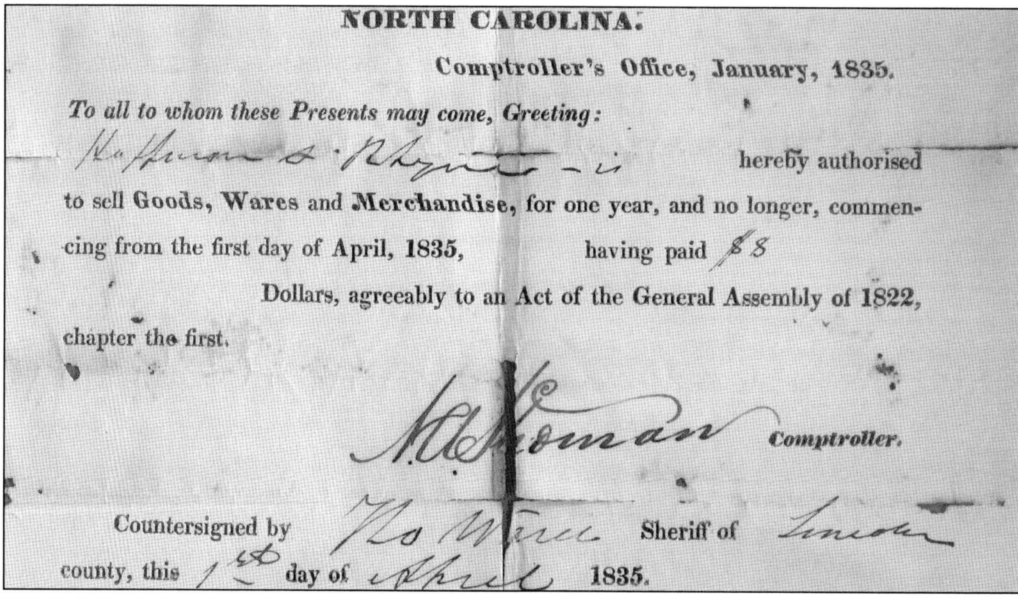

NORTH CAROLINA.

Comptroller's Office, January, 1835.

*To all to whom these Presents may come, Greeting:*

Hoffman & Rhyne is hereby authorised to sell Goods, Wares and Merchandise, for one year, and no longer, commencing from the first day of April, 1835, having paid $8 Dollars, agreeably to an Act of the General Assembly of 1822, chapter the first.

[illegible] Comptroller.

Countersigned by Tho Ward Sheriff of Lincoln county, this 1st day of April 1835.

**1835 Tax Receipt.** The earliest record of the historic Hoffman-Rhyne General Store is a tax receipt dated the "1st day of April, 1835, having paid $8 Dollars" and signed by Thomas Ward, sheriff of Lincoln County. This document gave authorization to the general store to "sell Goods, Wares and Merchandise, for one year and no longer." (Photograph by Rick Hauser.)

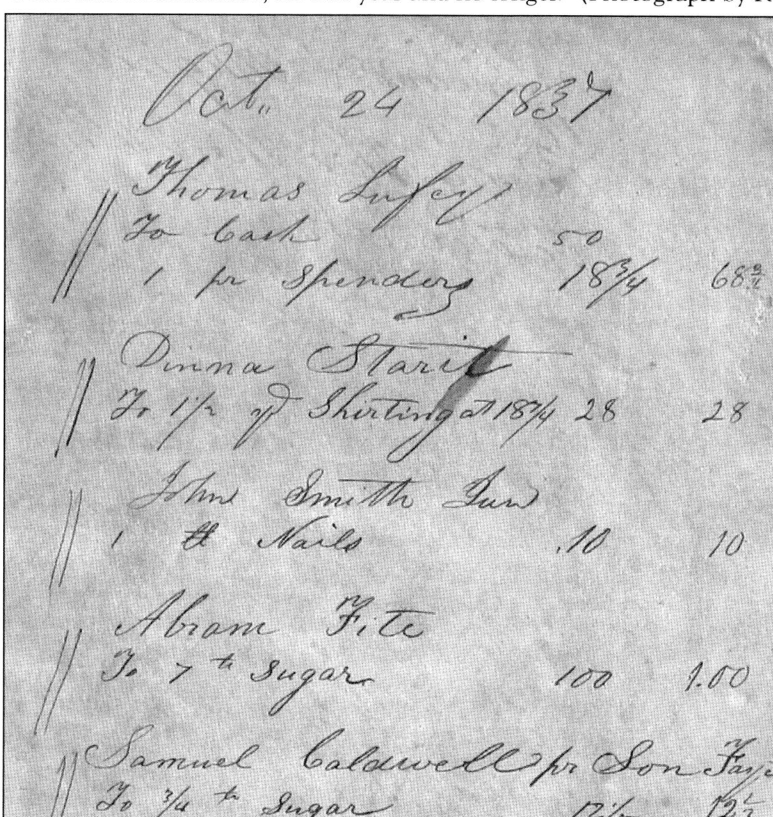

Oct. 24 1837

Thomas Lufey
To Cash 50
1 pr Spenders 18¾ 68¾

Dinna Starit
To 1½ yd Shirting at 18¾ 28 28

John Smith Jun
1 lb Nails .10 10

Abram Fite
To 7 lb Sugar 100 1.00

Samuel Caldwell pr Son Fay
To ¾ lb Sugar 12½ 12½

**Hoffman-Rhyne Store Journals.** October 1837 is the first date of the oldest remaining journal. The modern concept of the one-price system had not yet been invented. When the customer wanted to make a purchase, he or she asked to see the entire stock and rarely bought anything until the price had been dickered down. Barter and haggle were the market methods of the day. (Photograph by Rick Hauser.)

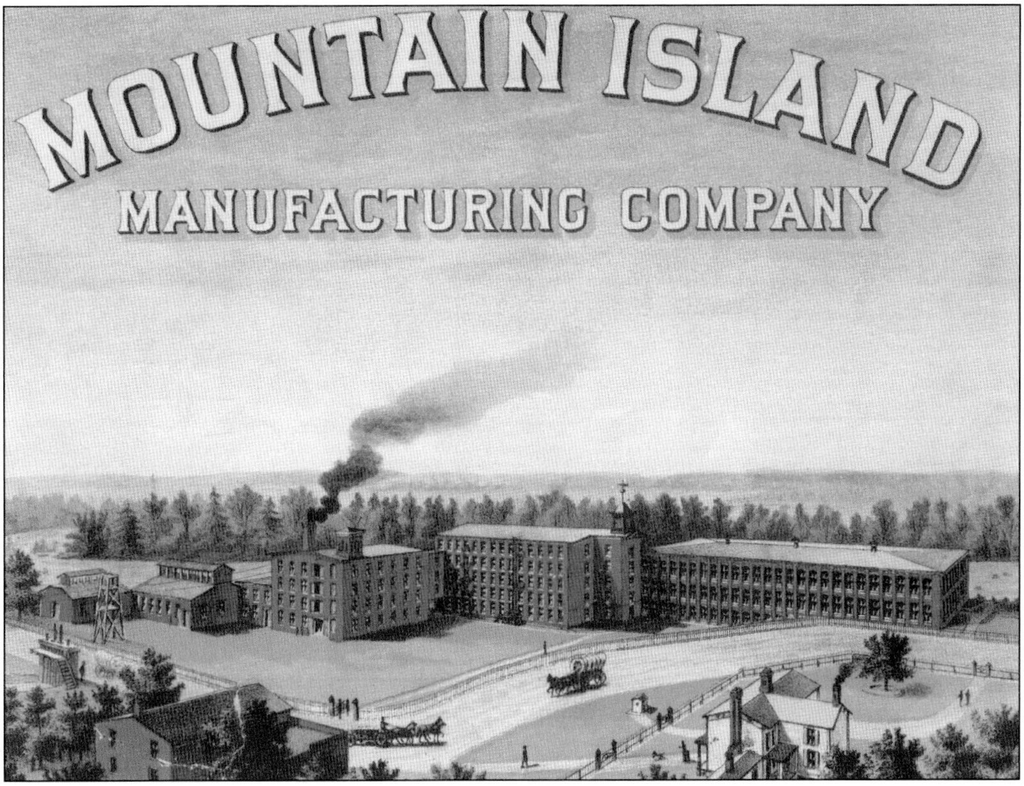


**First Cotton Mill in Gaston County.** Mountain Island Manufacturing Company was built in 1848 by Thomas Randolph Tate, who was from Greensboro. It was located a few miles north of Mount Holly beside the swift, rocky Catawba River, which provided its power. Men's wages were 25¢ to 40¢ per day for a 12-hour shift. Women and children were paid less. The large mill was completely destroyed by the flood of 1916, a transformative event in the life of Mount Holly and the region. (Both, courtesy of the Gaston County Museum of Art and History.)

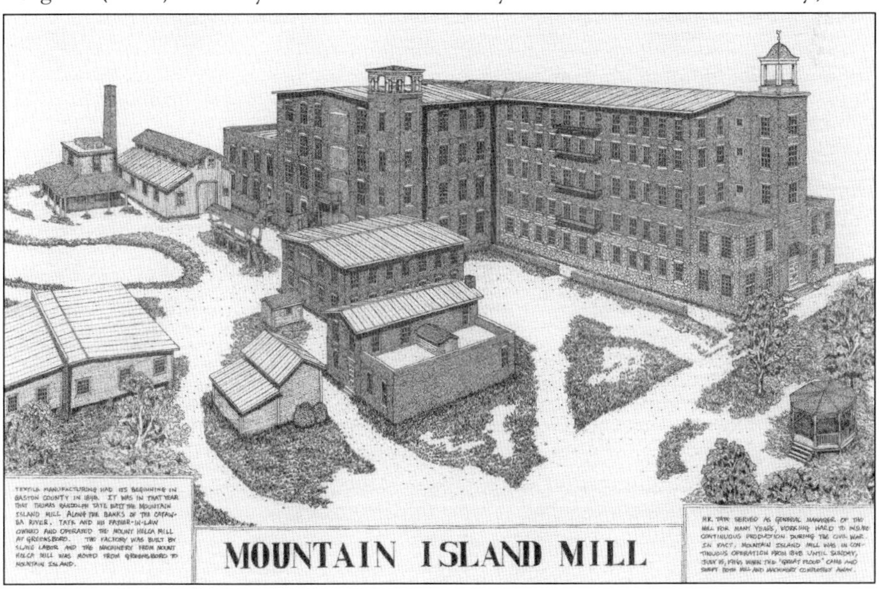

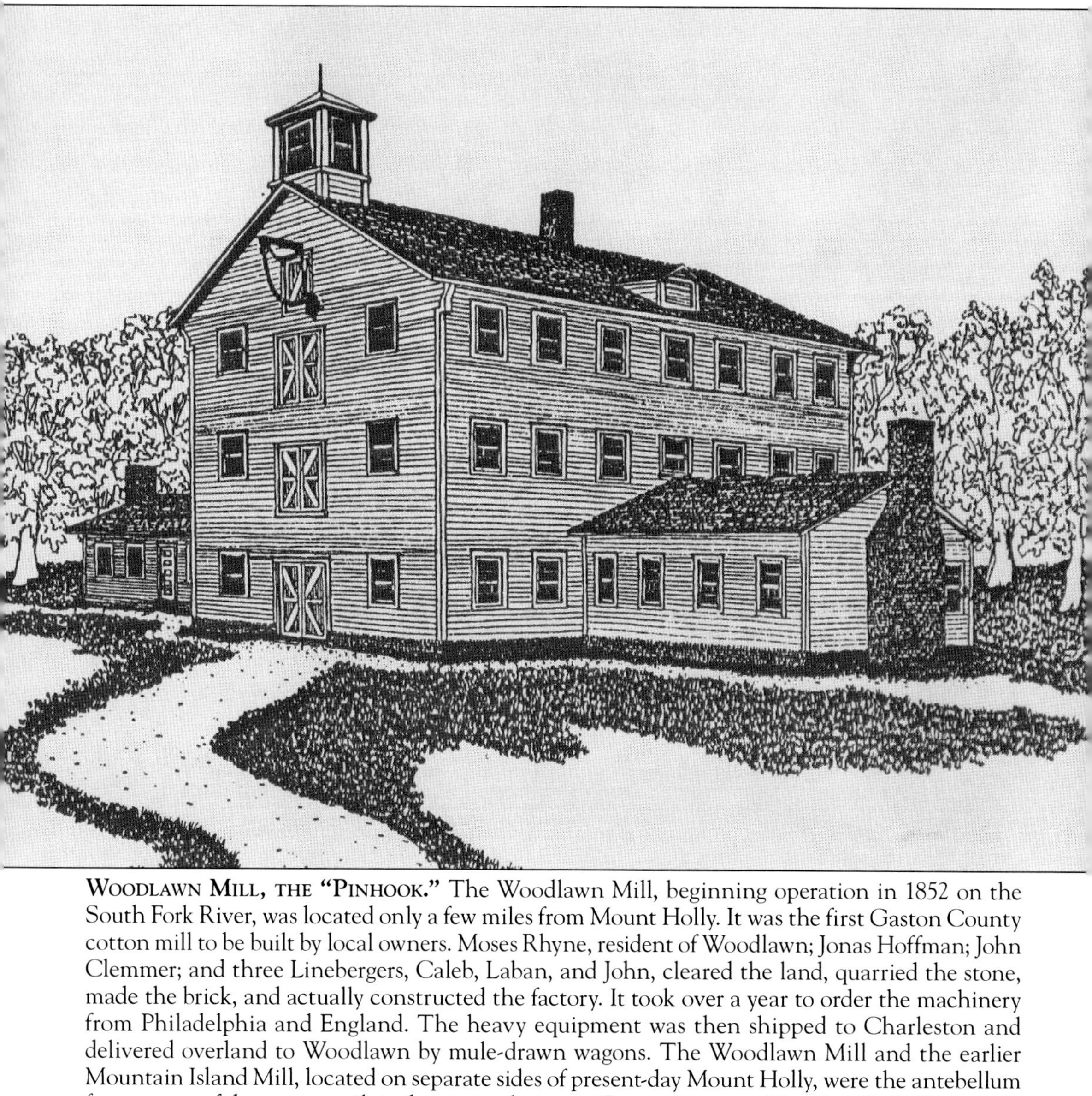

**Woodlawn Mill, the "Pinhook."** The Woodlawn Mill, beginning operation in 1852 on the South Fork River, was located only a few miles from Mount Holly. It was the first Gaston County cotton mill to be built by local owners. Moses Rhyne, resident of Woodlawn; Jonas Hoffman; John Clemmer; and three Linebergers, Caleb, Laban, and John, cleared the land, quarried the stone, made the brick, and actually constructed the factory. It took over a year to order the machinery from Philadelphia and England. The heavy equipment was then shipped to Charleston and delivered overland to Woodlawn by mule-drawn wagons. The Woodlawn Mill and the earlier Mountain Island Mill, located on separate sides of present-day Mount Holly, were the antebellum forerunners of the great textile industry revolution in Gaston County. After the Civil War, textile development in Gaston County took off with the founding of a little mill on Dutchman's Creek in 1874. (Courtesy of the Gaston County Museum of Art and History.)

**The Hoffman Dower Plat and House.** The 1857 dower plat of Mary Smith Hoffman (right) shows the location of her Woodlawn farm, which was willed to her by her husband, Fredrick Hoffman. The map shows the main roads of that time—the Tuckaseege Ford Road going northwest and the Armstrong Ford Road, which traveled south. Fredrick Hoffman was brother-in-law to Moses H. Rhyne, his partner in the Hoffman and Rhyne Store. The store was located at the intersection of Tuckaseege Road and South Main Street, and Hoffman's house (below) was across the road. The store was razed in the 1950s, and the Hoffman house was demolished in the 1980s. The footprint of the old store is located near a present-day retail complex, still a commercial center after 150 years. (Plat document courtesy of Pauline Jones; photograph courtesy of James F. Love III.)

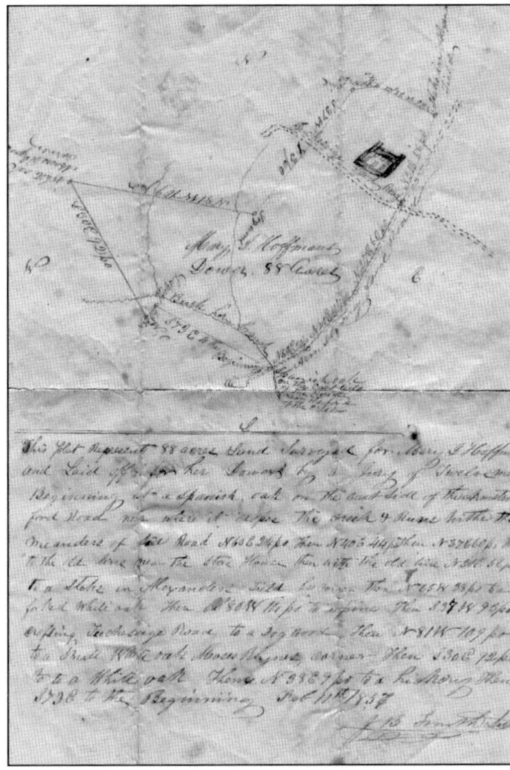

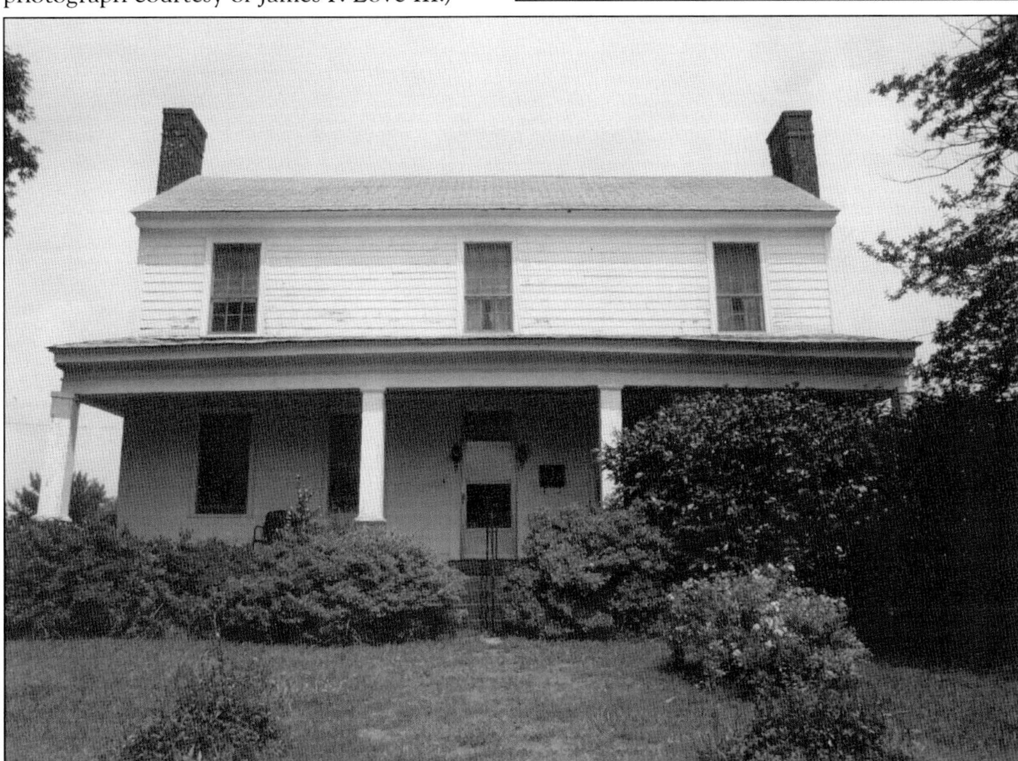

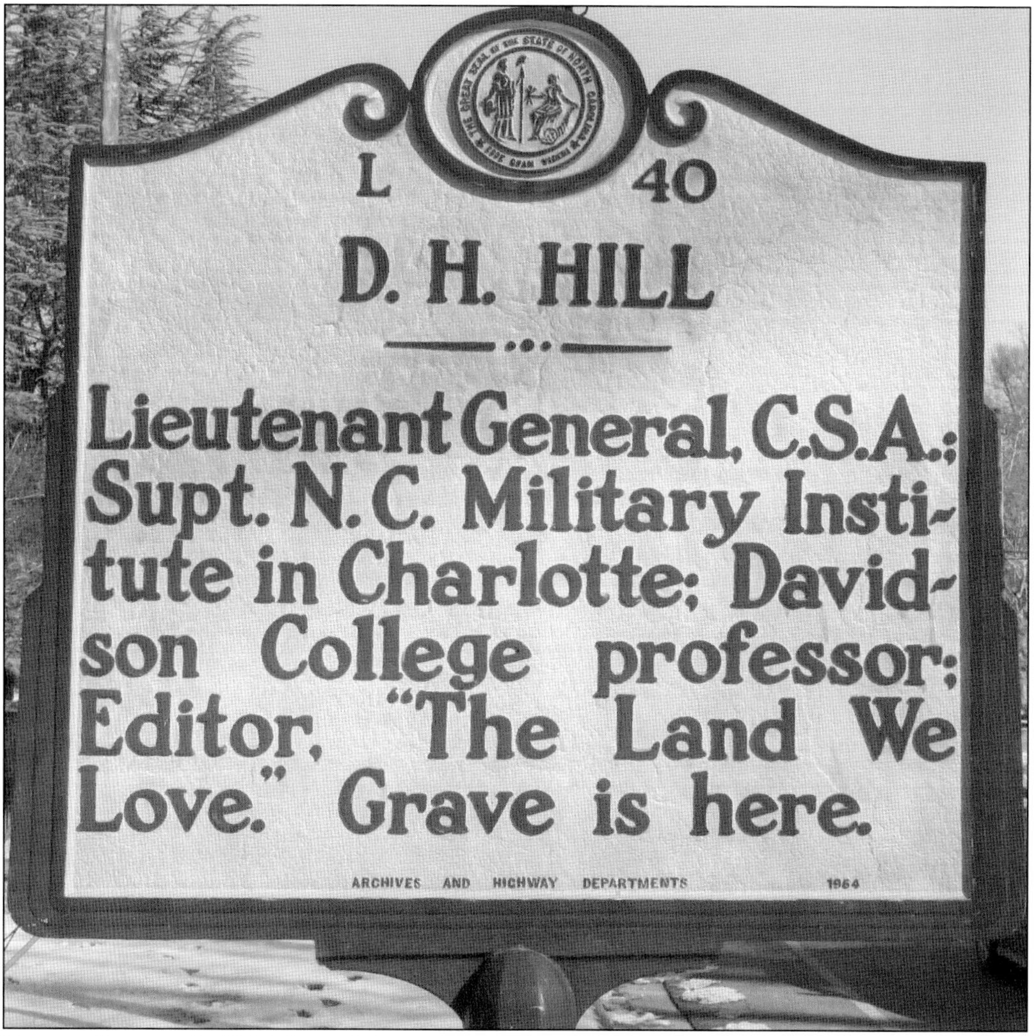


**DANIEL HARVEY (D.H.) HILL, 1821–1889.** A Confederate general during the American Civil War, Hill was also recognized as a Southern scholar. Hill and Thomas "Stonewall" Jackson married sisters who were the daughters of Rev. Hall Morrison, first president of Davidson College. General Hill was educated at West Point and was promoted to major during the Mexican-American War. He joined the faculty at Davidson College in 1854 and became the superintendent of the North Carolina Military Institute in Charlotte in 1859. After the Civil War, General Hill briefly moved to a farm in Mount Holly, intending to spend the rest of his days there. However, it turned out he was more of a scholar than a farmer. After the crops failed, Hill moved to Charlotte as editor of *The Land We Love*. In 1877, Hill became the first president of the University of Arkansas. General Hill is buried in the Davidson College Cemetery. (Courtesy of C. Alexander.)

# *Two*

# The Ties that Bind
## Formative Churches

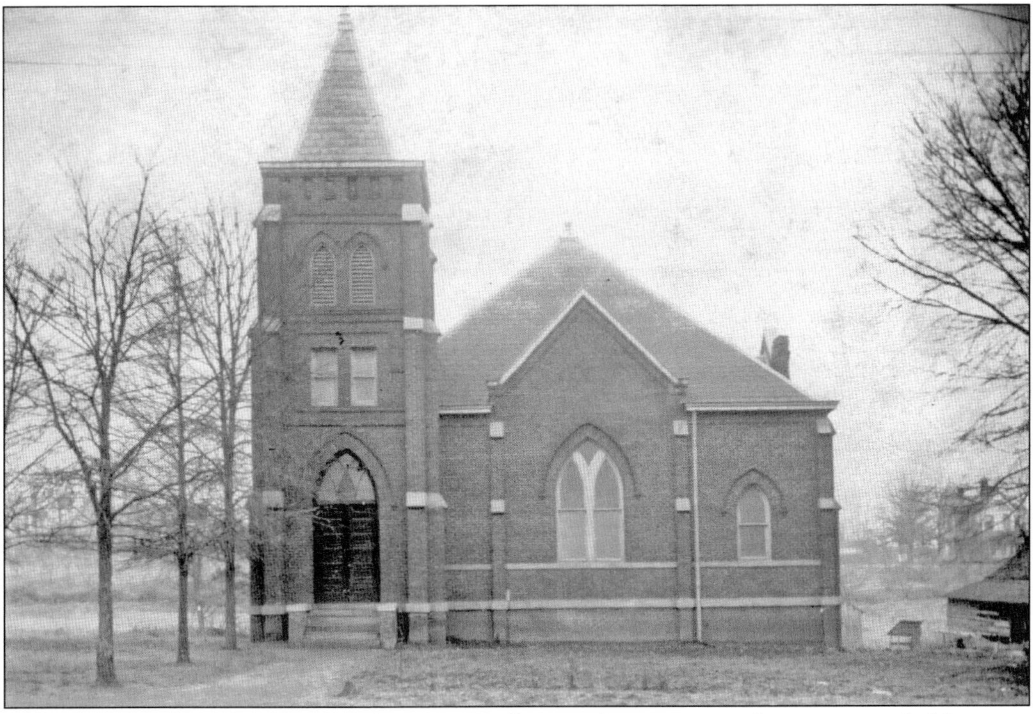

**Shepherding the Faithful.** In early Mount Holly, interdenominational services were held at store buildings. In 1881, these interfaith members decided to construct a church building that would be deeded to the denomination that paid the most for development. The Lutherans pledged the most money, but by agreement, all denominations could use the structure until they built their own. This Lutheran sanctuary was constructed in 1903. (Courtesy of the Evangelical Lutheran Church of the Good Shepherd.)

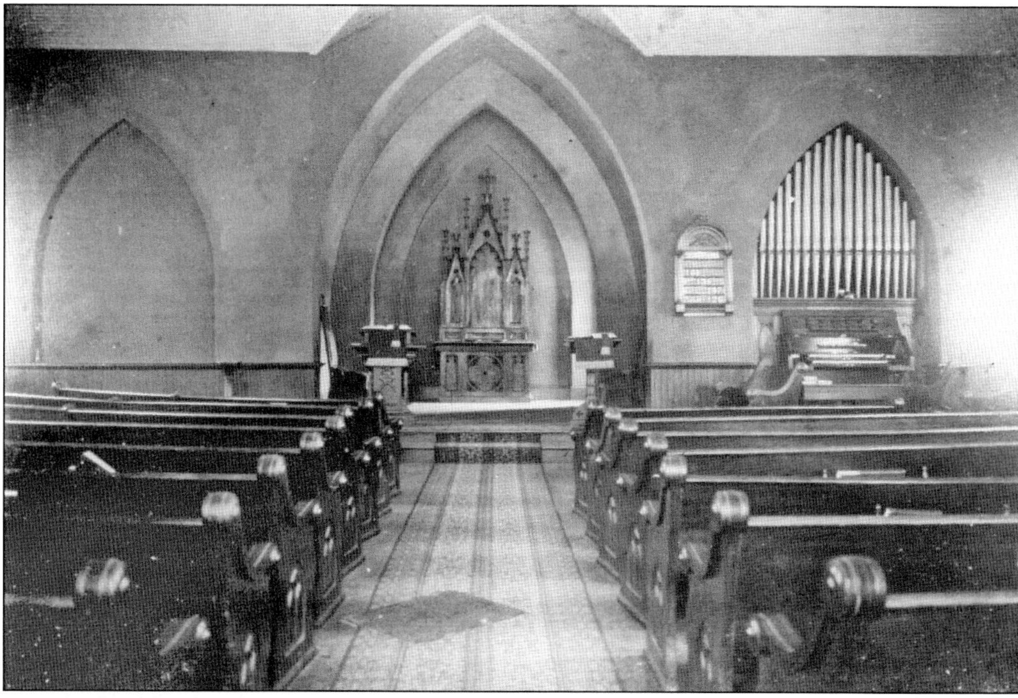

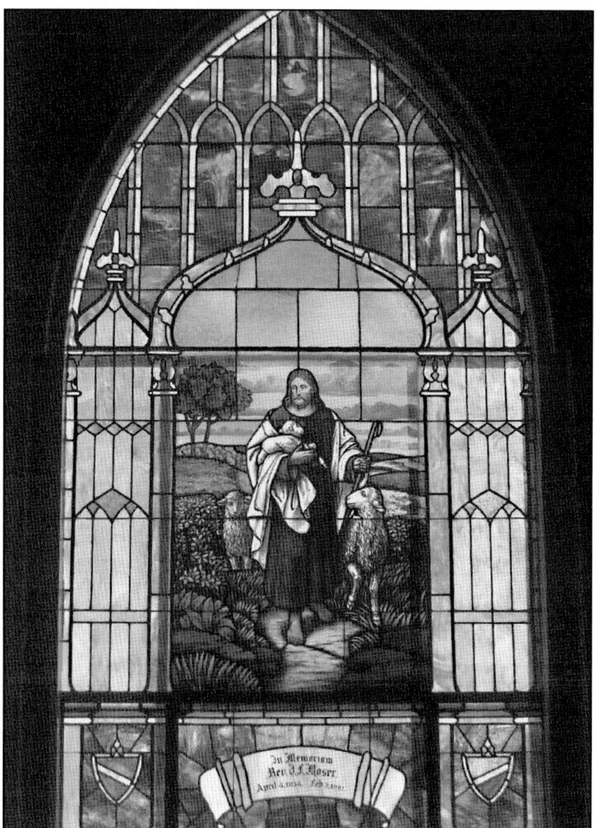

**GOOD SHEPHERD INTERIOR.** This view is from the Good Shepherd window. Note that the Holy Trinity is represented twice in the interior design—in the three side-by-side Gothic arches and in the three progressively smaller central arches that accentuate the altar. (Courtesy of the Evangelical Lutheran Church of the Good Shepherd.)

**GOOD SHEPHERD STAINED GLASS.** The Rhyne family commissioned three glass windows for a renovation of the Lutheran church sanctuary in 1916. The central window, showing the Good Shepherd tending his flock, faces east. During Sunday services, the morning sun streams through the image of Christ, illuminating the pulpit and congregation within. (Courtesy of the Evangelical Lutheran Church of the Good Shepherd.)

**St. Joseph's Catholic Church, c. 1843.** Gaston County's first Catholic church, the fourth Catholic church in North Carolina, is located north of downtown. In 1830, Irish Catholic families moved to the Riverbend area during Gaston County's gold rush. St. Joseph's Church was restored in 1975. (Courtesy of Belmont Abbey Archives.)

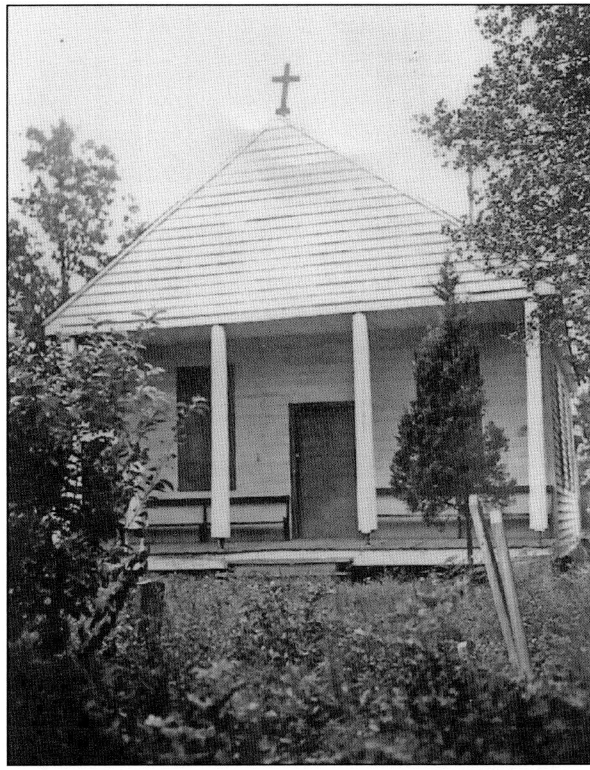

**St. Joseph's Cemetery, 1842.** The first pastor, Fr. T.J. Cronin, died of yellow fever before the church was built. He was the first to be buried in the cemetery. The names on the cemetery's tombstones, including Cahill, Duffey, and Lonergan, reflect their Irish heritage. The church and cemetery are located at the corner of state highway 273 and Sandy Ford Road. (Courtesy of Belmont Abbey Archives.)

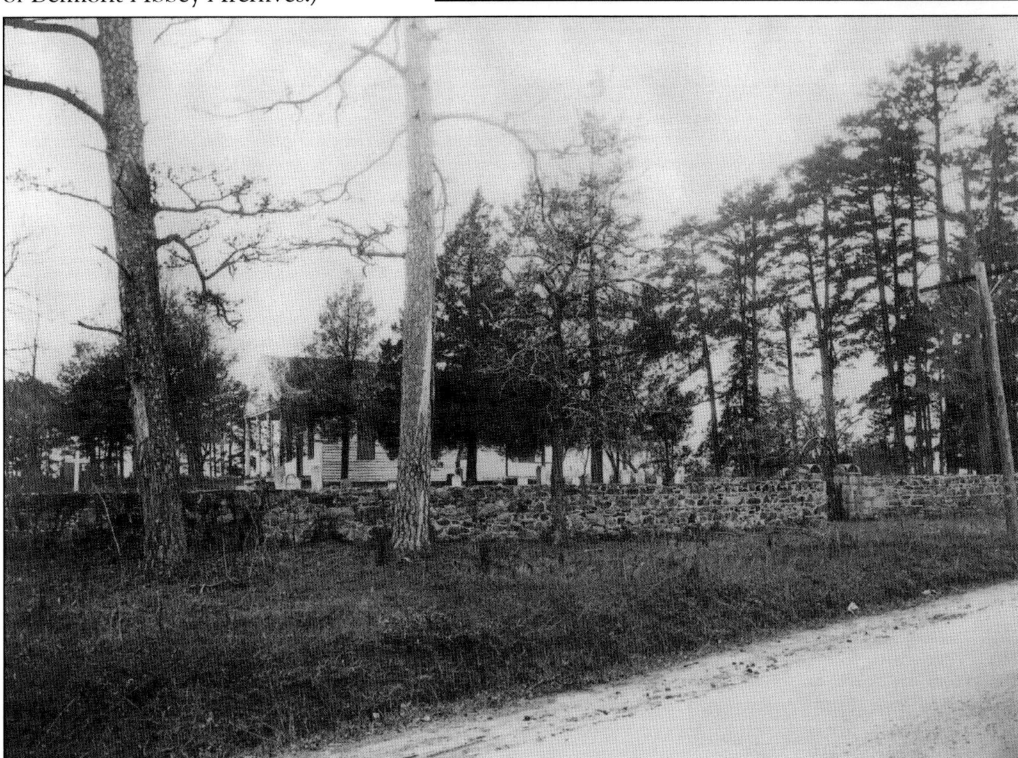

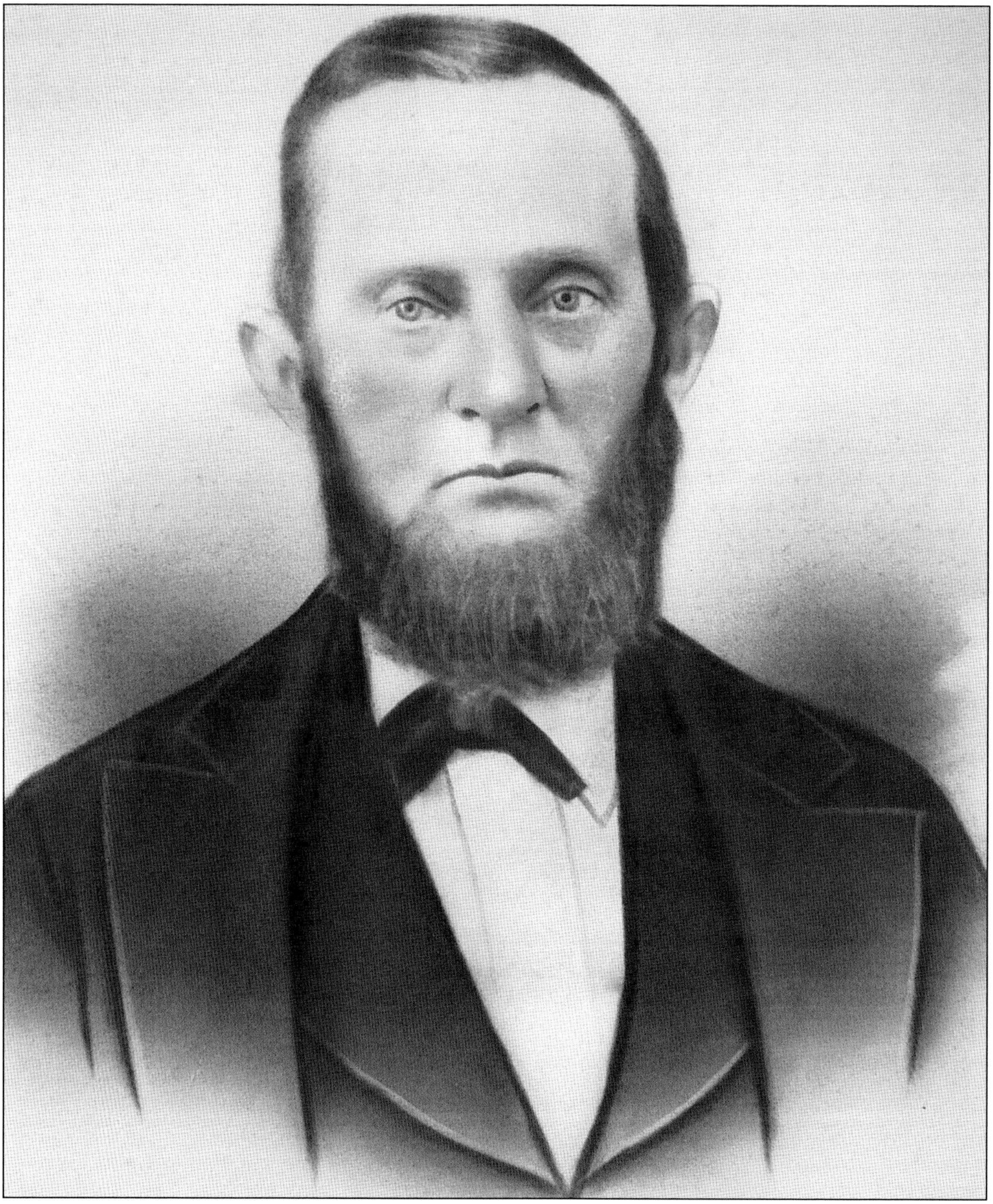

**FATHER PETERSON, 1821–1897.** Jesse Rueben Peterson was born in what is now Gaston County and spent his life in service to the Lutheran Church. It was under his leadership that the articles of agreement for organizing the first Mount Holly Lutheran Church were developed. The articles are recorded in his handwriting and dated the spring of 1881. He served as pastor of the Lutheran Church of the Good Shepherd from 1884 until 1892, but his influence went well beyond the borders of Mount Holly. Father Peterson was also pastor at Lutheran Chapel, Gastonia; Philadelphia Lutheran, Dallas; St. Mark Lutheran, Crouse; Christ Lutheran, Stanley; St. Luke Lutheran, Lincoln County; and St. Matthews Lutheran, Kings Mountain. In addition, he served as secretary of the Tennessee Synod from 1849 until 1873. (Courtesy of Christ Lutheran Church, Stanley; photograph by Rick Hauser.)

**FIRST BAPTIST CHURCH, THE FIRST SANCTUARY.** This building was on the west side of Main Street, between Central Avenue and Catawba Avenue. The sanctuary was dedicated in March 1890 by the 68 charter members. In 1915, a parsonage was built on Main Street south of Glendale Avenue. The present sanctuary was built beside the parsonage in 1924. (Courtesy of Millican Pictorial History Museum.)

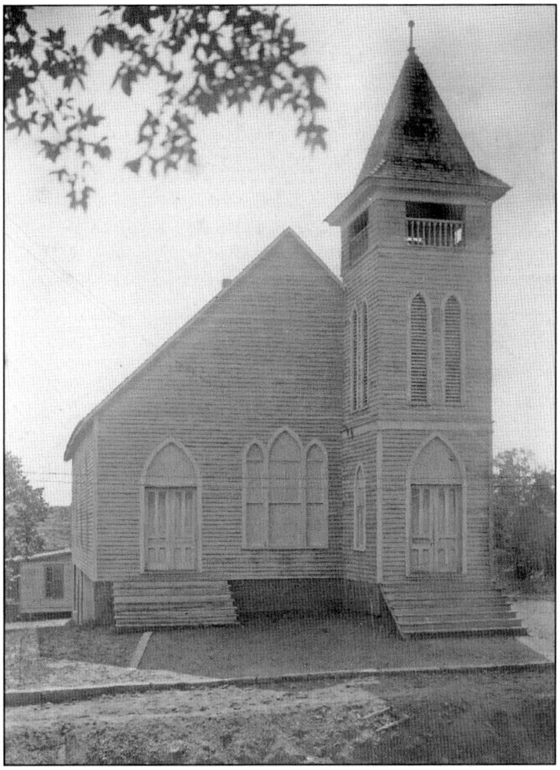

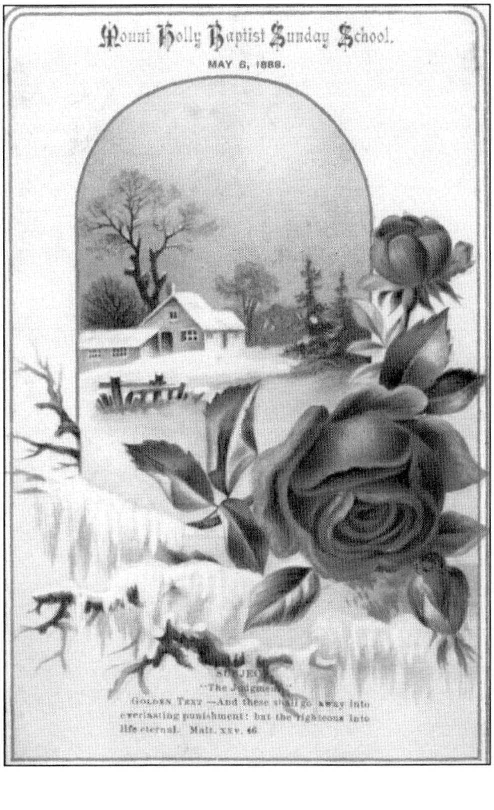


**SUNDAY SCHOOL CARD, 1888.** "Reward of Merit" lithographed cards were popular tokens given to Sunday school students in the late 19th century. The verse reads, "And these shall go away into everlasting punishment, but the righteous into life eternal." Although the Baptist church did not officially organize until 1890, Mount Holly Baptists had met at the Lutheran church since 1881. (Courtesy of the City of Mount Holly Archives.)

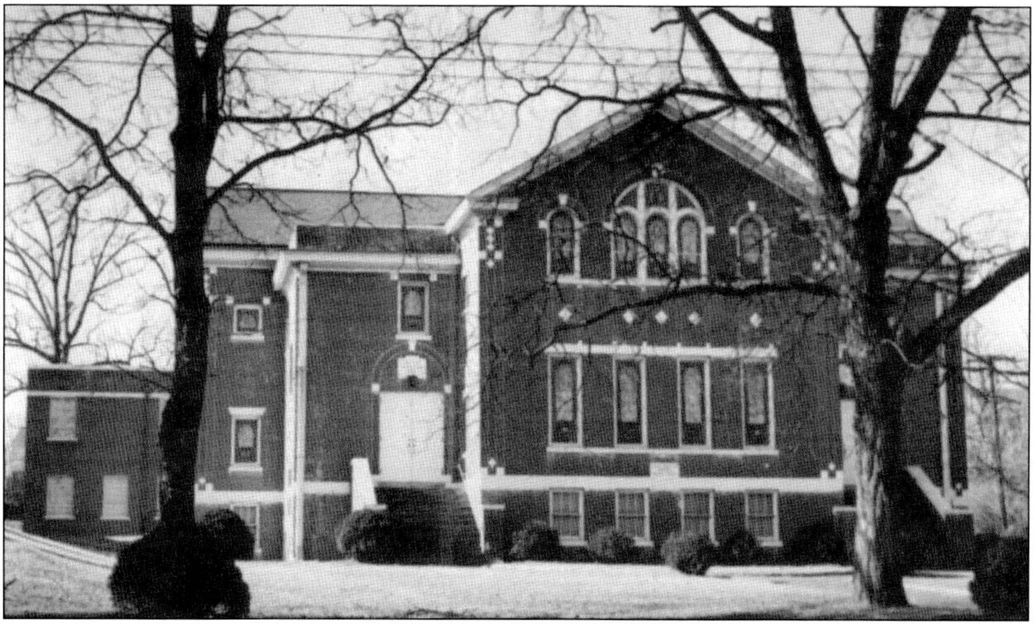

**First Baptist Church, 1950s.** Tall ash trees shaded South Main Street. Shown on the left of the photograph, an education building behind the church sanctuary was added in 1955. Above the education building's Glendale Avenue entrance, carved in stone, is the enduring directive, "Study to Show Thyself Approved unto God." (Courtesy of C. Alexander.)

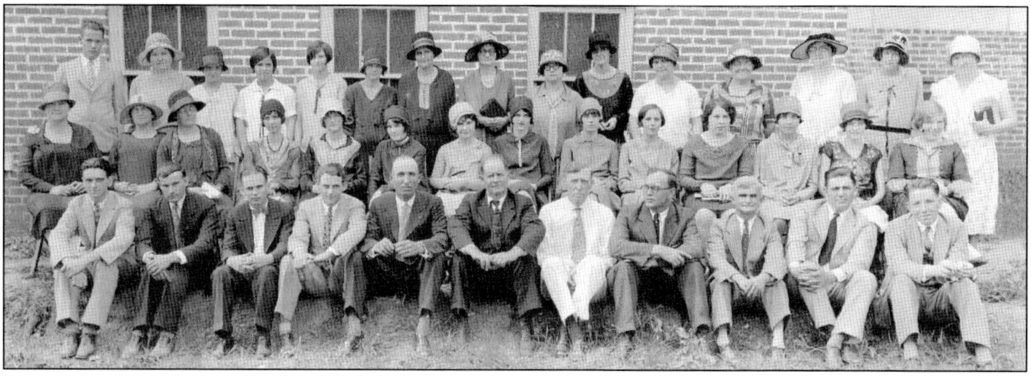

**Church Members, First Baptist Church.** This photograph was taken from the side of the church. Most men in the picture are wearing ankle-high brogans, and many of the young women are wearing cloche (helmet-like) hats, very popular in the late 1920s. These folks must have been quite proud of their new sanctuary, designed in an auditorium style with three balconies. (Courtesy of Millican Pictorial History Museum.)

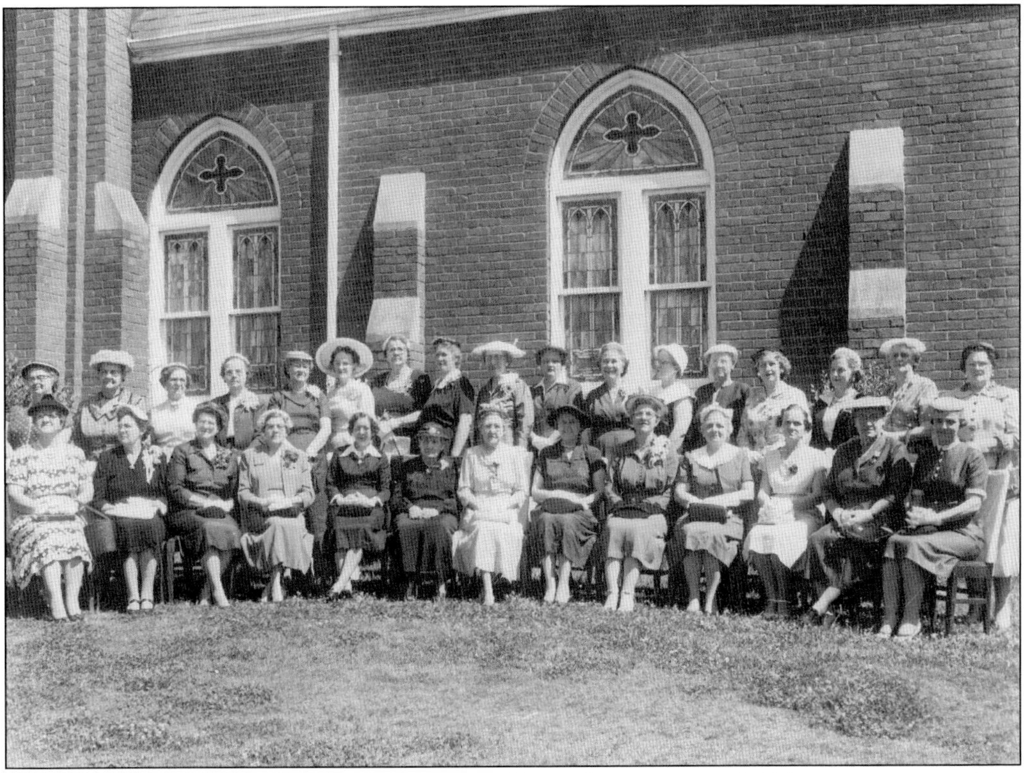

**First Methodist Women.** This photograph affirms that in the mid-20th century, a good hat was required fashion for Sunday services. This view is the south side of the church, facing East Catawba Avenue. Note the Gothic accents of the window shapes and wall buttresses. The education building, not seen in this view, was briefly an apartment building after the church moved to North Main Street. (Courtesy of Linda Thompson Sherrill.)

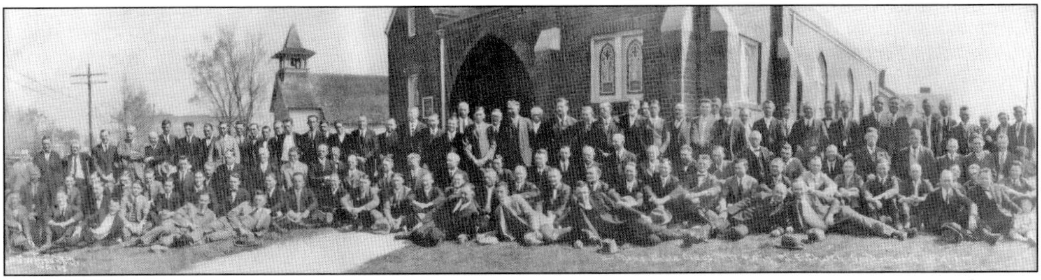

**First Methodist Men.** The Methodist men's Bible class is out in force in this panoramic photograph from the early 1920s. The First Presbyterian Church building is in the background on the left side. The wooden Presbyterian structure and brick Methodist building were both located on South Main Street. (Courtesy of the City of Mount Holly Archives.)

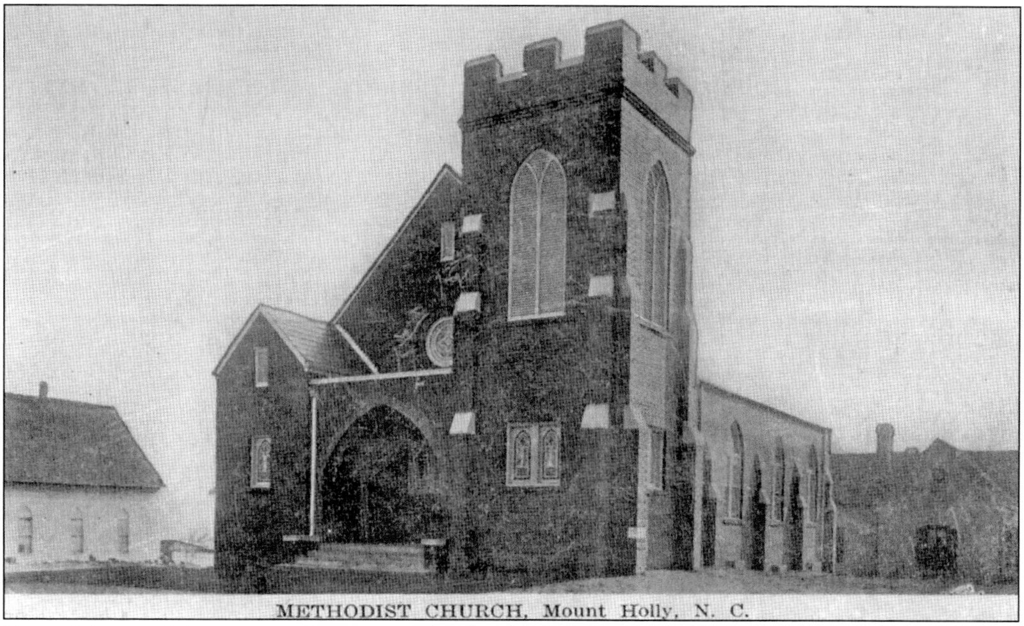


**First United Methodist Church.** This brick church was built in 1912. It was preceded by the original frame structure occupying the same site, built in 1890. The congregation must have been a persistent and steadfast group, for in 1896 and again in 1912, the frame sanctuaries were destroyed by storms. (Courtesy of the City of Mount Holly Archives.)

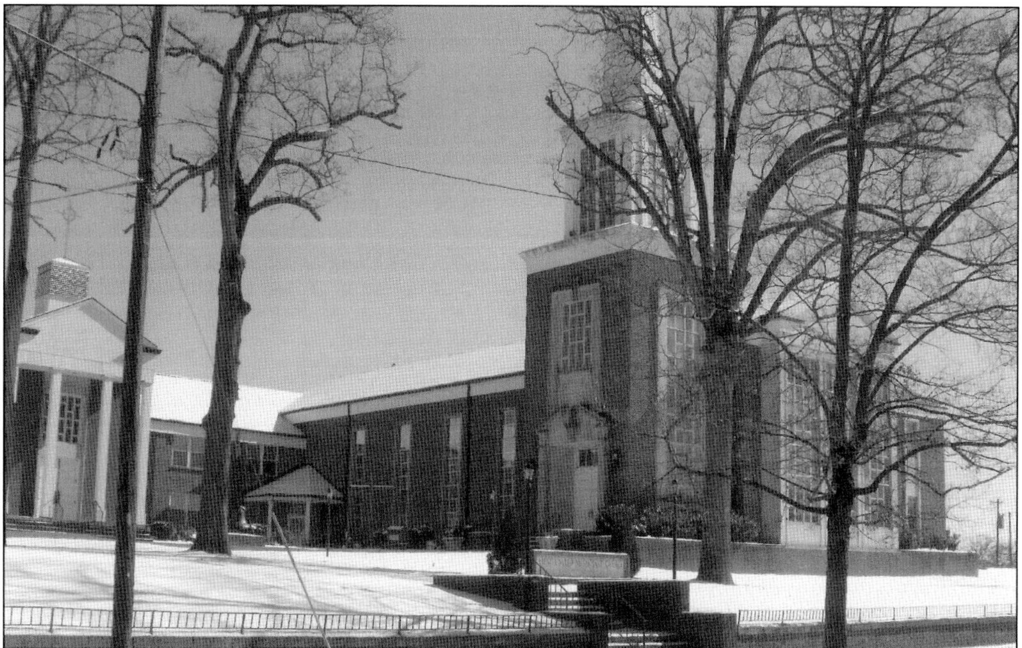

**First United Methodist Church, December 2010.** The chapel on the left and the education building were built in 1960 at the old A.P. Rhyne house site on North Main Street. More than a decade later, the church built the large sanctuary with the tall white spire that rises above downtown. (Courtesy of the First United Methodist Church.)

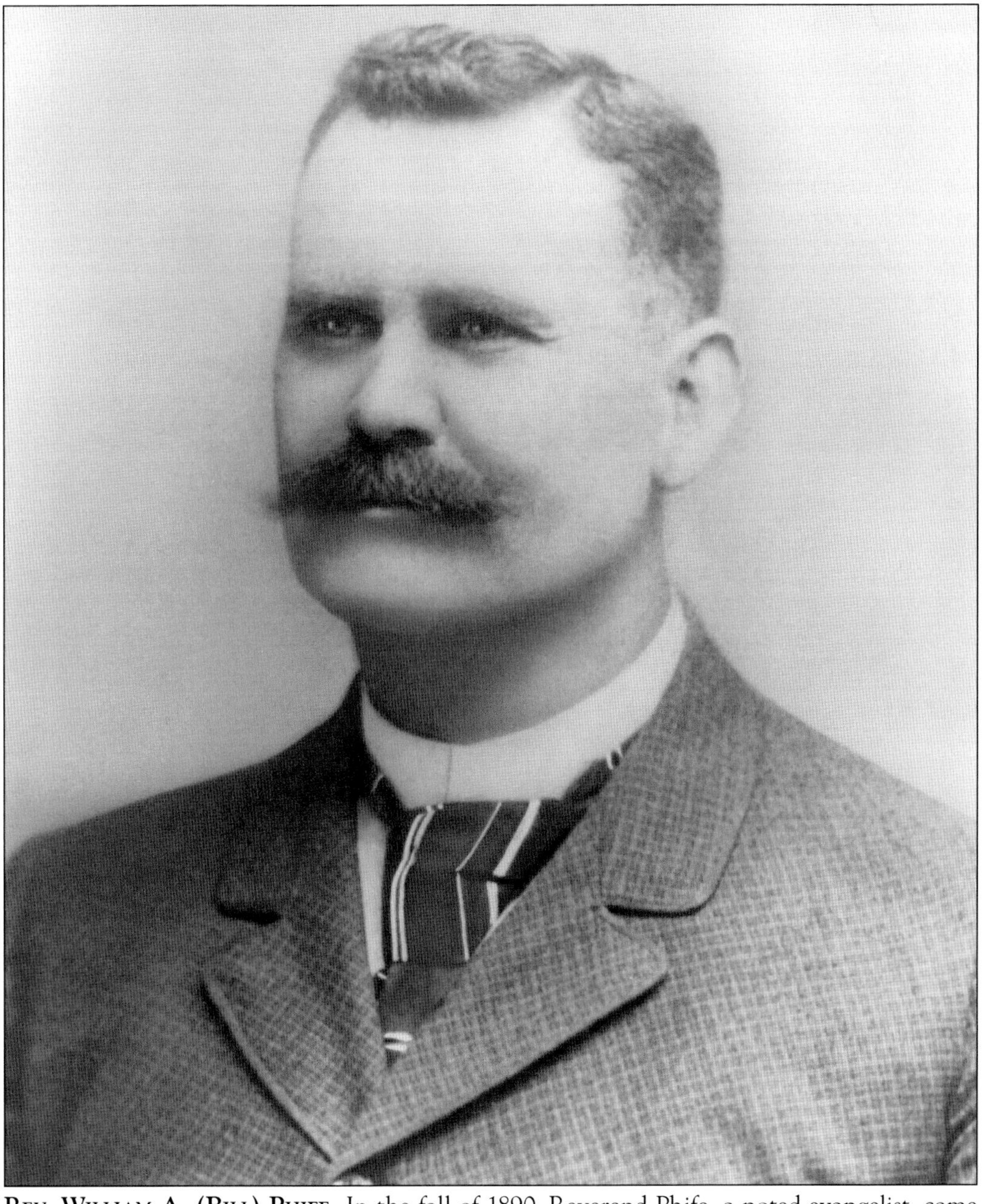

**REV. WILLIAM A. (BILL) PHIFE.** In the fall of 1890, Reverend Phife, a noted evangelist, came to Mount Holly for a revival meeting. He stirred some souls during a series of services that took place in an old sawmill building on East Central Avenue. Reverend Phife was intent on building a Presbyterian church in Mount Holly. A congregational meeting held on January 4, 1891, at Goshen Presbyterian Church resolved to form a congregation and build a church in downtown Mount Holly. Reverend Phife purchased a lot on South Main Street and presented it to the Mount Holly Presbyterians for their new sanctuary. Soon after Phife donated the land, lumber was ordered and placed at the job site. The materials sat there unused for some time because of an epidemic of typhoid fever, and the church was not built until the summer of 1894. (Courtesy of First Presbyterian Church Archives.)

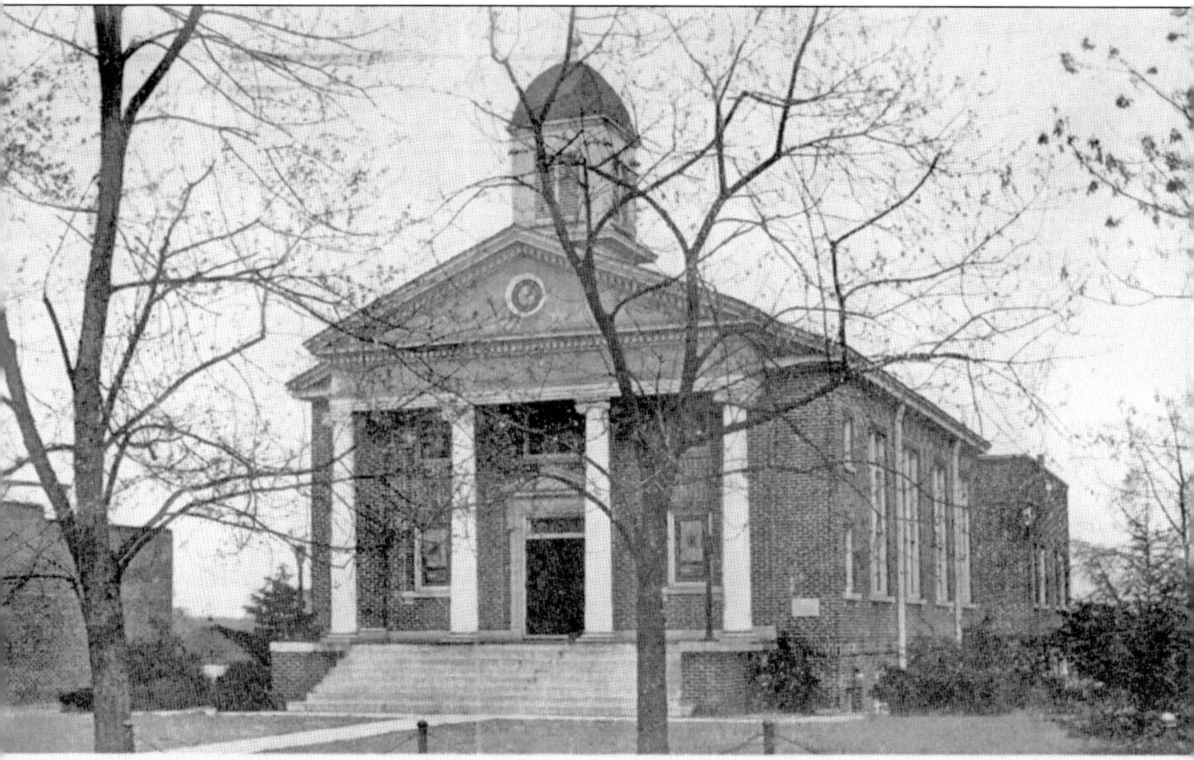


**FIRST PRESBYTERIAN CHURCH, C. 1930S.** This is the second church building that has been on this site at 133 South Main Street. Mount Holly Presbyterian members relocated from both the Goshen Presbyterian Church and the community church that had previously met in the Lutheran church on the other side of Main Street. Church historians do not believe that a full photograph of the early frame sanctuary exists. The brick sanctuary built in 1927 has a distinctive columned portico with a large triangular pediment. The first marriage in the new sanctuary was that of Thomas W. Springs Jr. and Willie Dunn on August 19, 1936. The church constructed an education building in 1959. The sanctuary exterior was restored in the 1980s to its original color scheme, and the interior underwent extensive restoration and improvements in 2010. (Courtesy of the First Presbyterian Church Archives.)

**SHILOH AFRICAN METHODIST EPISCOPAL ZION CHURCH.** The current church building was constructed in the mid-20th century, though the church was founded soon after the Civil War. This local church has served as a center of African American culture in Mount Holly for close to 150 years. The African Methodist Episcopal Zion Church was founded nationally in 1796. (Courtesy of Essie Mae McGill.)

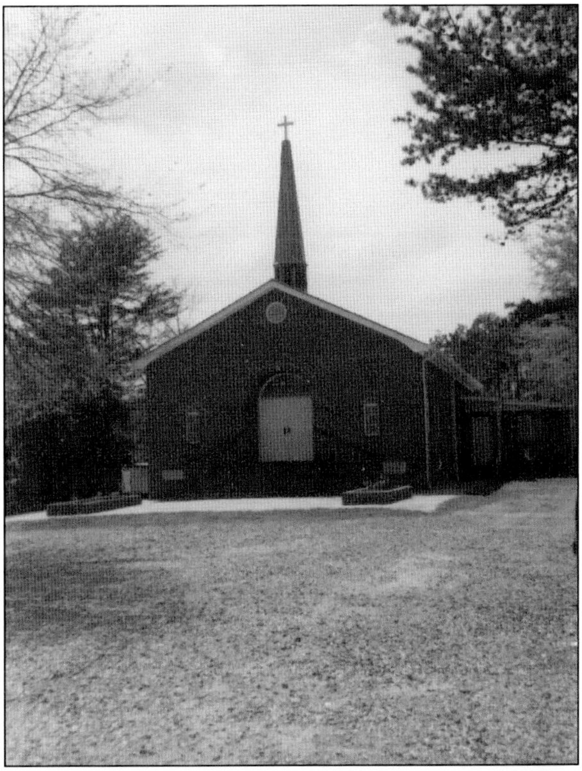

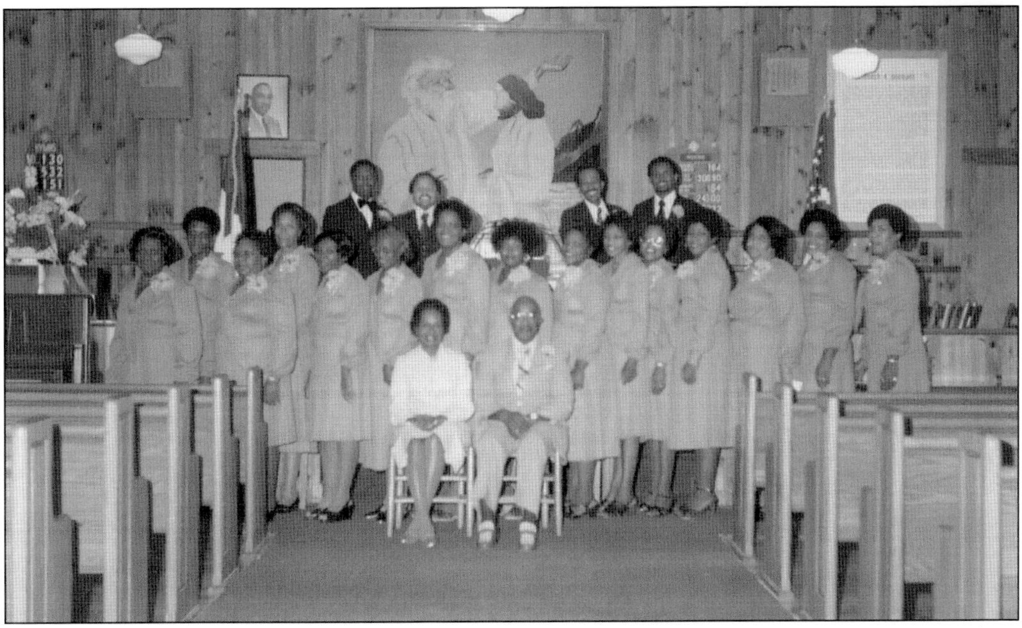

**A 25TH WEDDING ANNIVERSARY.** Essie Mae and Jack McGill had been married 25 years when this picture was taken in 1972 at Shiloh AME Zion Church on Old Highway 27. Jack McGill was a World War II veteran of the European theater. Essie Mae McGill has been a devoted volunteer, both at her church and at community organizations, including the Mount Holly Black History Forum. (Courtesy of Essie Mae McGill.)

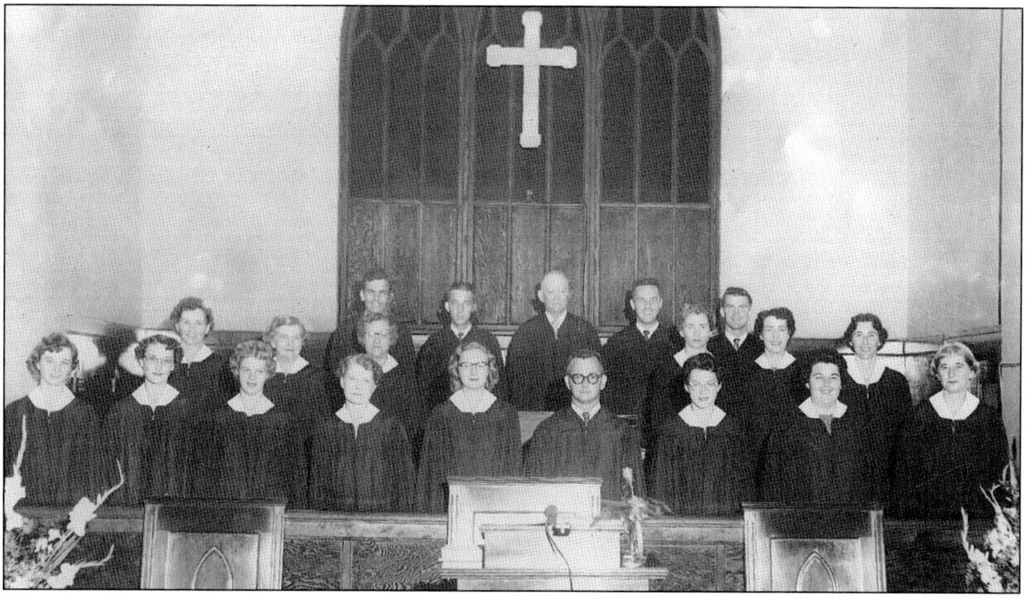

**CHURCH CHOIR.** The choir of First Methodist is pictured in the old sanctuary. Choir members included in this photograph are, from left to right, (first row) Abbie Fortner, Evelyn Painter, Lenora Arthur, Dot H. Beatty, Shirley Robinson, Bob Black, unidentified, June Garrett, and Martha Benfield; (second row) Mary Fortner, Macie Henson, Jett Black, Grace Cloninger, Pudgie Jones, and Wrene Benfield; (third row) Gene Painter, Benny Carpenter, W.G. Henson, Gene Hendrix, and Ralph Hamilton. (Courtesy of First United Methodist Church.)

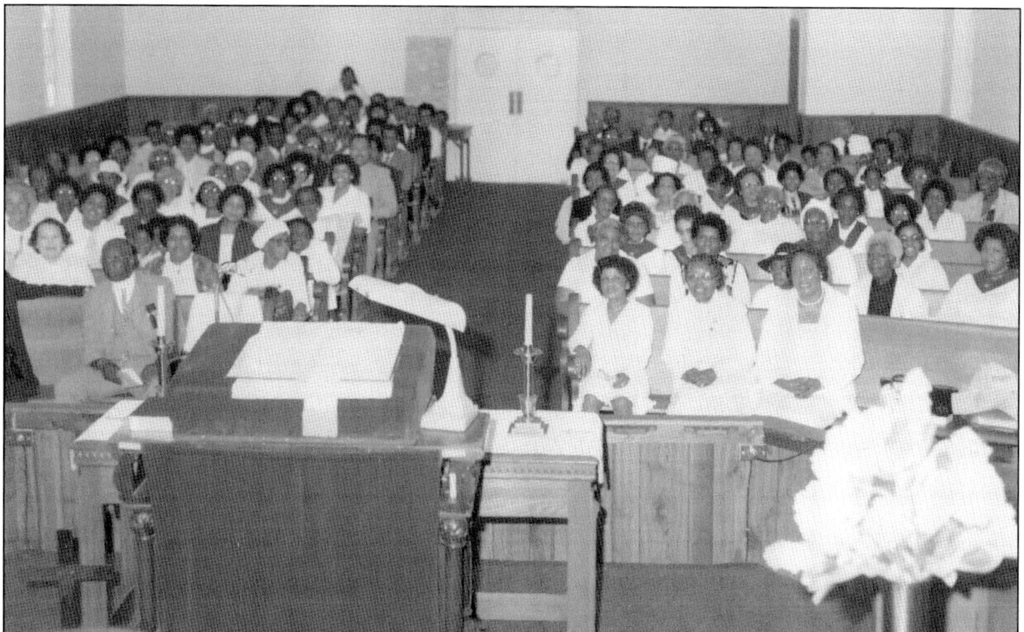

**AWAITING THE PASTOR.** A full house of congregants awaits the beginning of services at Shiloh African Methodist Episcopal Zion Church, west of downtown Mount Holly near Lowland Dairy Farm Road. Through the years, Frederick Douglass, Harriet Tubman, and Sojourner Truth were all members of the AME Zion denomination. (Courtesy of Essie Mae McGill.)

*Three*

# Harnessing the River

## Local Industry

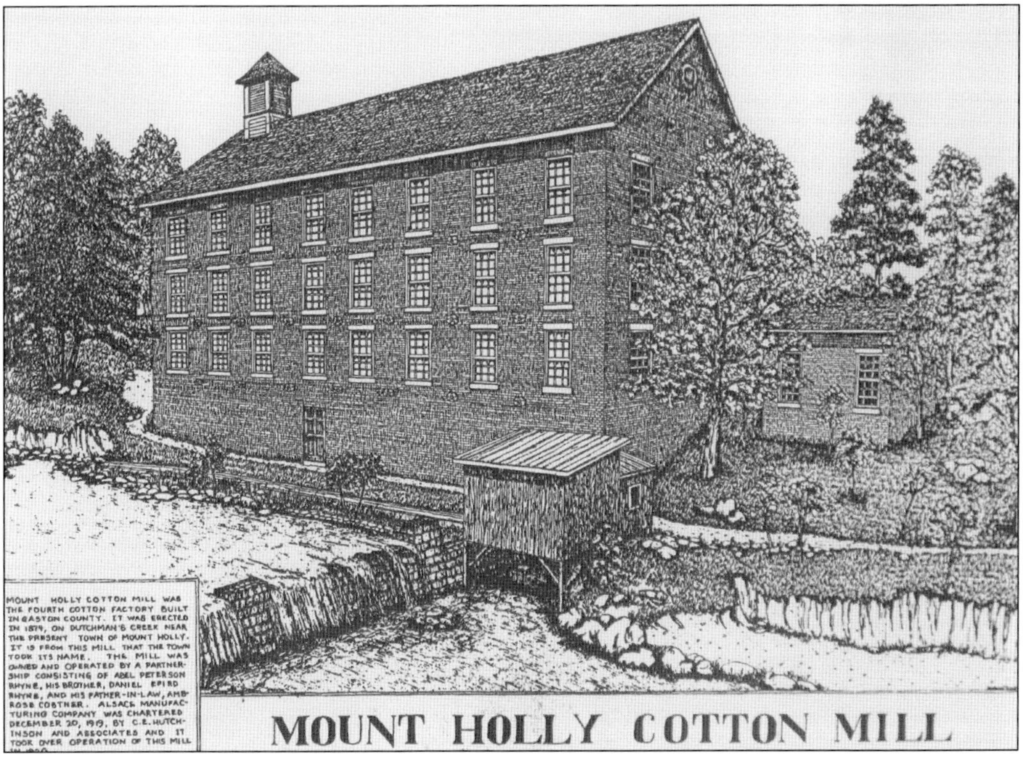


**The Spark that Started It All.** Completed in 1875, the Mount Holly Cotton Mill was the first mill built in Gaston County after the Civil War. This mill ignited the textile revolution in Gaston County and beyond. It acted as the model for other early textile entrepreneurs, including Charles E. Hutchison, Robert L. Stowe, Abel C. Lineberger, and Robert C.G. Love. It still stands on Dutchman's Creek. (Courtesy of the Gaston County Museum of Art and History.)

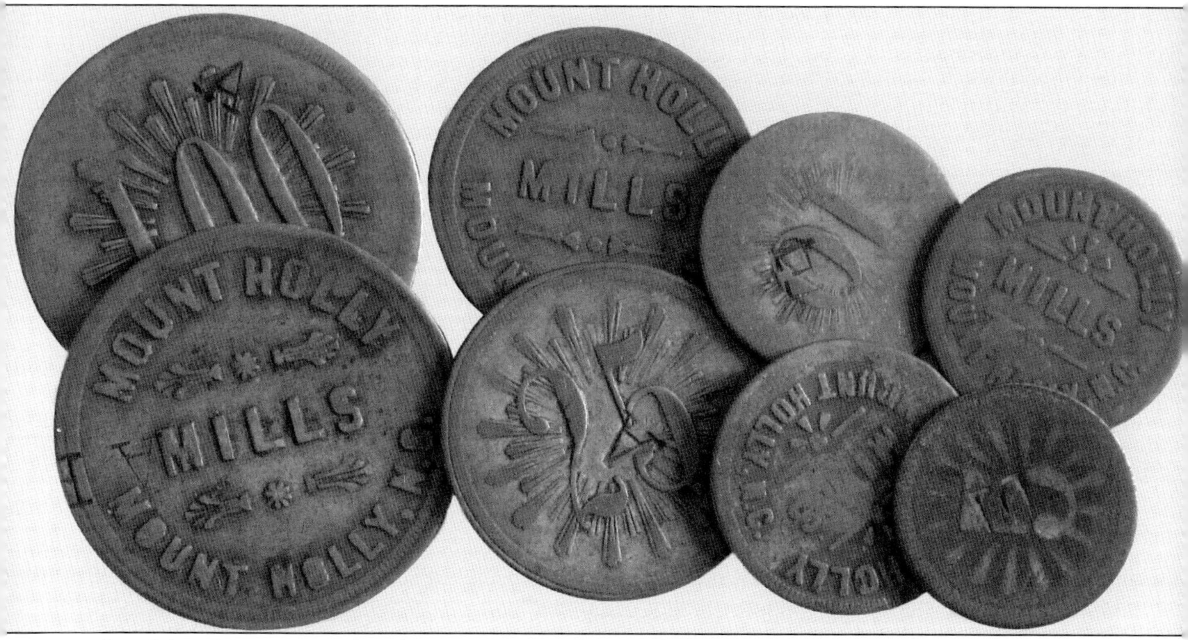

**Old Mill Money.** Hard cash was scarce in the South following the devastation from the Civil War and the postwar period called Reconstruction. The coins pictured above were issued by the Mount Holly Mills to be used as a medium of exchange. This Mount Holly Mills money was paid to employees, and in turn, it was accepted by most, if not all, of the merchants in the community. On March 14, 1879, the North Carolina Legislature ratified the incorporation of the Woodlawn village, which changed its name to Mount Holly. By 1883, the Rhyne brothers, Abel P. and Daniel, had two mills in Mount Holly, the Mount Holly Mill on Dutchman's Creek and the Tuckaseege Manufacturing Company on the Catawba River. Pictured are tokens with values of 100 ($1), 25¢, 10¢, and 5¢. (Photograph by Rick Hauser.)

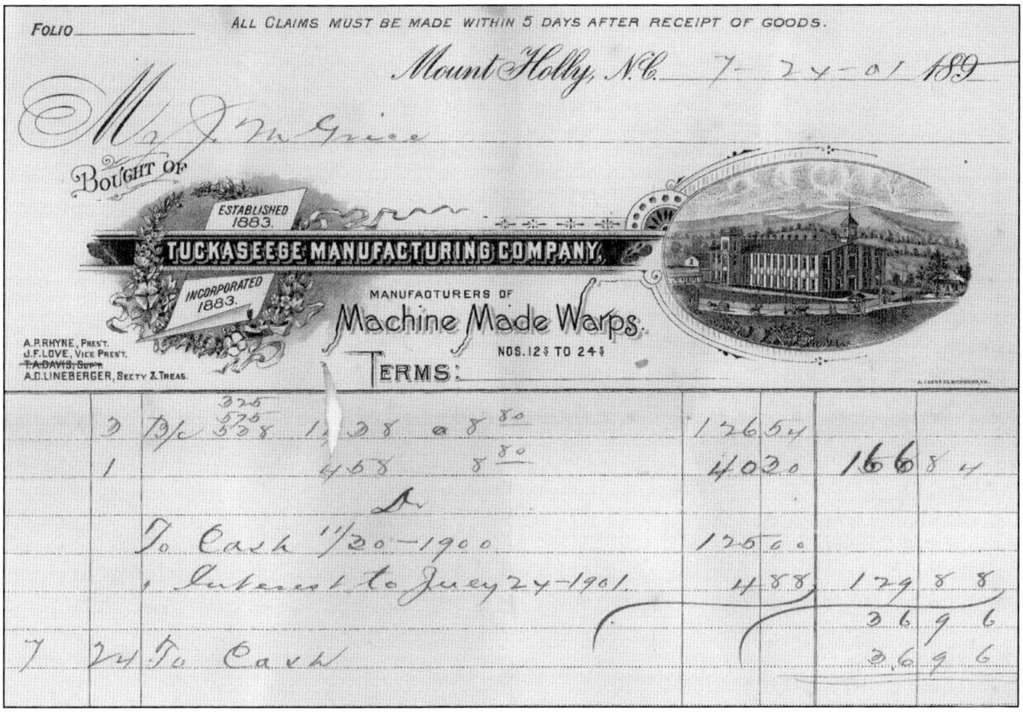

FOLIO

ALL CLAIMS MUST BE MADE WITHIN 5 DAYS AFTER RECEIPT OF GOODS.

Mount Holly, N.C. 7-24-01 ~~189~~

M Mr J. McGrice

BOUGHT OF

ESTABLISHED 1883.

TUCKASEEGE MANUFACTURING COMPANY.

INCORPORATED 1883.

MANUFACTURERS OF

Machine Made Warps.

NOS. 12S TO 24S

A.P. RHYNE, PRES'T.
J.F. LOVE, VICE PRES'T.
~~T.A. DAVIS, SUP'T.~~
A.C. LINEBERGER, SECTY & TREAS.

TERMS:

| | | | | |
|---|---|---|---|---|
| 3 | B/C 1,438 @ 8 80 | | 126 54 | |
| 1 | 458 8 80 | | 40 30 | 166 84 |
| | Cr | | | |
| | To Cash 11/20-1900 | | 125 00 | |
| | " Interest to July 24-1901 | | 4 88 | 129 88 |
| | | | | 36 96 |
| 7 | 24 To Cash | | | 36 96 |

**TUCKASEEGE MANUFACTURING COMPANY.** Tuckaseege Manufacturing Company's invoice (above) had an engraved, stylized image (below) that depicted the building's architectural details, the beautiful site, the horse-drawn wagons, and one rider on horseback. The Tuckaseege mill was built in 1883, the second factory in the new town of Mount Holly. It was built by the Rhyne brothers (Abel P. and "Uncle Dan") and T.A. Davis. Abel C. Lineberger, who became a textile legend, was hired as superintendent in 1884 and worked there until 1910. The Tuckaseege mill looked like a wilderness after the flood of 1916. Mud on the floor was eight inches deep, and all the machinery had to be sandpapered. Hanging on the wall of the mill was the coat of Stowe Huffstetler, just as he had left it—except the pockets were full of river mud. (Courtesy of C. Alexander.)

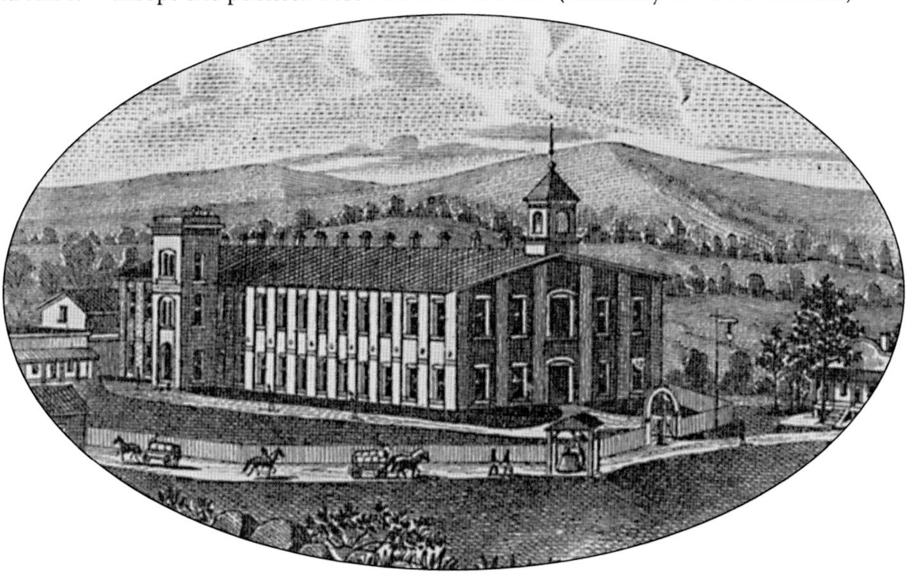

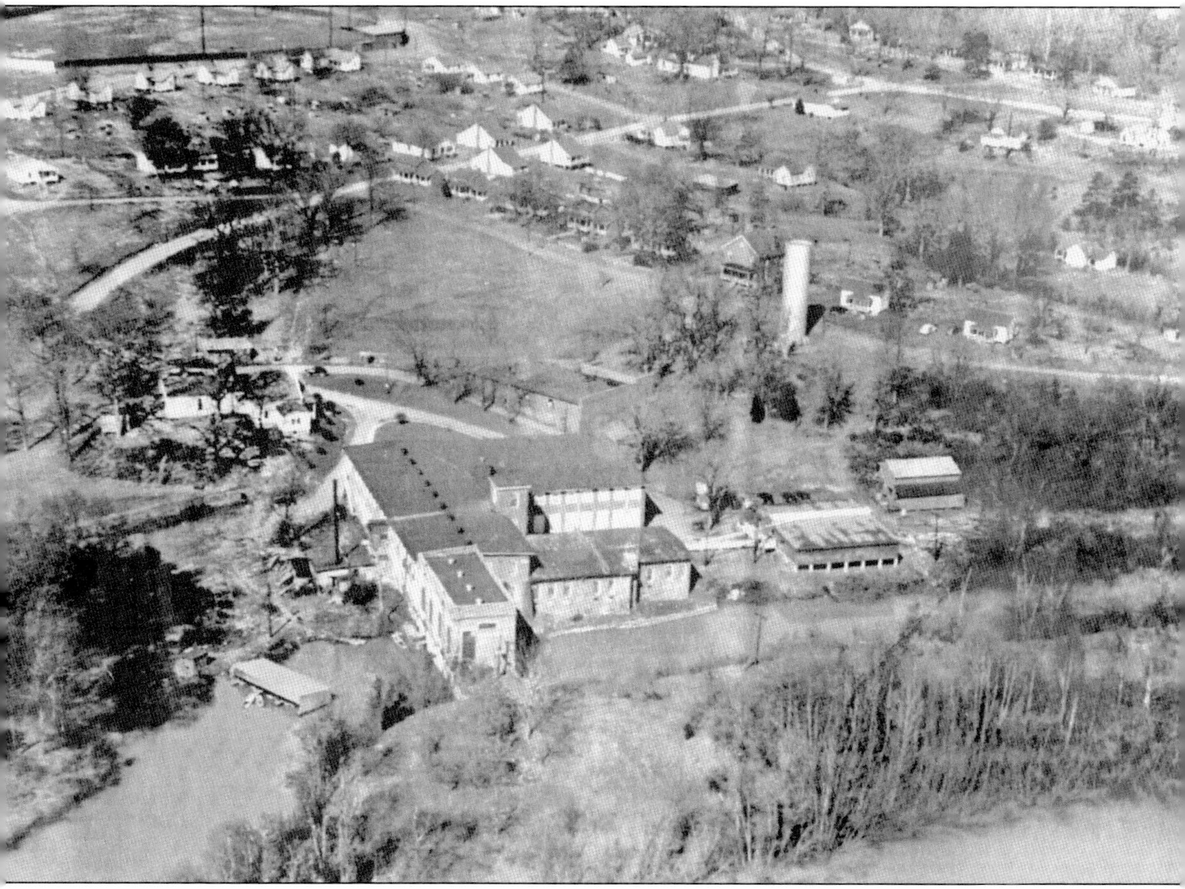

**Tuckaseege Mill and Village.** This mill, the seventh in the county, was located near the western landing of historic Tuckaseege Ford. The plant was greatly damaged by the flood of 1916, which completely swept away the Mountain Island Mill to the north. Note the power plant that extends over the water mill race at bottom left. Over the years, the Tuckaseege mill changed hands a number of times, and it became Superior Yarn Mills in 1929. A large, close-knit community developed around the factory, the mill store, and the mill village, informally named Tuckaseege. In 1890, the mill store was managed by the son of Robert C.G. Love, Edgar Love, who later co-owned two mills and a store in Lincolnton. As this photograph shows, the large mill was the centerpiece of the entire village community. Today, the property closest to the river is the Riverfront residential development and marina. (Courtesy of Millican Pictorial History Museum.)

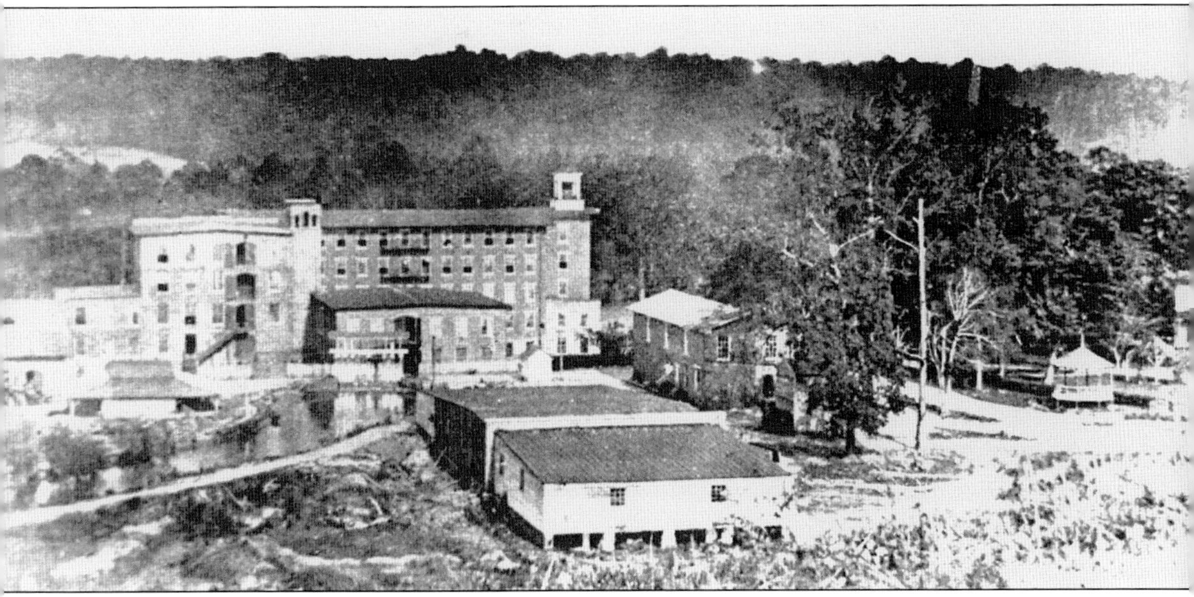

**Swept Away by the Flood.** Built in 1848, Mountain Island Manufacturing was a colossal complex. By the early 20th century, it was five stories high and employed hundreds of workers. It is hard to imagine the unpredictable, awesome power of the river before dams were introduced. Consider the following excerpt from the journal of Jim Parker, a mill supervisor for the Mountain Island Mill: "May 22, 1901. High water again. Catawba on rampage rising rapidly. Highest last night about one o'clock. Water up to top sills of cotton warehouse, dry and warp room. Lots of Indian skeletons washed up in Beatty's Bottoms." In 1916, the Catawba unleashed its full fury, as a flood, stoked by hurricanes dropping two feet of rain over Asheville, swept through the mill and then further downstream swept through the town of Mount Holly. Locals recovered the tower bell, which now sits silent in the Mount Holly Municipal Complex. (Courtesy of Millican Pictorial History Museum.)

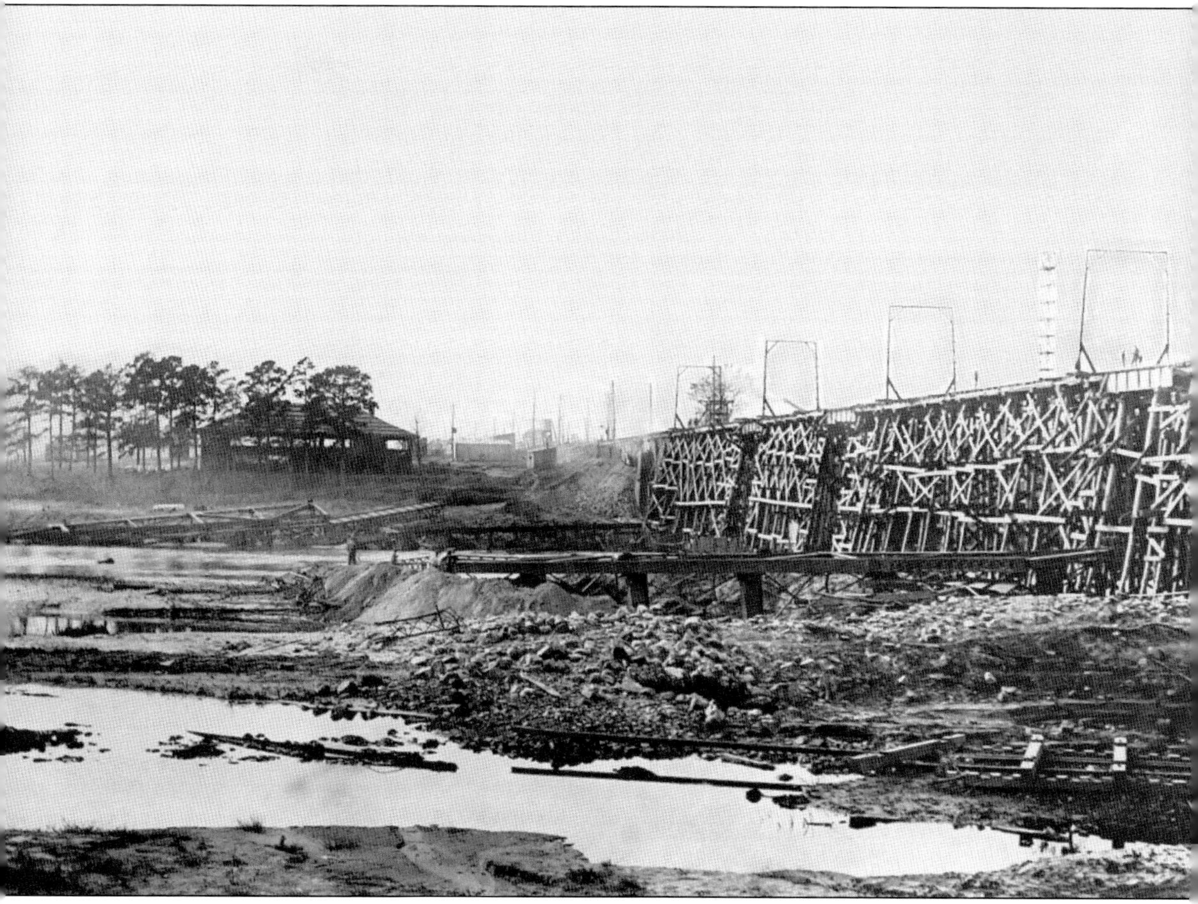

**1916 Flood.** The Catawba River railroad trestle had to be rebuilt after the flood of 1916 washed the bridge away, along with rail workers who were there trying to strengthen it against the floodwaters. Some of the men were rescued clinging to trees downstream, but 19 died. A 1997 *Mount Holly News* article by Willie Springs mentioned the "beautiful big park down by the River, just below the Piedmont and Northern bridge, where many teachers would treat their students, once a year, to a march down to the park to eat their lunches. On the bank above the river there was a large pavilion with a big dance floor." The pavilion can be seen in this photograph, to the left of the wooden bridge within the trees. Notice the tall masts over the tracks, indicating the electric lines of the Piedmont and Northern train. (Courtesy of Millican Pictorial History Museum.)

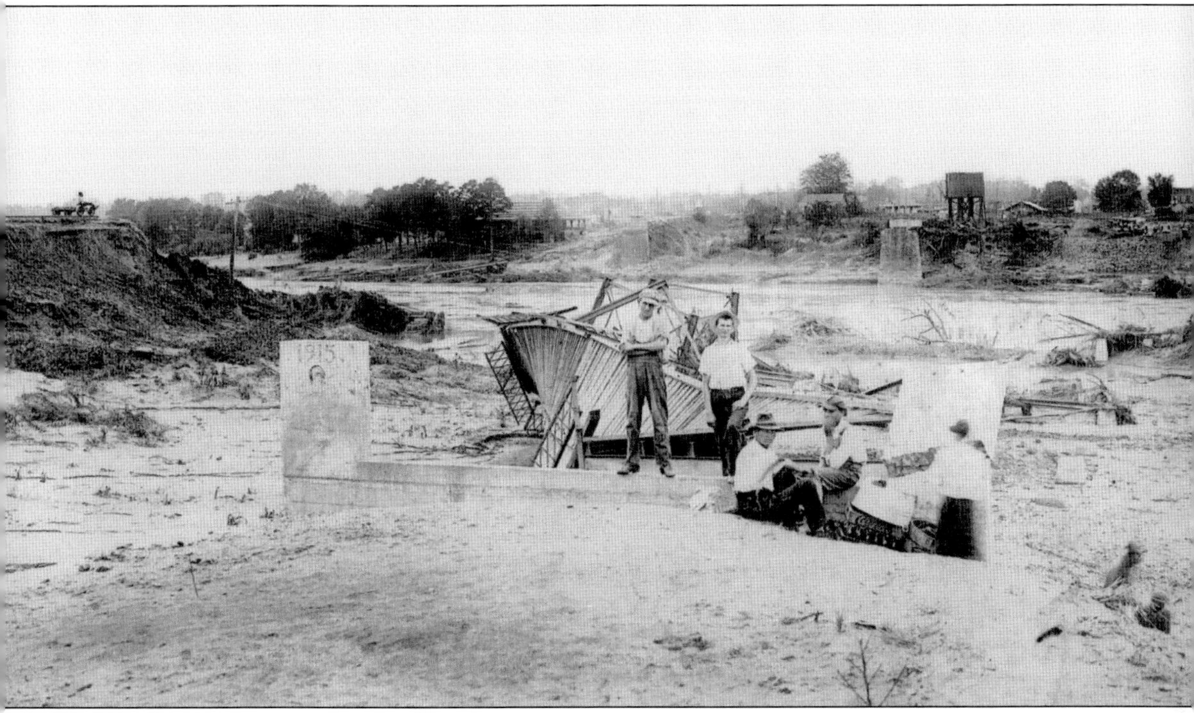

**CATAWBA RIVER HAVOC.** Two Category 4 hurricanes converged over North Carolina, causing more than three days of downpours. Southern Railway reported that all 24-hour records for rainfall in the United States were exceeded. The flood made a clean sweep of all railroad and highway bridges that crossed the Catawba River. Cotton bales swept away from Mountain Island Mill were snared in midstream by large trees and bridge timbers. According to eyewitnesses, local boys risked life and limb for pocket change pulling the bales out of the logjams. This photograph was shot looking across the river toward Mount Holly, where the water rose all the way into what is now downtown. It was two years before a new highway bridge was constructed. At first, the people of Mount Holly had to be satisfied with a ferry service; then, a pine-pole toll bridge was erected. (Courtesy of Millican Pictorial History Museum.)

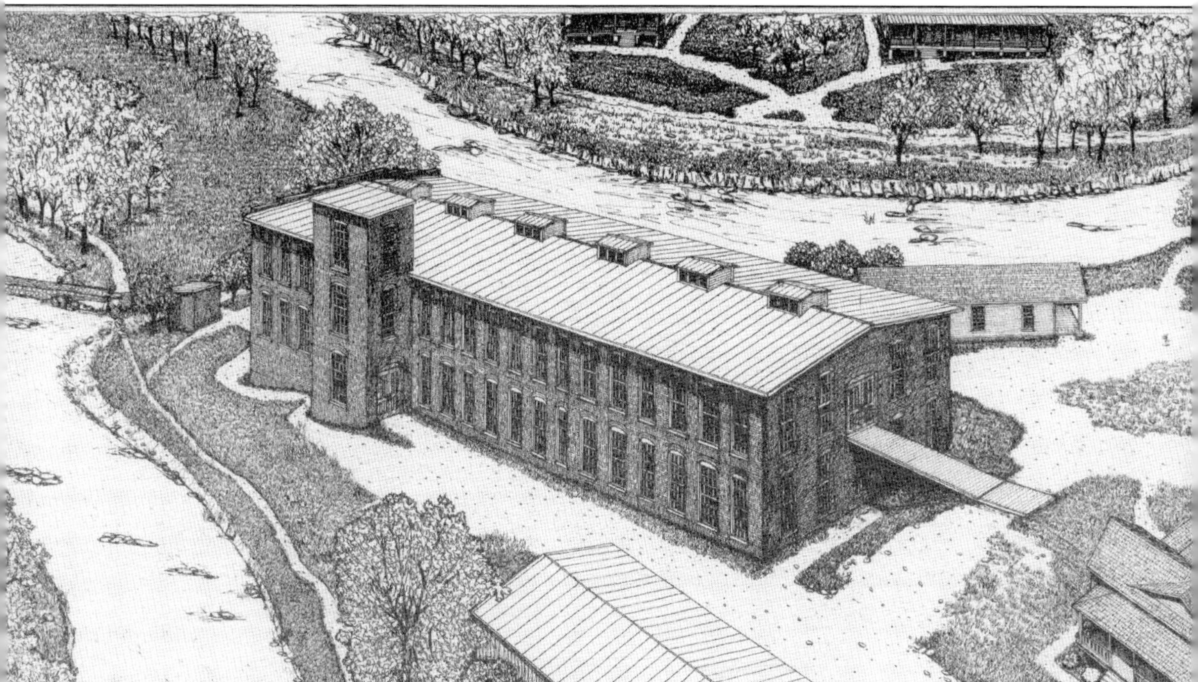


**Nims Manufacturing Company.** The partners Charles E. Hutchison, Ike Lowe, Luther Nims, Richard K. Davenport, M.R. Dewstoe, J. Alonzo Abernathy, and John C. Rankin established the Nims Manufacturing Company in 1891. Only one of the men, Dewstoe, had any previous textile experience. The plant was located at the oxbow (Nim's Shoals) of Dutchman's Creek, about one mile north of the center of Mount Holly. To power the mill, the owners dammed the creek and installed a narrow canal—a millrace—to accelerate the water. To house the workers, the partnership built a village of home-like cottages, each incorporating a front porch with a distinctive gabled roof. Some of these houses still exist along Woodlawn Avenue. Later called the Rush Plant, named for Rush Dickson, Nims Mill was the first mill in the now global textile enterprise of American and Efird, Inc. (Courtesy Gaston County Museum of Art and History.)

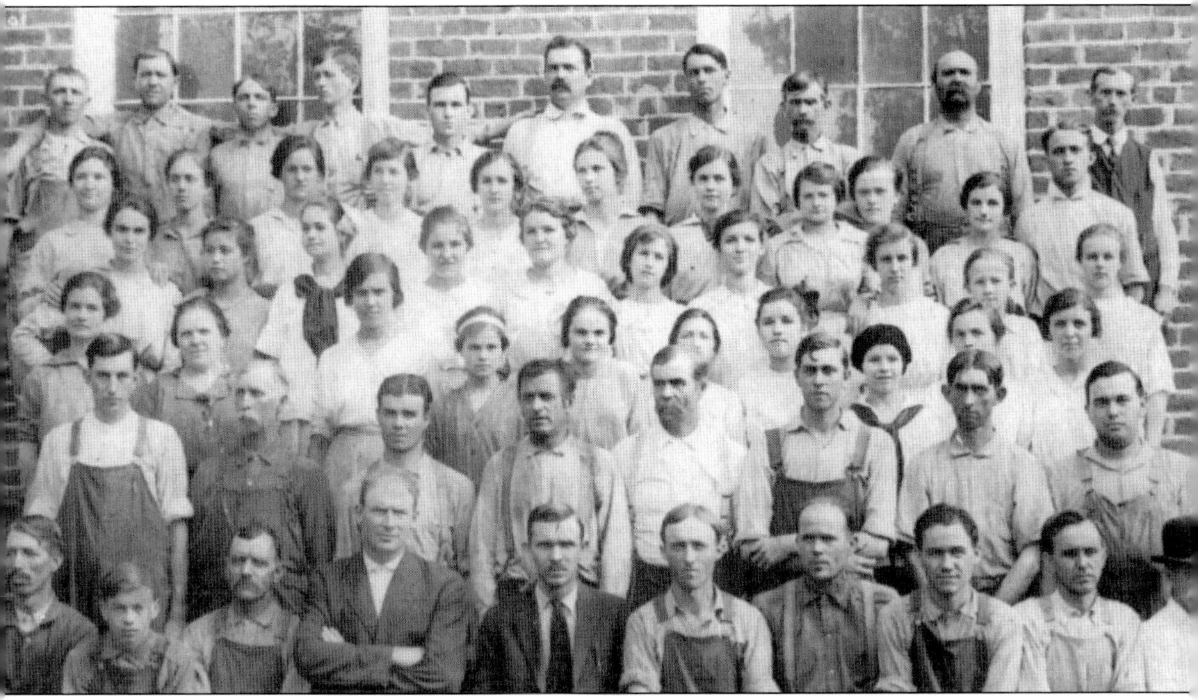

**TEXTILE WORKERS AT NIMS MILL, 1915.** The *Southern Textile Bulletin* of December 1918 stated, "The Nims Manufacturing Company has 8,100 spindles and is operated by electric power." Note the youth of the women workers. The authors of *Like A Family, the Making of a Southern Cotton Mill World* state that "before World War I, the typical female laborer was either a widow working until her children could take her place in the mill or a young woman earning an income until she could marry and start a family of her own. . . . With the decline of child labor, however, adult women returned to the mills to stay. In 1920 the majority of women workers were between the ages of fifteen and twenty-four; in 1940 they were between twenty-five and forty-four." Many of these workers were recruited from poor mountain communities. (Courtesy of Millican Pictorial History Museum.)

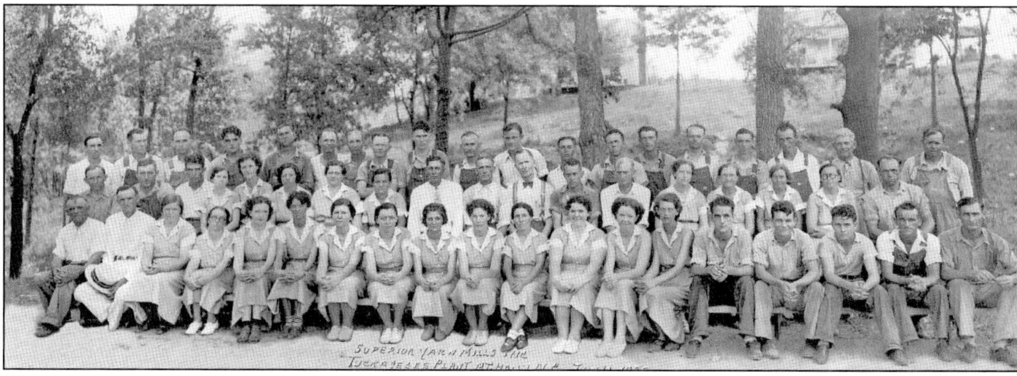

**SUPERIOR YARNS, MOUNT HOLLY, 1935.** This photograph of workers was taken during the Great Depression. Unemployment still raged on a national basis. In 1935, Congress passed the Social Security Act, which set up a program to ensure an income for the elderly. (Courtesy of Millican Pictorial History Museum.)

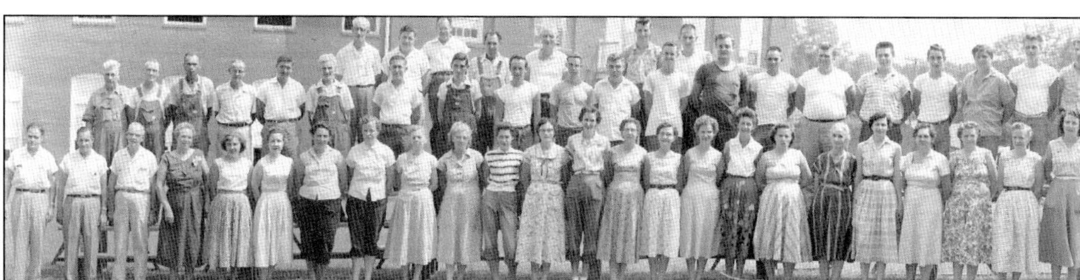

**SUPERIOR YARNS, MOUNT HOLLY, 1957.** Note the relatively older age of the women shown here as compared to those on page 43. After World War I, more women held jobs while raising families as well as after their families were grown. These women were certainly not the stay-at-home stereotypes portrayed in popular television shows of the time, such as *The Donna Reed Show* and *Leave It to Beaver.* (Courtesy of Millican Pictorial History Museum.)

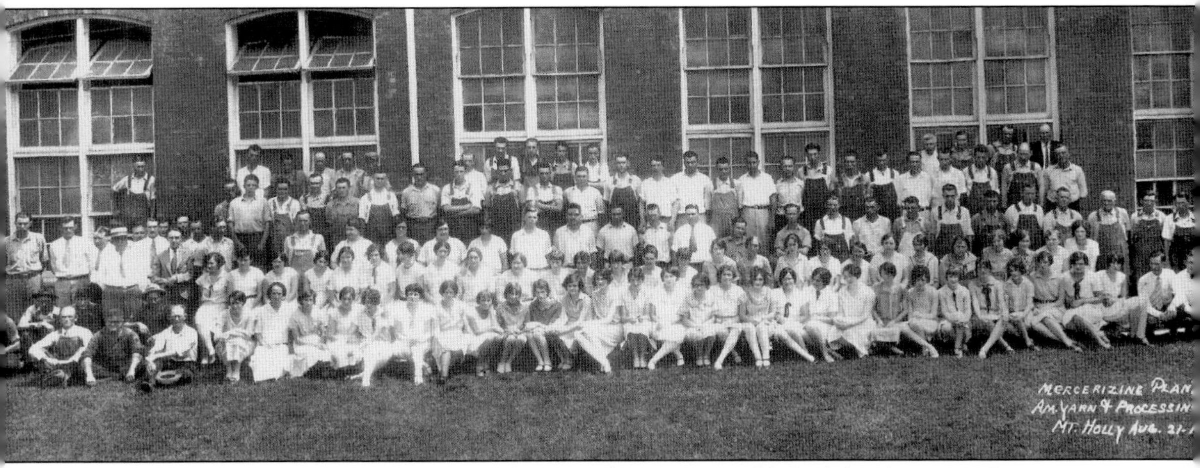

**AMERICAN PLANT, 1928.** Charles E. Hutchison and partners established the American Processing Company in 1918. All of their previous mills had manufactured yarn. To diversify their product line, they built a yarn processing plant to treat the yarn for various applications. By the 1890s, American manufacturers had significantly improved a cotton yarn process that made the yarn both lustrous and receptive to dye. This process, called mercerizing for its British inventor, John Mercer, required large water resources to wash the caustic chemical treatments from the yarn. Thus, the diversified mill corporation was now called the American Yarn and Processing Company. Mercerizing would become an integral part of the company over the years, and a brand of the mercerized cotton yarn product, Durene, would become a household name in Mount Holly and the nation. The photograph shows workers at the American Processing plant, still standing on American Street near the river. (Courtesy of Millican Pictorial History Museum.)

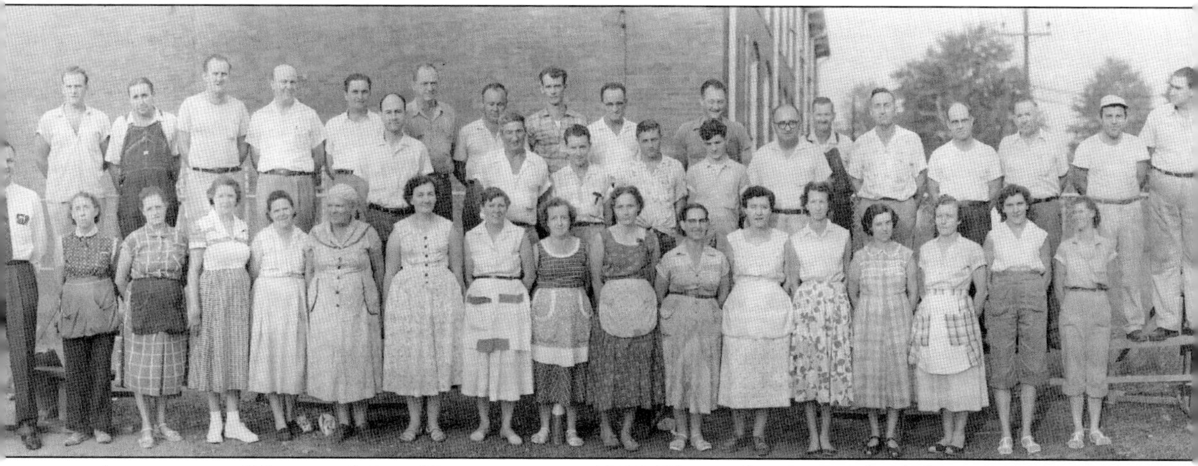

**ADRIAN AND MADORA MILLS EMPLOYEES, C. 1957.** These plants were built between 1916 and 1922 and were on each side of the Piedmont and Northern Railroad. The employees are standing in front of the Adrian facility. J. Frank Love Jr., superintendent of both plants, is on the left in the first row. He went on to become president of American and Efird Mills, Inc., from 1973 to 1984. Bill Rogers was overseer of the Adrian spinning, twisting, and winding departments and soon after became assistant superintendent of the Adrian plant. Rogers is at left in the second row that starts in the middle. Gib Pressley is at right in the second row. Pressley was overseer of the card room. The Adrian-Madora village is known for its tall oak trees and the Bright-Star drive-in restaurant. (Courtesy of the City of Mount Holly Archives.)

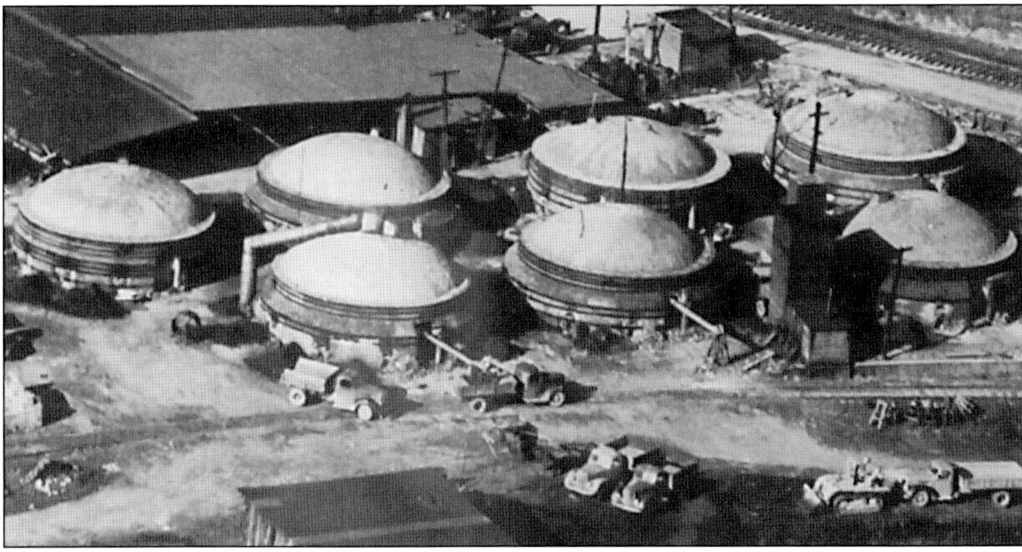

**KENDRICK BRICK AND TILE, C. 1950S.** In 1900, brothers J.W. and N.B. Kendrick began making bricks in Cleveland County, North Carolina. In 1915, a new site was purchased in Mount Holly, where they formally organized Kendrick Brick and Tile. Bricks from this facility were used in the building that housed Central Bank and Hotel Juliette (page 59). G.L. Kendrick was elected president in 1948. Kendrick Brick and Tile merged all subsidiaries with Boren Clay Products Company in 1961. The Mount Holly plant pictured below was located on West Central Avenue and operated until 1973. In the photograph above, notice the giant scale of the brick kilns towering over the large trucks. (Both, courtesy of Anne Kendrick Brinkley.)

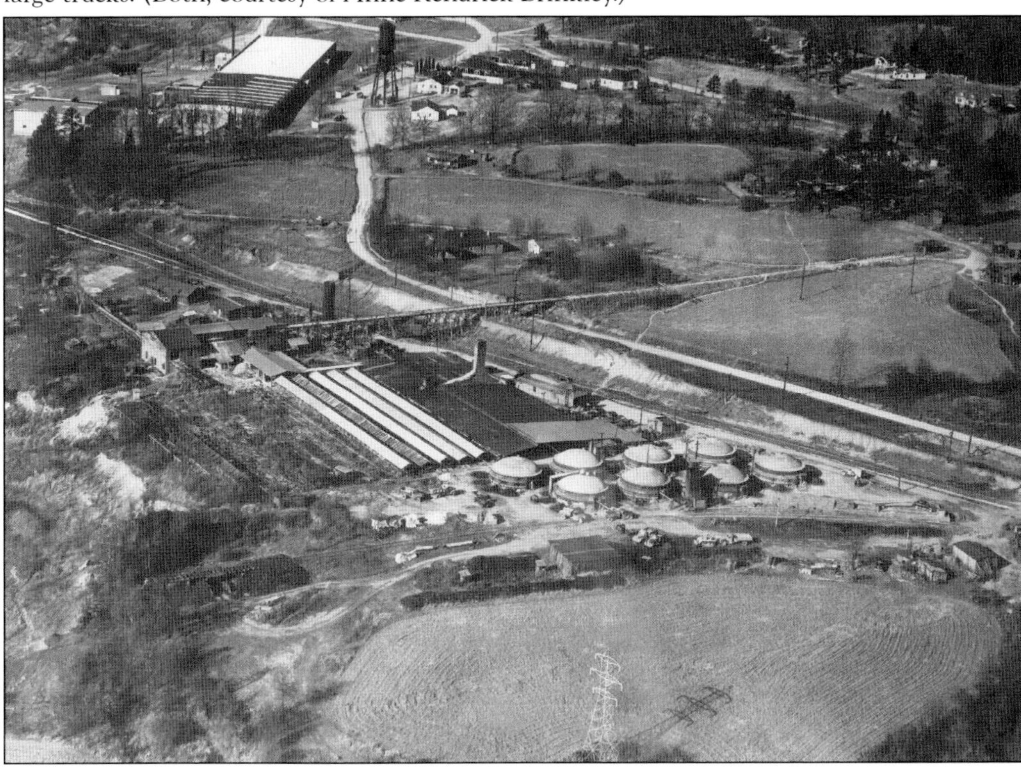

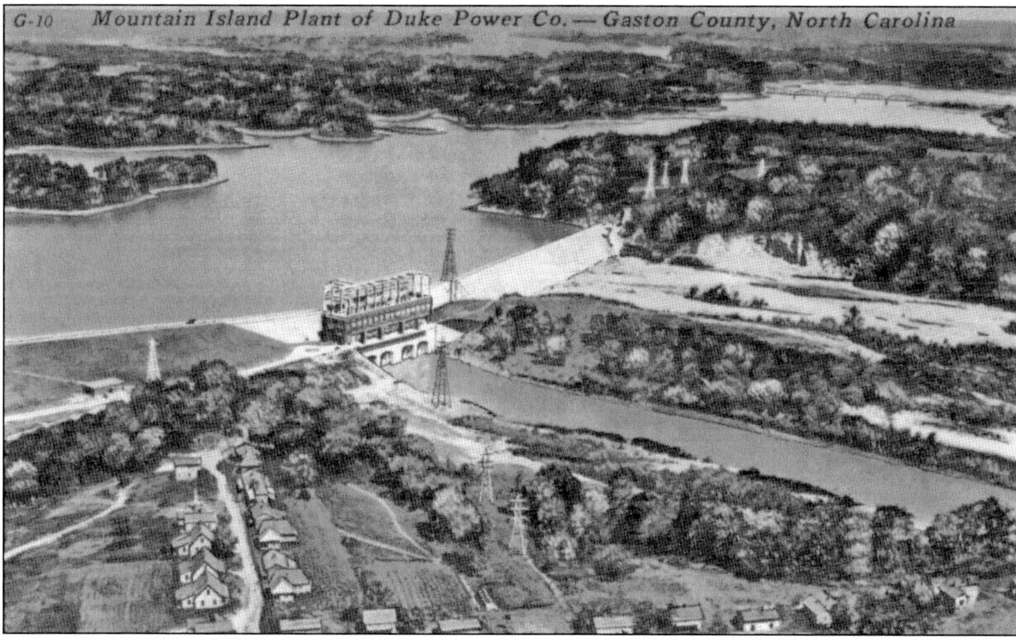


**Mountain Island Hydroelectric Plant.** The Duke Power dam formally came into service December 1923, seven years after the devastating flood that wiped out nearby Mountain Island Mill. Note the Duke employee village, which no longer exists. Oak trees planted by the villagers survive to this day. (Courtesy of C. Alexander.)

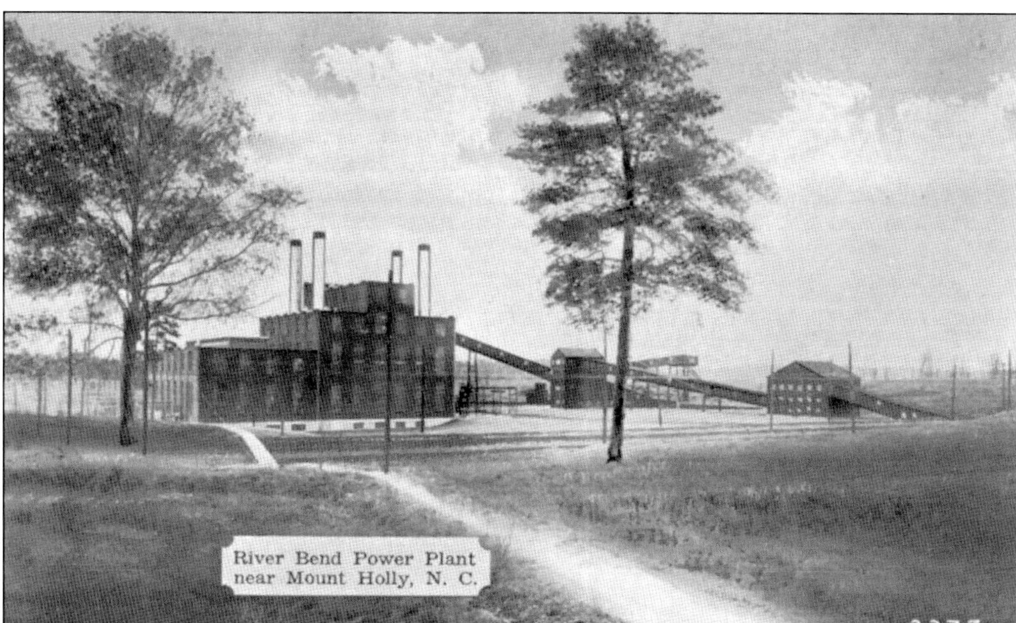


**River Bend Steam Station.** The River Bend Steam Station was completed in 1929. For decades, this was a base load plant that produced power for homes and industry 24 hours a day. It is named for a bend in the Catawba River on which it is located. (Courtesy of C. Alexander.)

*Four*

# THE BACKDROP OF LIFE
## TOWN LANDSCAPES

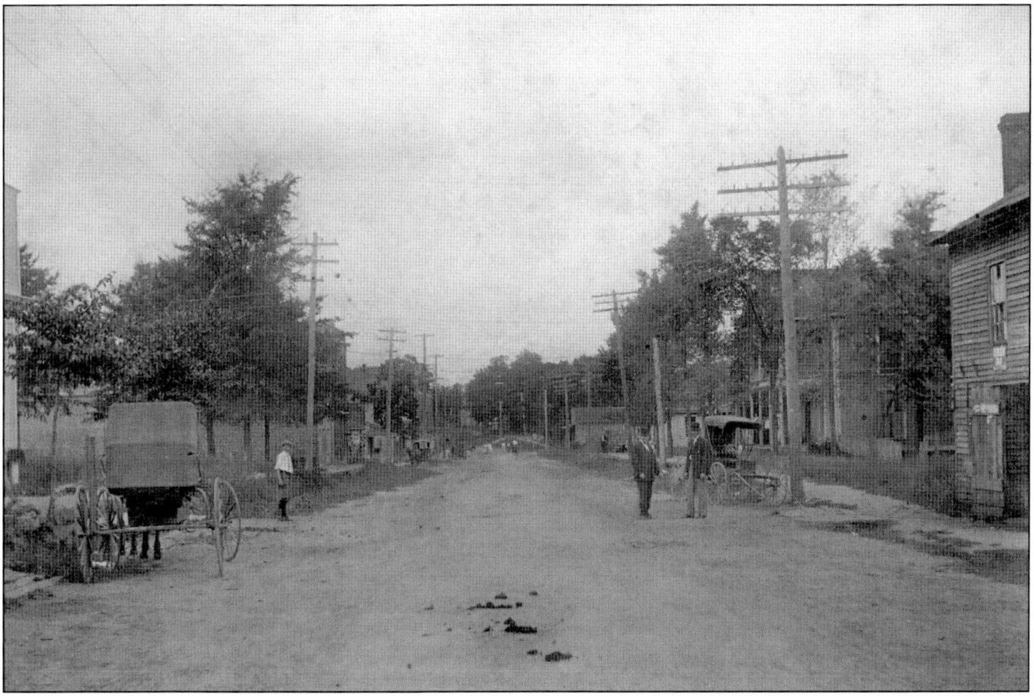

**A CENTURY AGO.** This early-1900s photograph shows South Main Street, looking north. The residue of horsepower is evident in the center of the street. The far left side of the photograph includes the edge of the Tucker-Springs store. The Central Hotel is second building, moving north on the right side of the street. The Hutchison-Davenport Store is in the distance on the left side. (Courtesy of Millican Pictorial History Museum.)

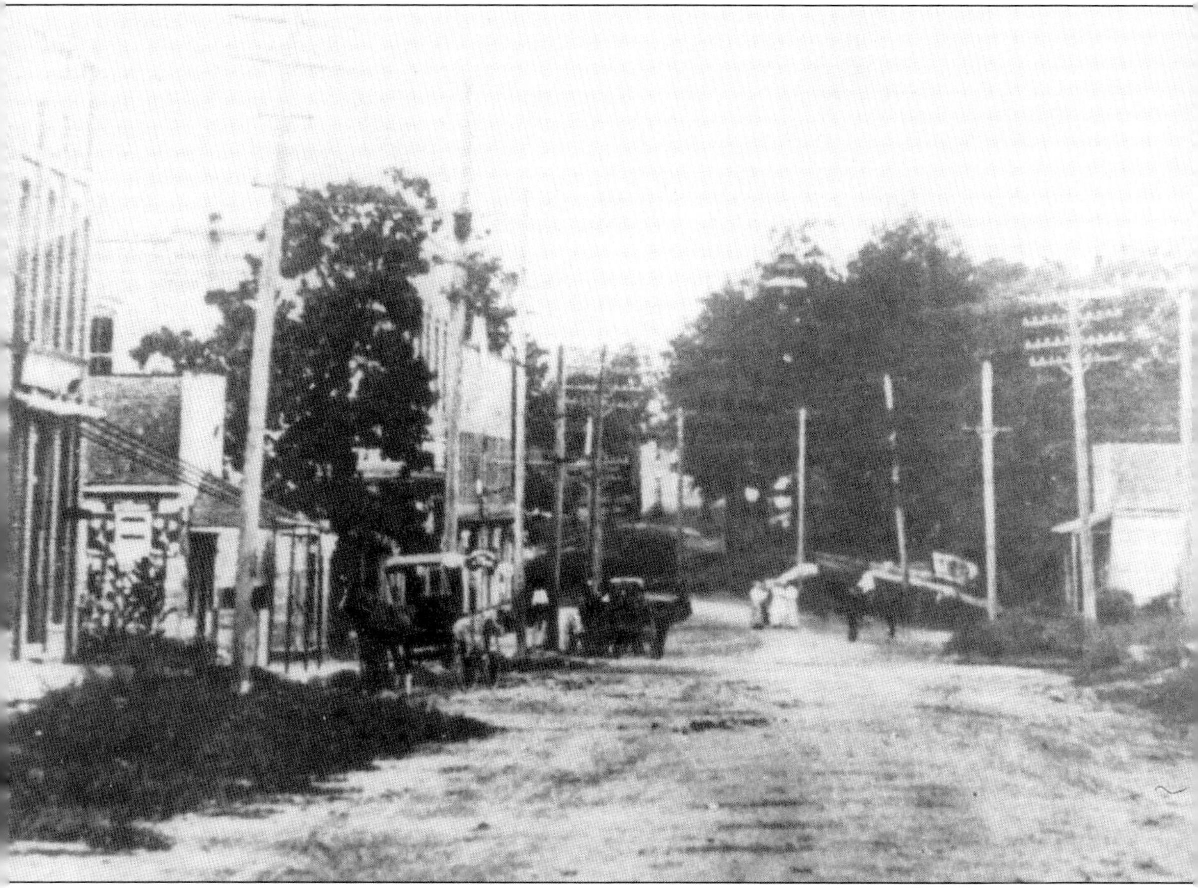

**SOUTH MAIN STREET, C. 1900.** Similar to the photograph on page 49, this image is of Main Street, looking farther north. The two-story Hutchison-Davenport Store, now 106 South Main Street, is on the left. Going north, the next building on the left, a frame structure with a porch, was replaced about 1905 by the Mount Holly Bank building, which still stands at the corner of South Main Street and West Central Avenue. Partially obscured by the tree, the Rhyne building and Farrar building are across the railroad tracks on the left. Note the center round arch parapet on the roof of the Farrar building. This central parapet was a special and recurring architectural theme in Mount Holly's downtown commercial buildings in the early part of the 20th century, topping the later Holland building on both east and west sides. (Courtesy of Millican Pictorial History Museum.)

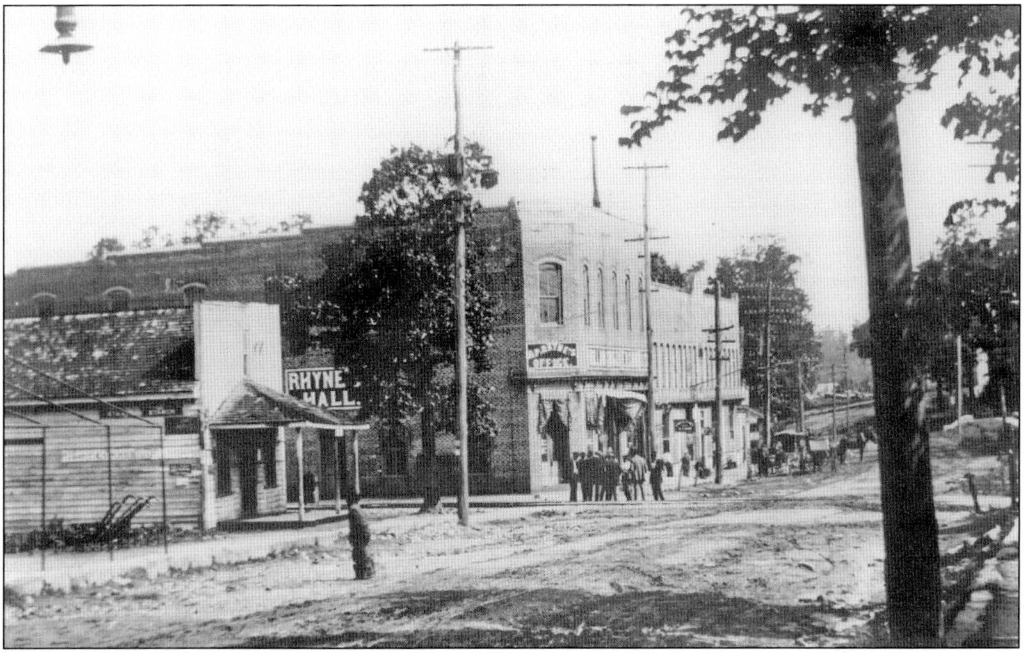


**RHYNE HALL.** The building in the center of the photograph contained Abel P. Rhyne's office and a general store. Local historian Mary Dunn Warren wrote, "In the upstairs of the Rhyne Building was a large auditorium, complete with a stage. The first high school graduations were held there." She continued, "The young people had dances and box suppers there." (Courtesy of C. Alexander.)

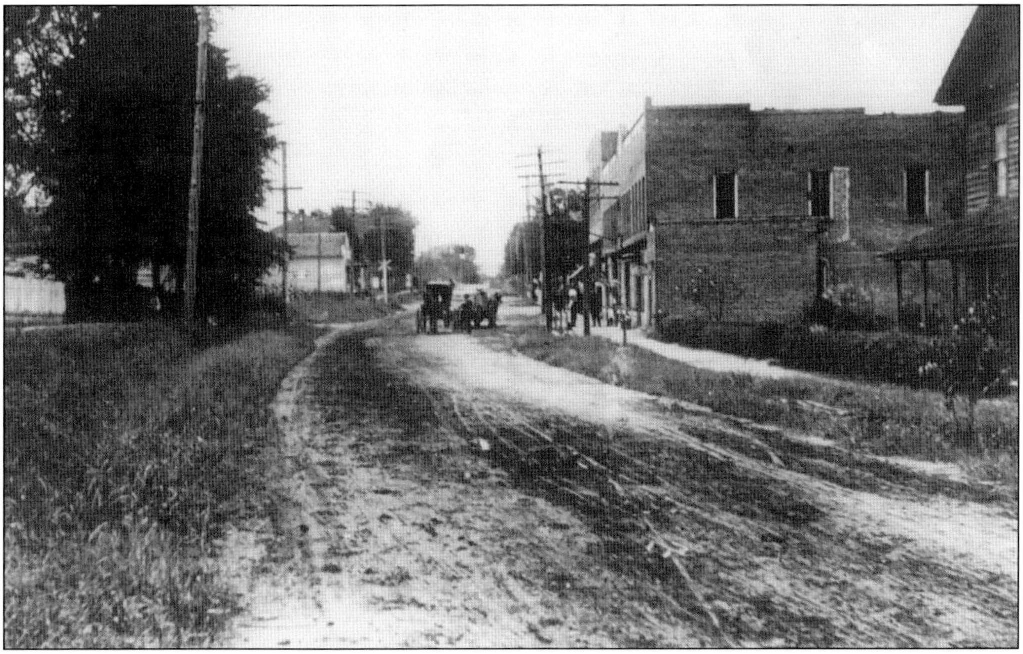

**NORTH MAIN STREET, LOOKING SOUTH, C. 1900.** The Farrar building is on the right, built less than a decade after the opening of the Mount Holly Cotton Mill. Note the dirt street and the rambling frame structure in the right foreground, now the location of the Kimbrell furniture building. (Courtesy of the City of Mount Holly Archives.)

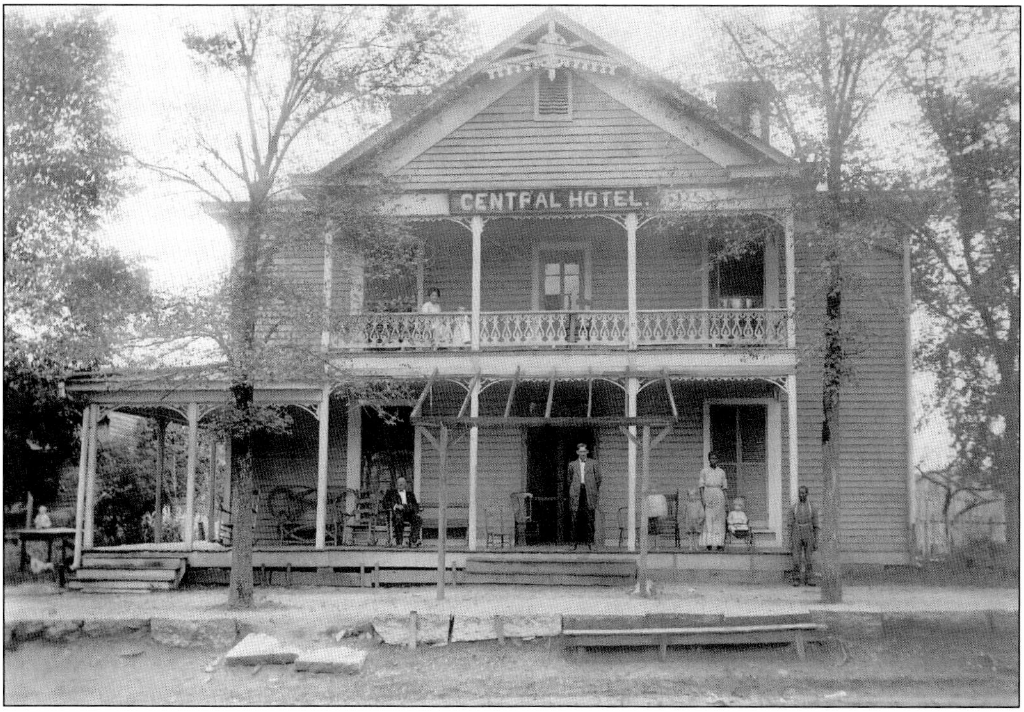


**CENTRAL HOTEL, C. 1900S.** The Central Hotel was built before 1900 and was located on the east side of South Main Street. The actual builder is unknown, but records indicate Margaret Hutchison, mother of textile magnate C.E. Hutchison, operated the hotel for several years after 1900. (Courtesy of Millican Pictorial History Museum.)

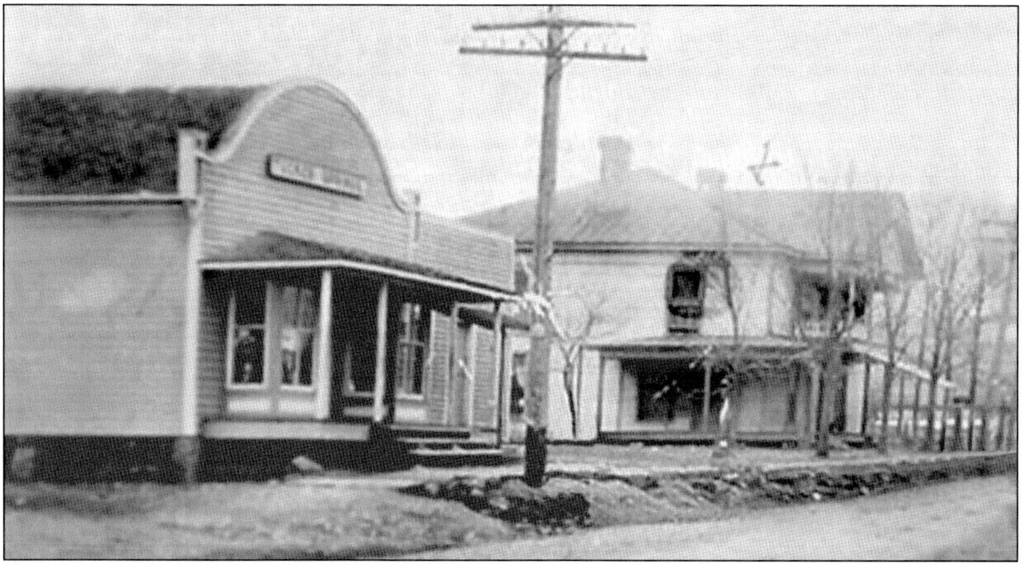

**TUCKER-SPRINGS STORE AND CENTRAL HOTEL.** The photograph was shot looking southeast along Main Street before 1915. The store in the foreground was one of two operated by Walter and John Tucker and Junius Springs. Mamie Tucker managed the hotel for a time after Margaret Hutchison. The store was near the east corner of Main Street and Central Avenue. (Courtesy of Millican Pictorial History Museum.)

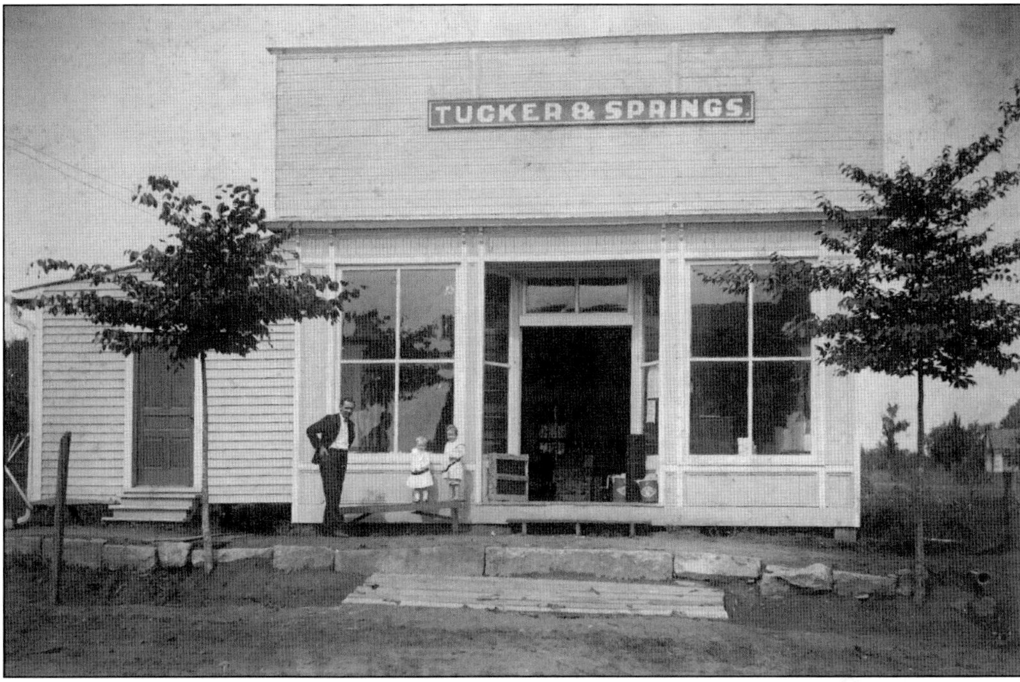


**TUCKER-SPRINGS STORE, WEST SIDE.** The busy merchants had two stores on the same block of South Main Street in the era before World War I. One store featured lighter merchandise, while the other had more substantial items, such as clothing and hardware. Note the young canopy trees, which have made a comeback on Main Street. (Courtesy of Millican Pictorial History Museum.)

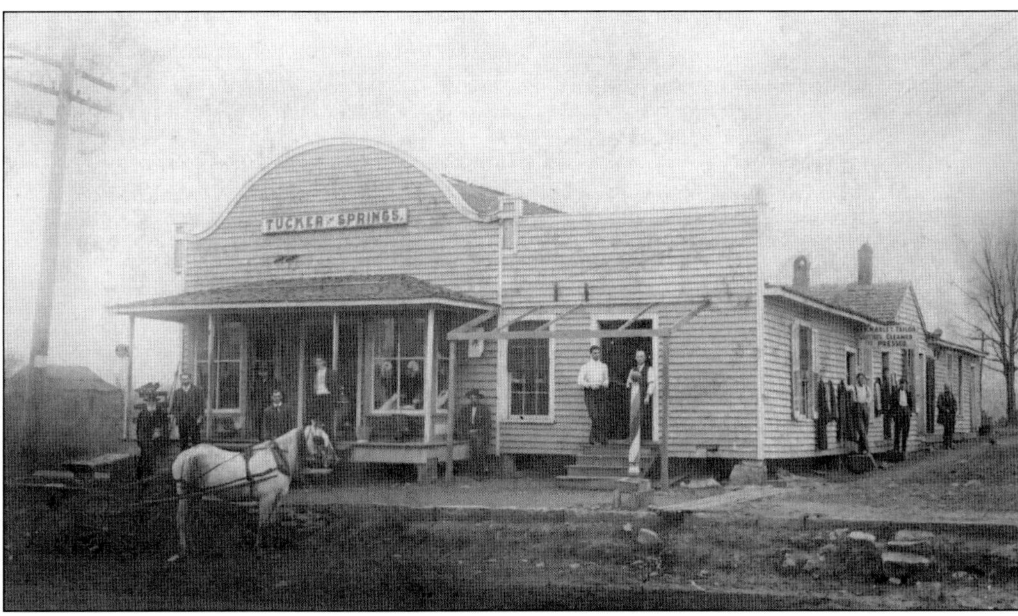

**TUCKER-SPRINGS STORE, EAST SIDE.** This store was just north of the Central Hotel. Note the laundry, with a sign that reads "Garments Cleaned and Pressed." By the 1920s, this store was replaced by brick structures that rose during the economic heyday of postwar America. (Courtesy of Millican Pictorial History Museum.)

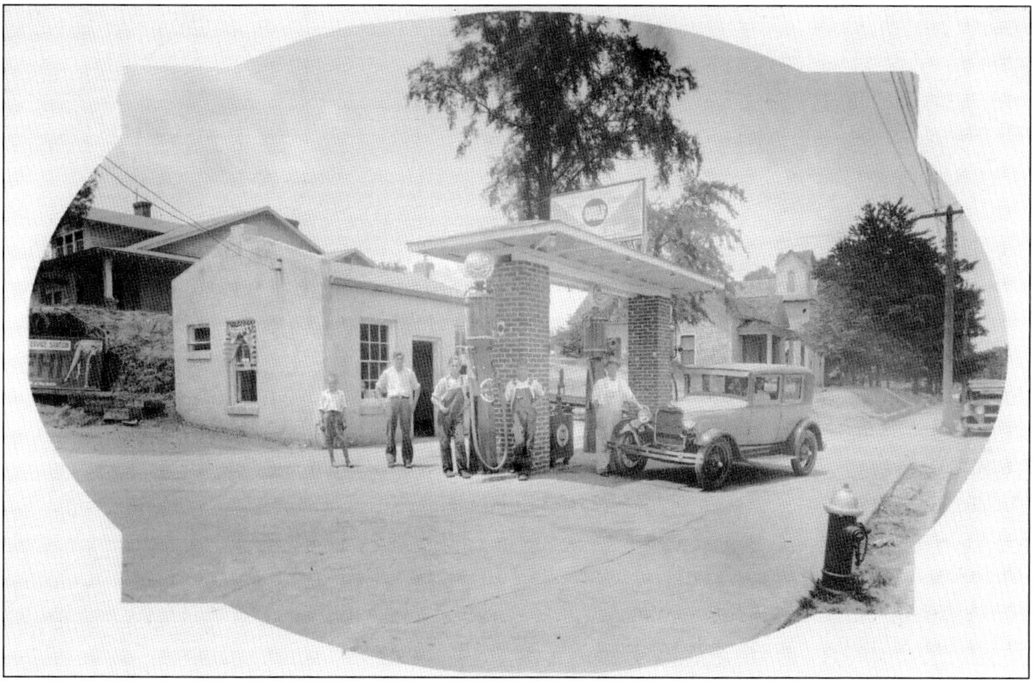

**TUCKER GASOLINE STATION, C. 1930S.** This scene is at the northwest corner of Main Street and Catawba Avenue. The man standing with his hand on the 1928 Chevrolet is Walter Tucker, the original owner of the station. Over the years, this station sold Gulf, Esso, and McCoy petroleum products. (Courtesy of the City of Mount Holly Archives.)

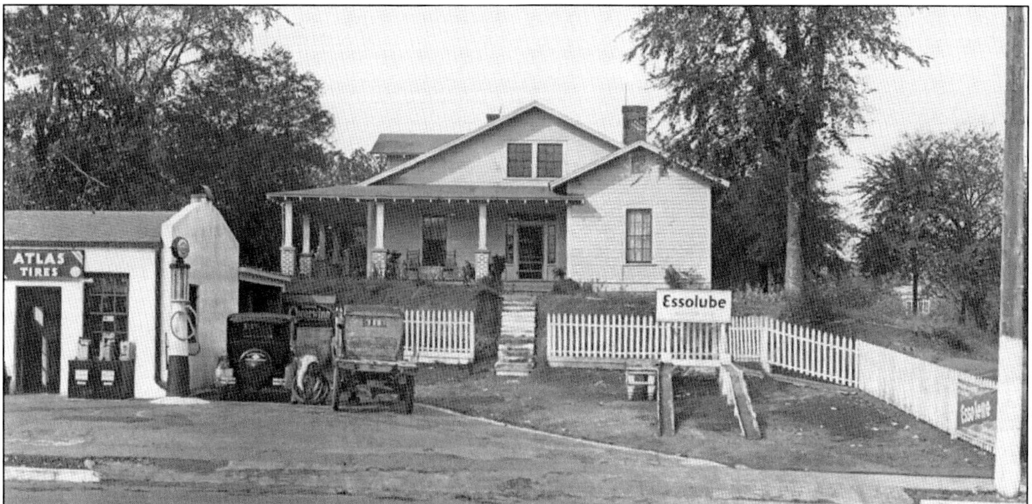


**TUCKER HOUSE AND GASOLINE STATION.** Legend says the house of Walter Tucker and family used to be closer to the corner and was moved by a large mule team to make way for the station. With the rapid expansion of automobiles in the 1920s, Tucker recognized that car service was the commercial business of the era. (Courtesy of Millican Pictorial History Museum.)

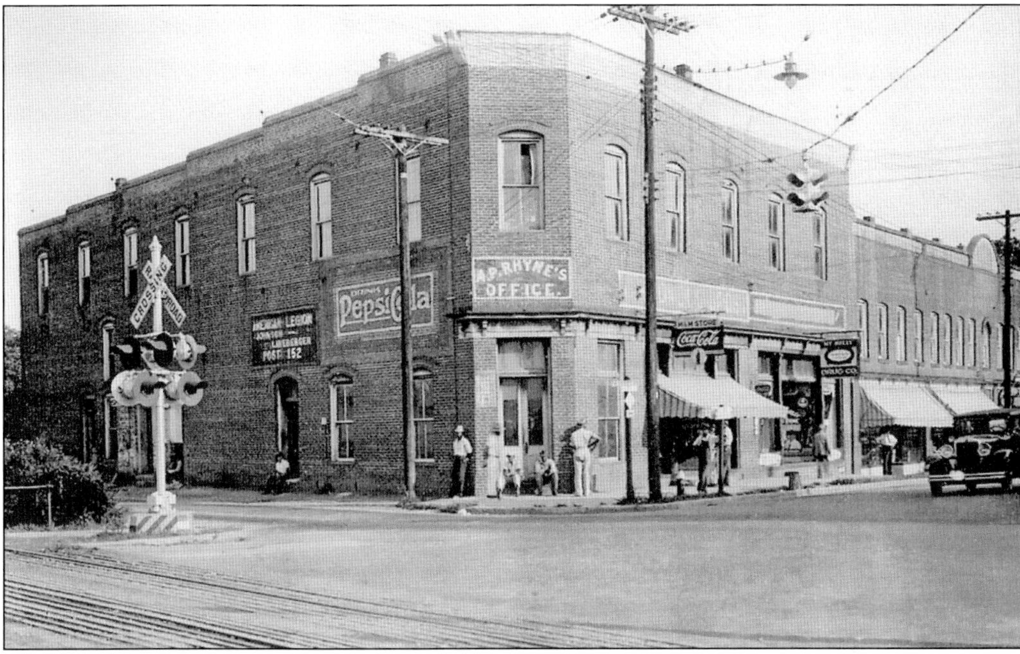


**Street Lights at the Rhyne Building, 1930.** Note the streetlight in front of the building. A.P. Rhyne owned the first electric system in Mount Holly. In 1893, a decade before Duke Power, Rhyne installed a generator at his mill on Dutchman's Creek. The generator supplied power to local businesses and town streetlights. (Courtesy of Millican Pictorial History Museum.)

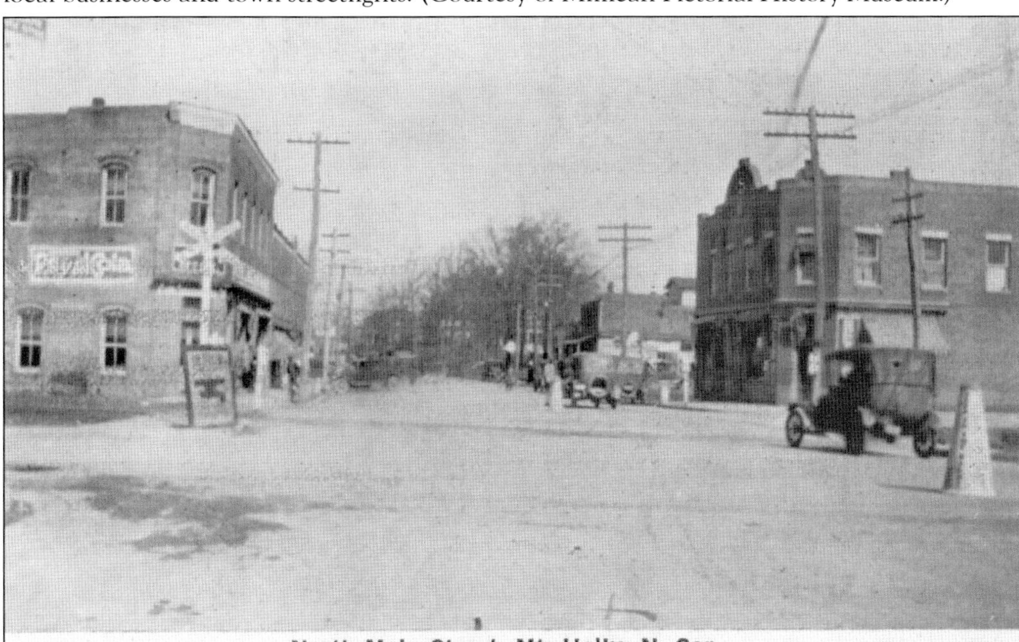


**North Main Street, c. 1920s.** The car in the foreground is crossing the railroad tracks. On the right is a good view of the central round arch parapet topping Holland Drug. Note the corner entrances of the buildings on both sides of the street. (Courtesy of the City of Mount Holly Archives.)

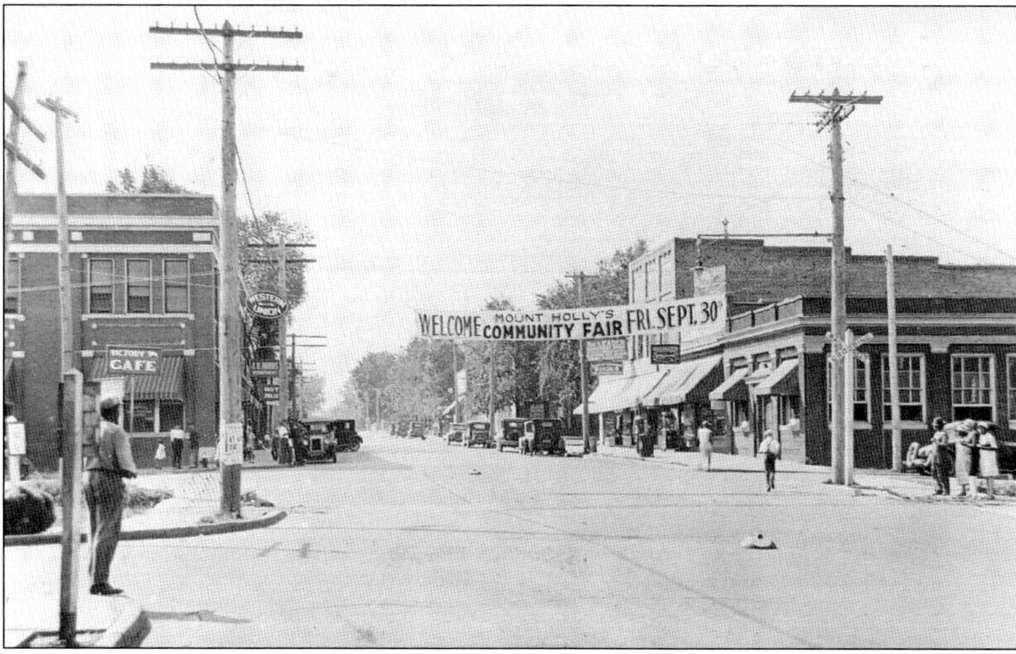


**TOWN SQUARE, 1920s.** This is a late-1920s photograph of South Main Street in downtown's center during a community fair. On the left is the building housing the Central Bank and Trust and Hotel Juliette. The Mount Holly Bank and the Leader Store are on the right side. (Courtesy of the City of Mount Holly Archives.)

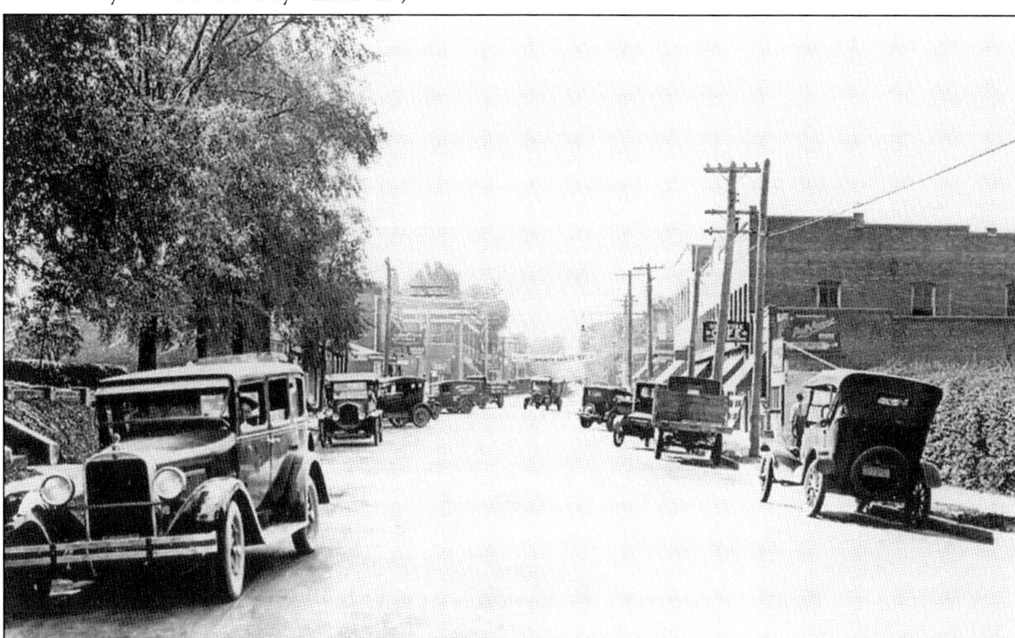

**DOWNTOWN MOUNT HOLLY, C. 1920s.** The c. 1880s Farrar building on the right contributes to the "brick block" of the early business hub of the town. An elegant sedan parked in front of A.P. Rhyne's house faces the camera. Compared to the early-1900s view on page 51, Mount Holly is now immersed in the age of the automobile. (Courtesy of the City of Mount Holly Archives.)

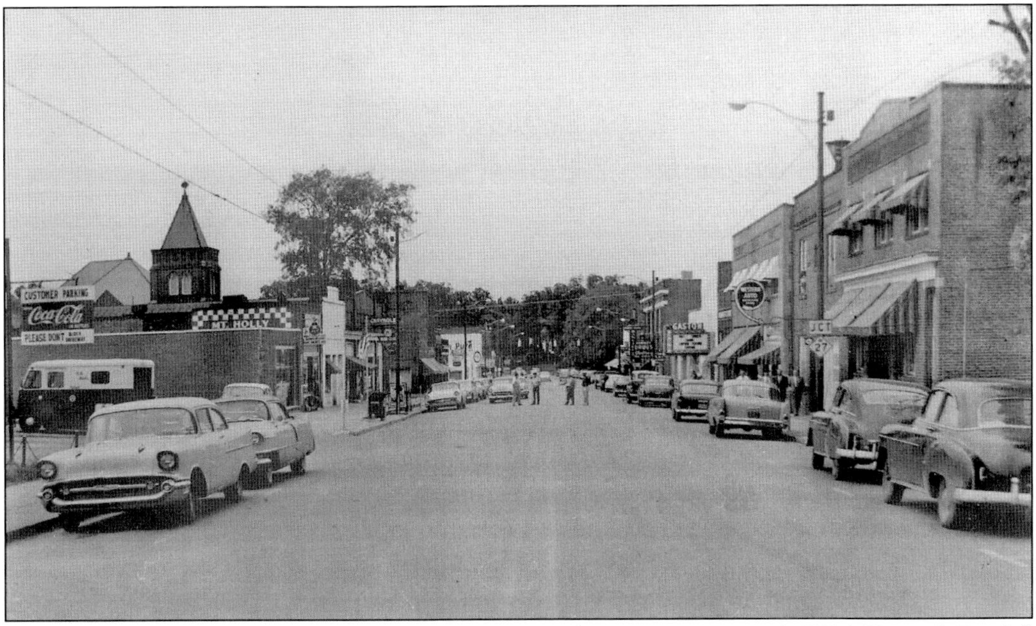


**South Main Street, Looking North.** The Gaston Theater marquee reads "Walt Disney's *Bambi*." The cars and the movie title indicate this picture was taken around 1957. Note the iconic Western Auto hardware sign on the right (east) side of the street. On the left, from the foreground, are the post office (with the American flag), Mount Holly Farm Supply (the Purina checkerboard), and River Valley Chevrolet. (Courtesy of the City of Mount Holly Archives.)

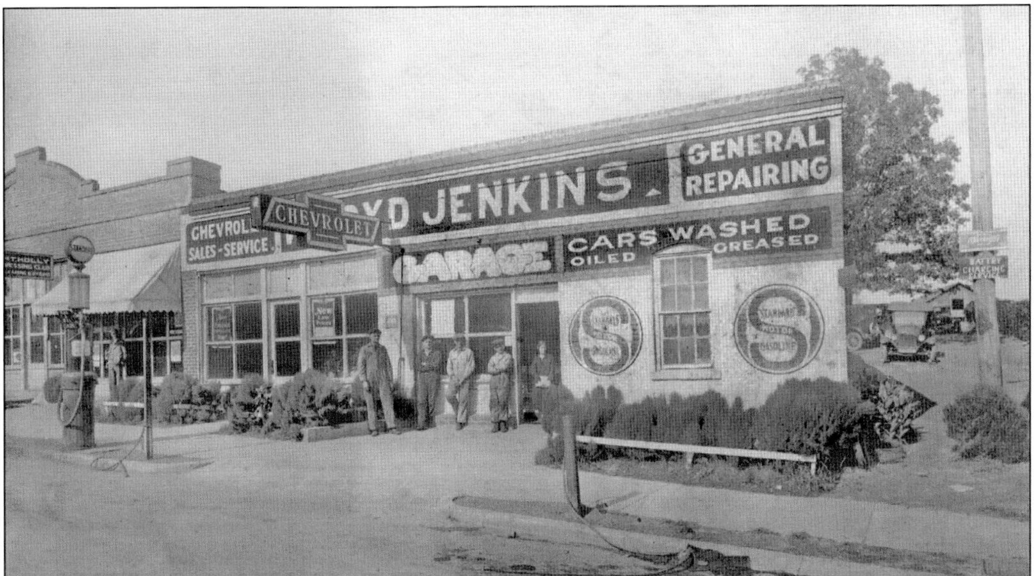


**W. Loyd Jenkins Chevrolet.** A town promotional brochure from around 1930 described the local Chevrolet dealership on East Charlotte Avenue as follows: "Mr. Jenkins has a well-equipped garage and is in a position to render service on all makes of cars. He sells automobile accessories, tires, tubes, gas, greases, and oils." A Ford dealership was on South Main Street at the time. (Courtesy of Reggie Henkle at Rabb Florist.)

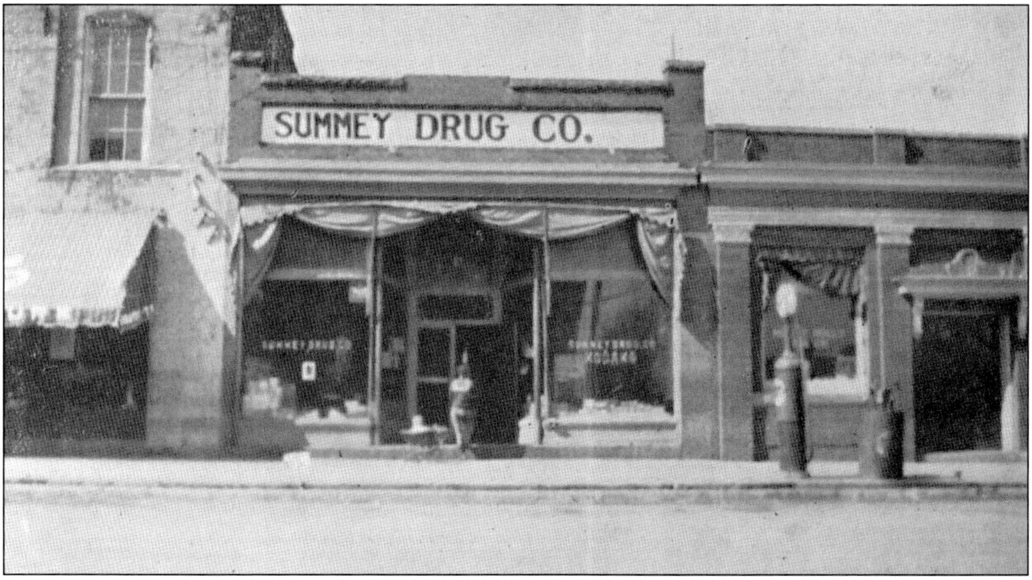


**SUMMEY DRUG COMPANY, C. 1920S.** This turn-of-the-20th-century commercial building housed Holland Drug Company until 1913. Note the gasoline pump on the sidewalk; pharmacies often sold automobile fuel in the early 1900s. Summey Drug later moved across the street to the two-story bank building. Summey Drug's last location, before closing in the 1970s, was in the Summey building. (Courtesy of C. Alexander.)

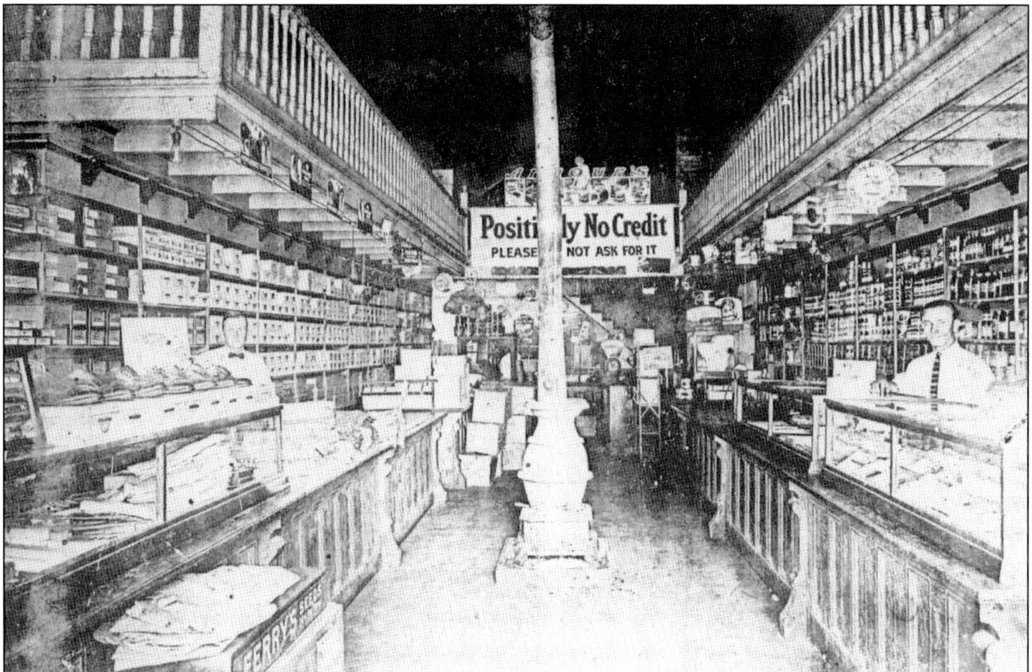


**CALDWELL GENERAL STORE.** Frank Caldwell General Store sold dry goods, notions, shoes, staples, and fancy groceries, but as the sign says, it offered no credit. The potbelly stove would have been a gathering place for local gossip to be shared during cold weather. (Courtesy of Millican Pictorial History Museum.)

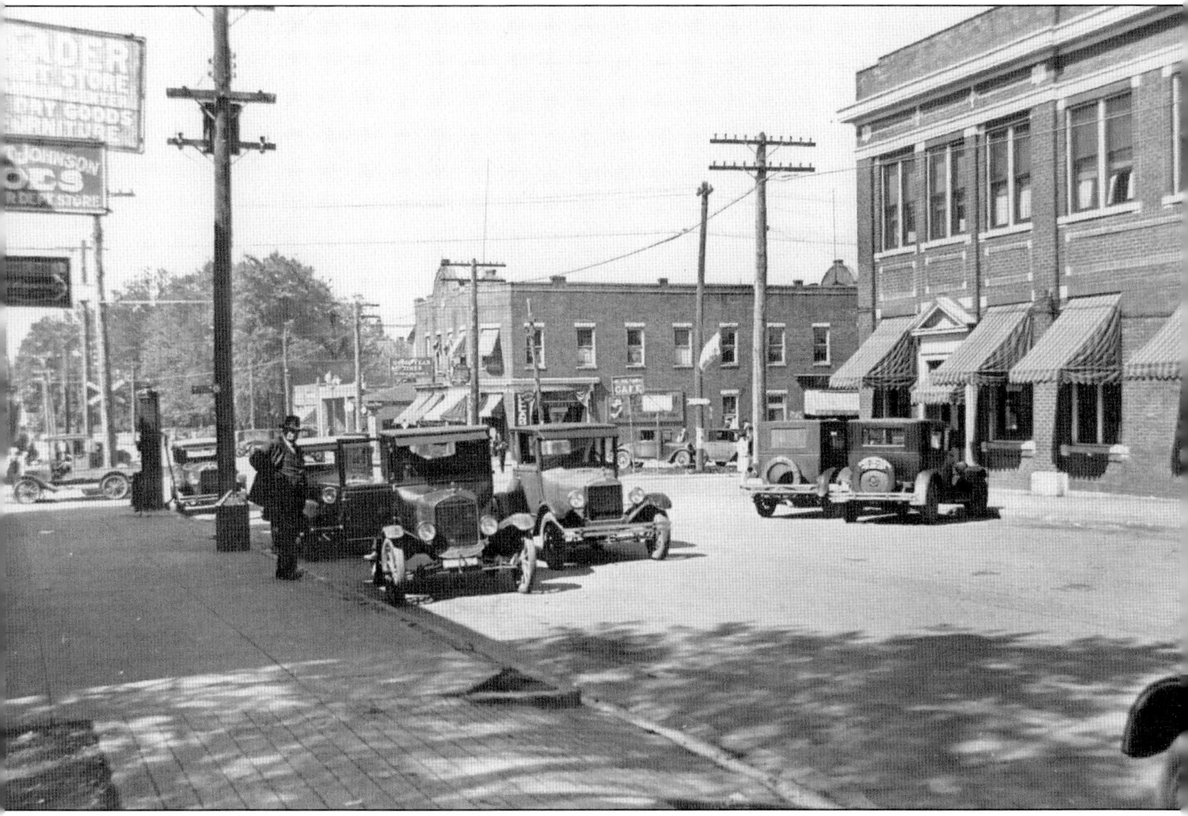

**A Bustling Downtown, c. 1920s.** This is an iconic image of downtown Mount Holly in its prime. The photograph was taken looking north on South Main Street. Commerce is so busy that cars are double-parked. Note the angle parking in front of the Central Bank and Trust building. On the second floor, the open windows indicate guests staying at the Hotel Juliette. Of course, no air-conditioning was available, just hand fans and window awnings. The Leader Department Store is on the left, selling Endicott Johnson shoes. Farther north on the sidewalk, Summey Drugs sells gasoline from a tall pump near the street. The flatbed truck on the left is heading down West Central Avenue. Framing the center of the photograph, the noble Holland Drug Company, with granite windowsills on the second floor, faces west and south. (Courtesy of the City of Mount Holly Archives.)

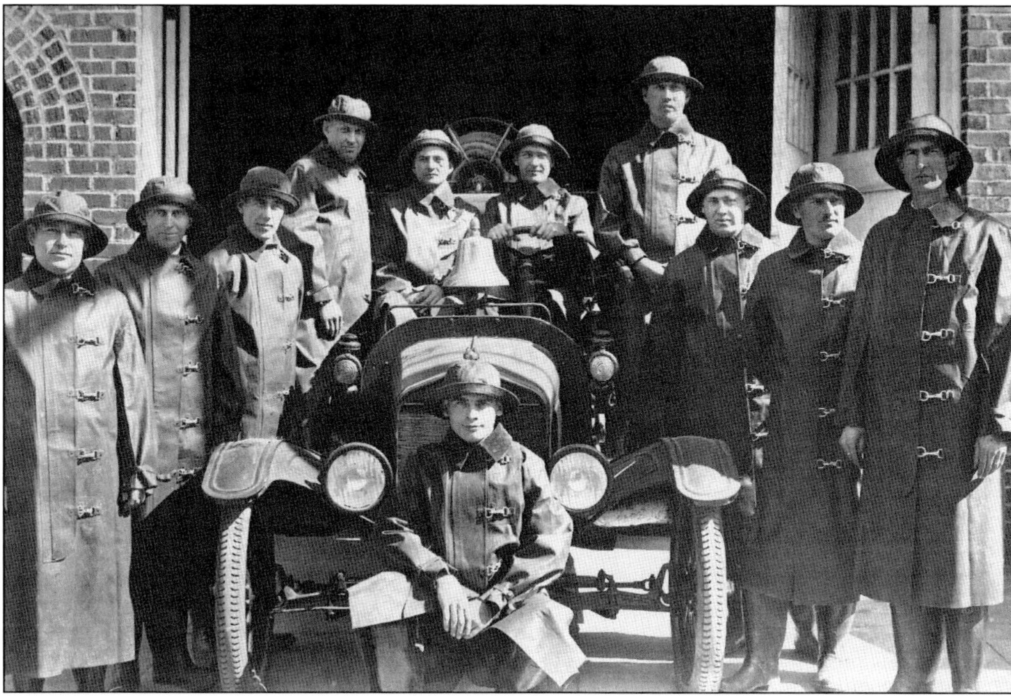

**MOUNT HOLLY FIRE DEPARTMENT, 1927 OR 1928.** The department was officially established on April 25, 1927, with seven charter volunteer members. This photograph was taken at the old city hall, located on South Main Street between the old American Yarn and Processing corporate offices and the Summey building. The old jail can still be seen in the alley east of Main Street. (Courtesy of Millican Pictorial History Museum.)

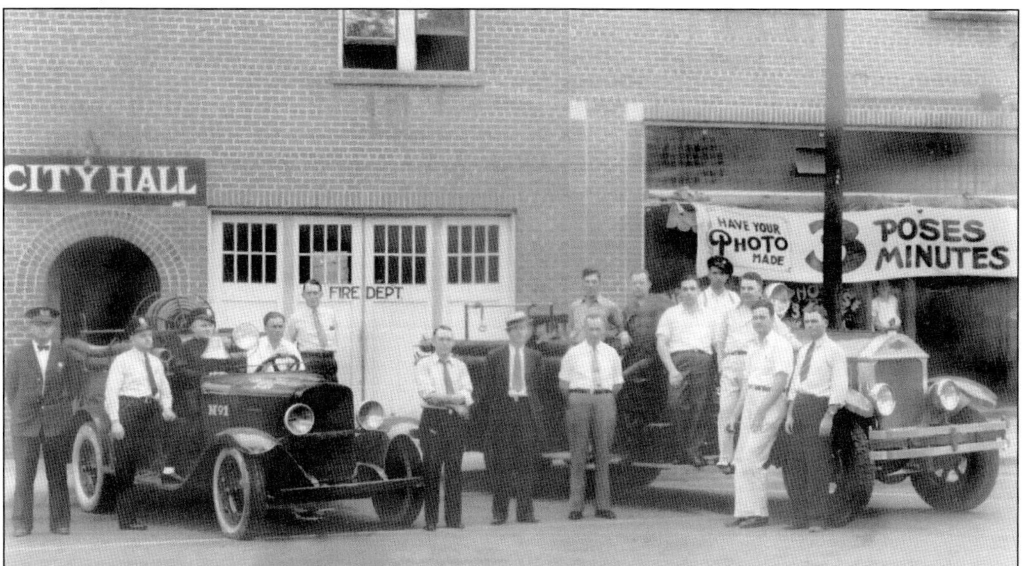


**FIRE DEPARTMENT, C. 1930S.** The firefighters now have two trucks. The upstairs of city hall housed the courtroom, presided over by a justice of the peace. Note that at the time of this photograph, there was a store in the building on the right. The building housed American and Efird corporate offices and a later version of city hall. (Courtesy of Millican Pictorial History Museum.)

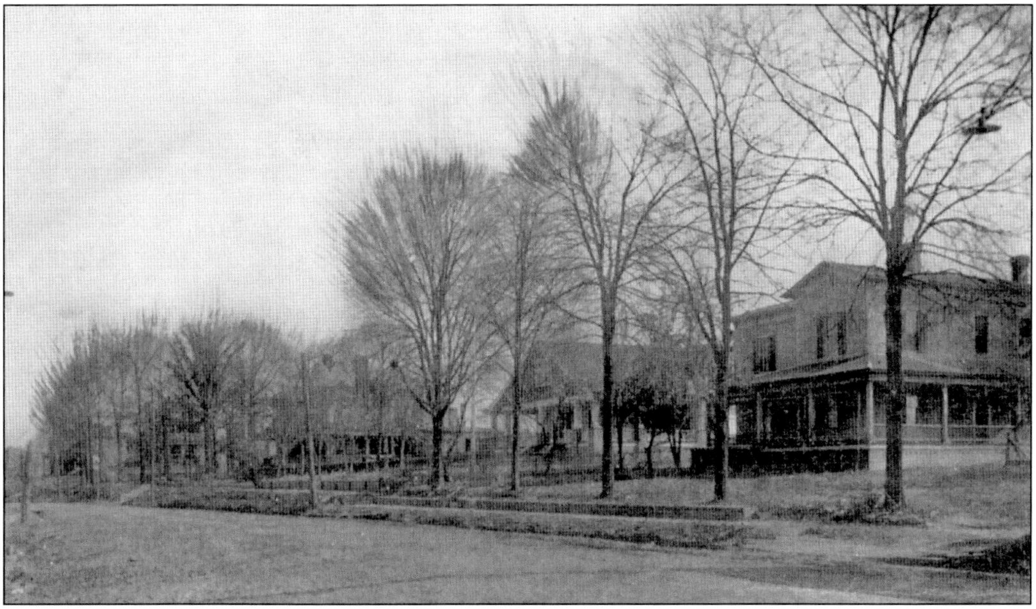

**North Main Street, c. 1920s.** Shady elm trees form a sun-dappled canopy. Elms were popular street trees in towns of the eastern United States. Note the low walls along the sidewalk that define the street border of the house lawns. Some of these walls are still present today, but the elegant residences are gone. (Courtesy of C. Alexander.)

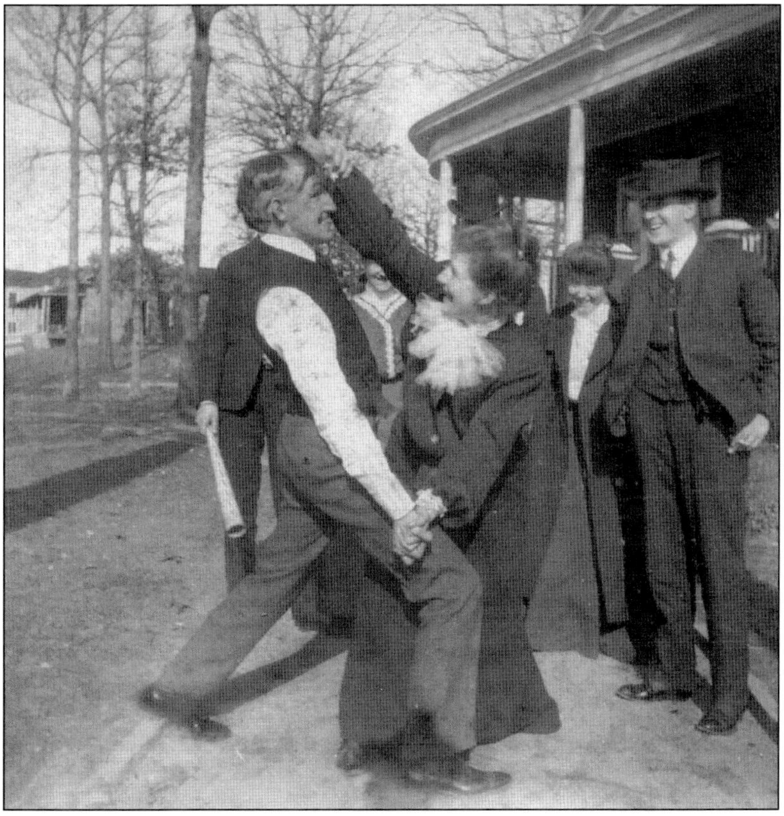

**Dancing under the Elms.** The famous Charleston dance grew popular during the 1920s as dance halls and nightclubs featured fast-paced jazz music. Here, Walter Rhyne is showing an audience how the dance requires both swaying arms and fast feet. This photograph was shot in front of 140 North Main Street, the home of his father, A.P. Rhyne. (Courtesy of C. Alexander.)

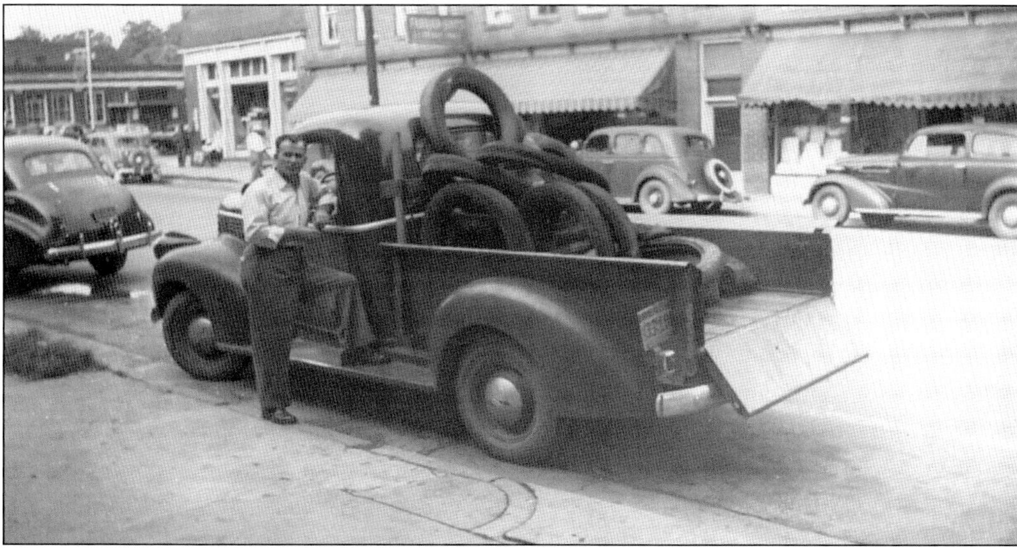

**Busy North Main Street, c. 1940s.** The Farrar building on North Main Street is in the background on the right. The Rhyne building, downsized in the 1930s to accommodate state highway 27, is on the left, featuring a white trim facade. The single door between the two awnings led upstairs, where a funeral home served Mount Holly in the early 1900s. (Courtesy of the City of Mount Holly Archives.)

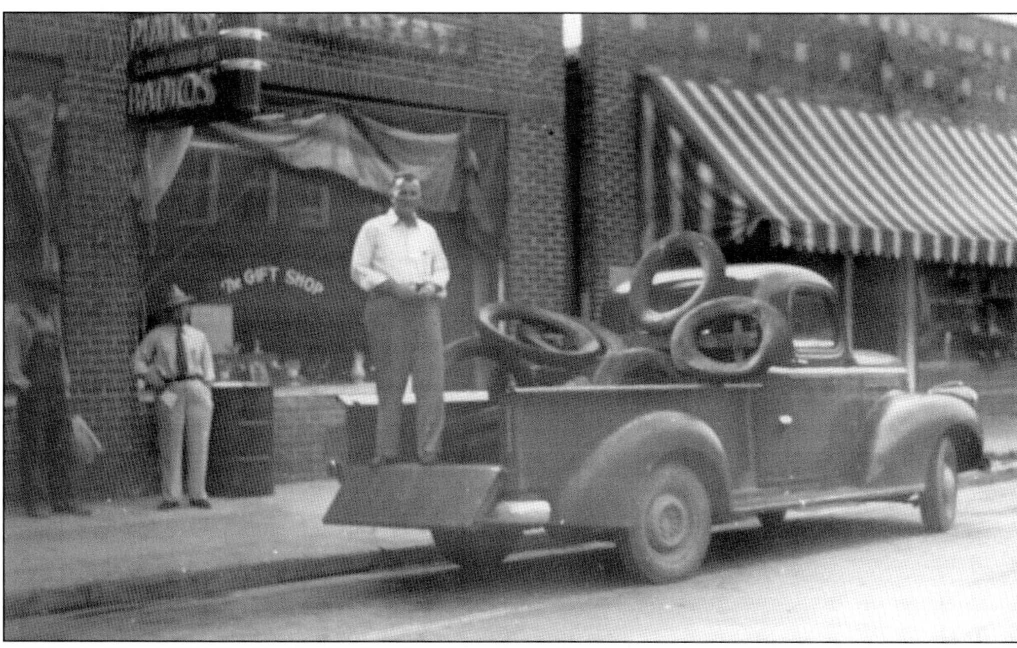



**Mount Holly Furniture and Clark Radio.** The original Mount Holly Furniture Store is on the right, started by Leo Fuller in the 1930s. In 1950, as his business expanded, he added a two-story building next door. Clark Radio Company is on the left, indicated by the attractive, pedestrian-friendly neon sign. (Courtesy of the City of Mount Holly Archives.)

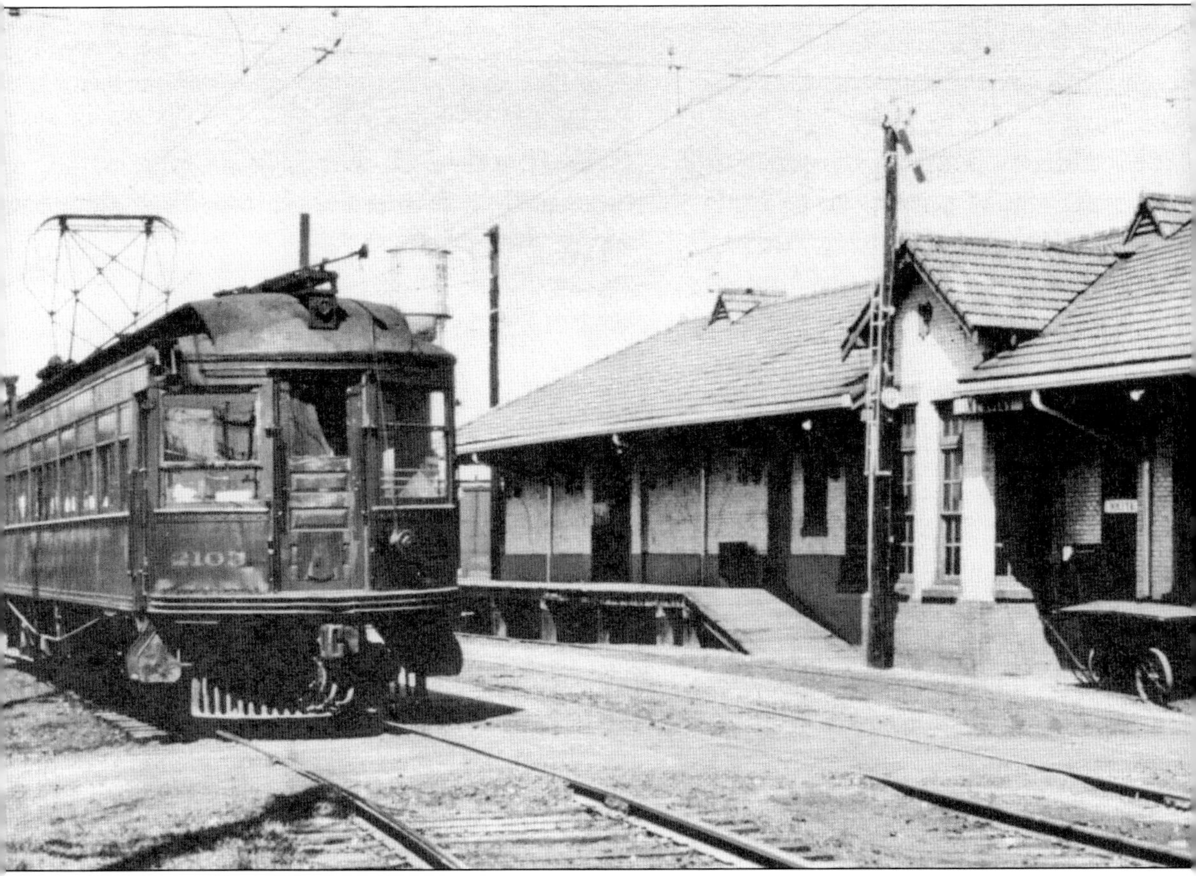


**Piedmont and Northern, May 1950.** The Piedmont and Northern Train Depot was built in 1911 and is located near the river on East Central Avenue. The distinctive red tile roof with yellow-tan brick was used on train depots throughout the railroad line's communities. Overhead electric lines powered the train car. In 1905, James Buchanan and Benjamin N. Duke, the Durham brothers of tobacco fame, incorporated Southern Power Company (later Duke Power Company), which provided the electricity for this passenger and freight carrier. The Duke brothers' plan was to access the "richest, fastest-growing, and most progressive section of the entire south." This portion of the line linked Charlotte to Gastonia, where the locals boasted of "a mill every mile" along the route. This view faces the building's south side. Today, the depot has been restored for offices and a salon and is the eastern terminus of the city's downtown linear park. (Courtesy of Millican Pictorial History Museum.)

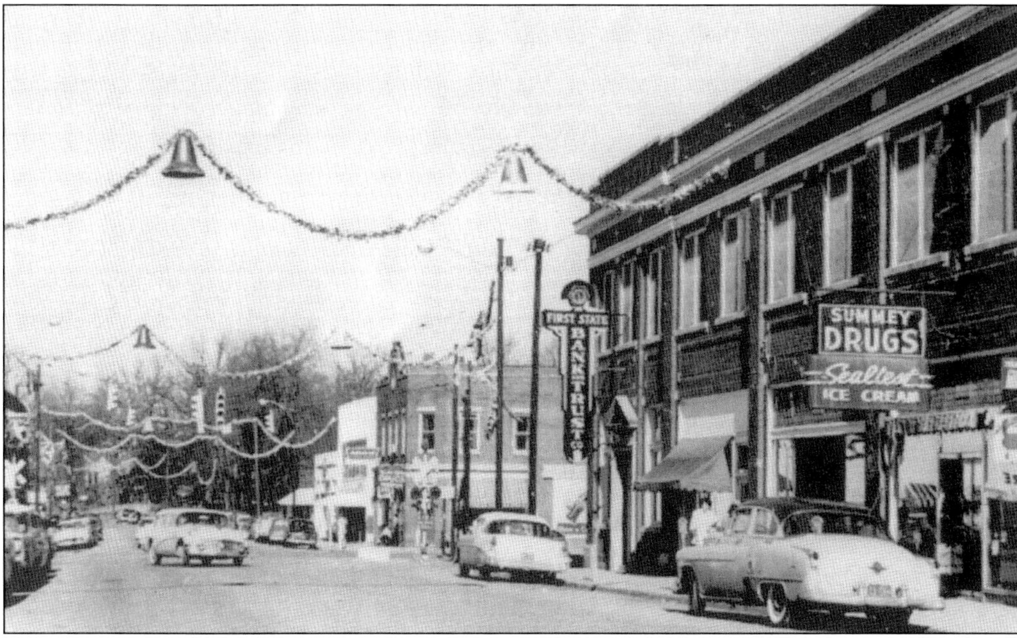


**CHRISTMAS IN DOWNTOWN.** This 1950s holiday image was shot looking north on South Main Street. To the right is the First State Bank and Trust, along with Summey Drug Company. Many baby boomers remember the Sealtest Ice Cream sign that drew folks into the soda fountain. (Courtesy of the City of Mount Holly Archives.)

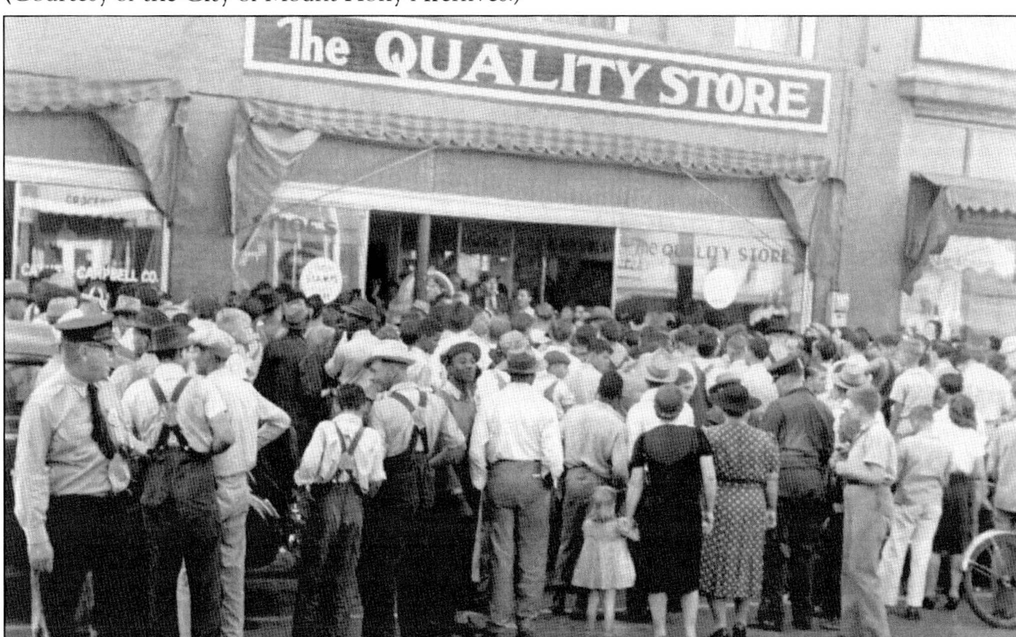


**QUALITY DEPARTMENT STORE, C. 1950S.** The store put on a major promotion. The store owner and his wife lived on the second floor. The building was originally constructed as a general store in the late 19th century. The Cathey and Campbell Grocery is to the left. (Courtesy of Millican Pictorial History Museum.)

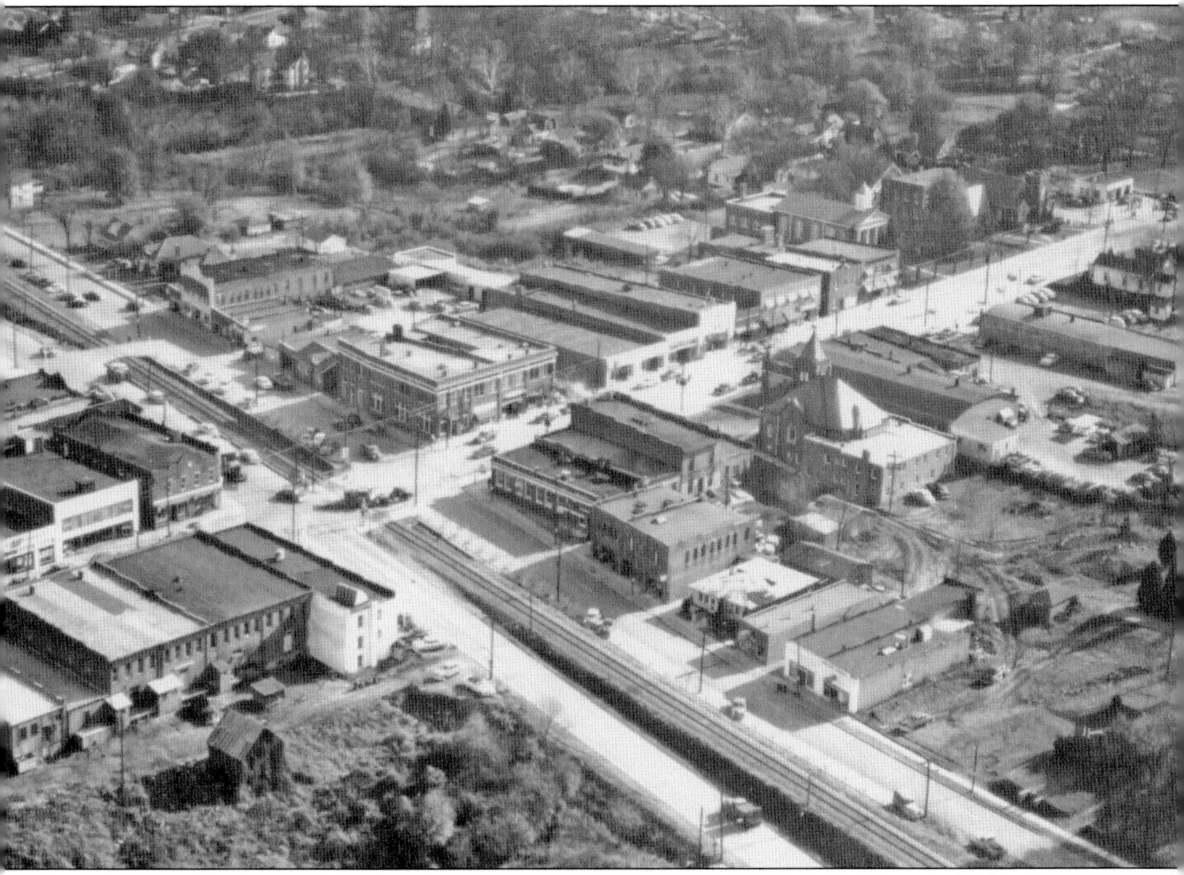

**Aerial View of Downtown, c. 1950s.** This view is looking south. Main Street is a walled corridor of continuous commercial buildings. Years before Interstate 85, Highway 27 was the primary east–west thoroughfare, connecting Mount Holly to Charlotte. Note the diagonal parking on Central Avenue, just south of the railroad tracks. Downtown then had three pharmacies, multiple clothing stores, five-and-dime stores, restaurants, a bank, three groceries, two hardware stores, one farm supply store, five gasoline stations, two theaters, and two automobile dealerships. Residents living in tree-lined neighborhoods around the central commercial area were the customers for downtown businesses. The grocery stores delivered to homes. Apartments were in the second floor of some downtown buildings, increasing the customer base for this expansive retail center. At the time of this photograph, there was no need for malls and shopping centers. (Courtesy of Millican Pictorial History Museum.)

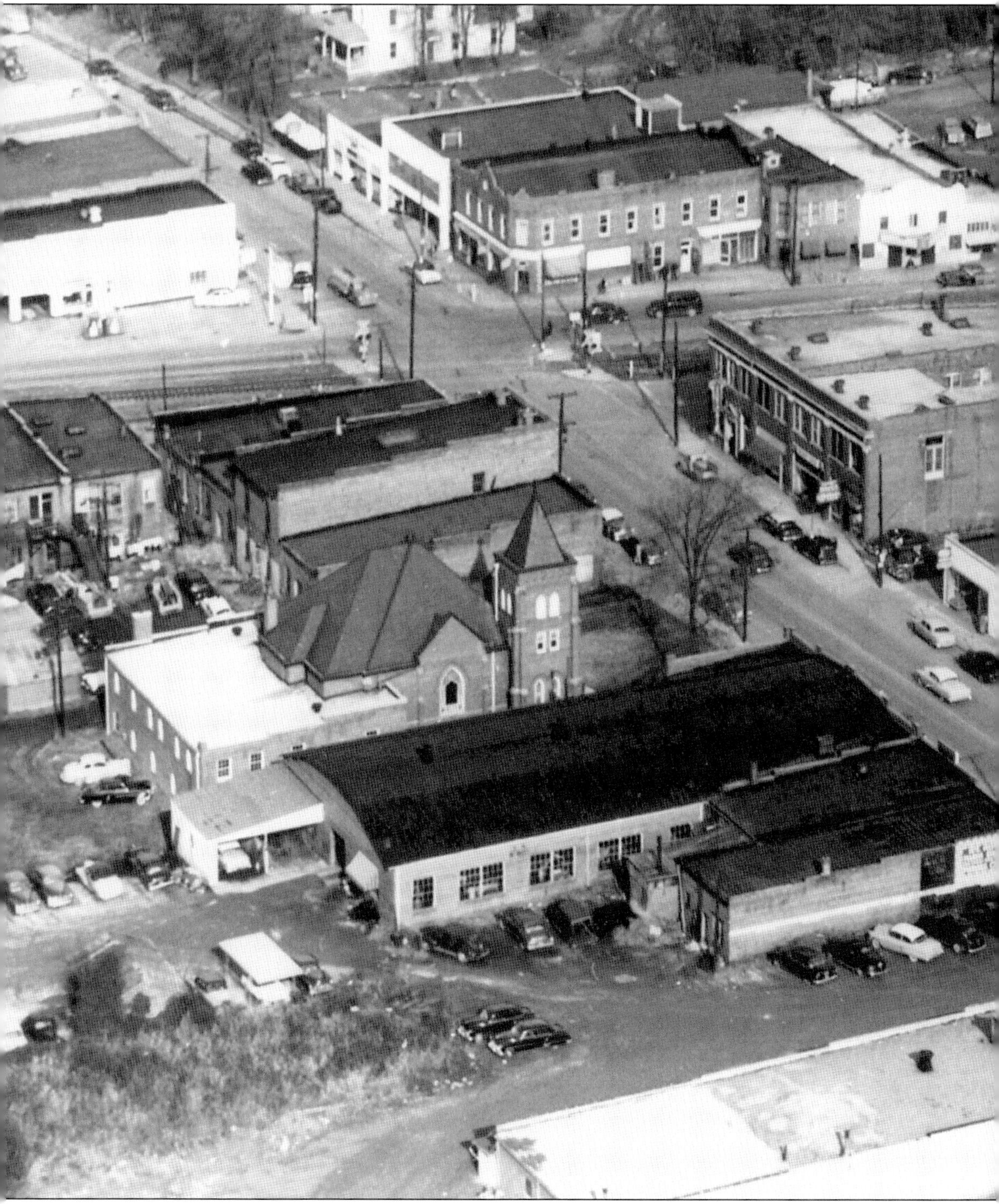

**Downtown Aerial View, Looking North, c. 1950s.** The density of commercial buildings downtown was far greater than in present-day Mount Holly. The central round arch parapets of many commercial buildings are still intact. Several large buildings pictured here were demolished in the 1970s, including First State Bank and Trust (center), Massey Hardware (just south of center),

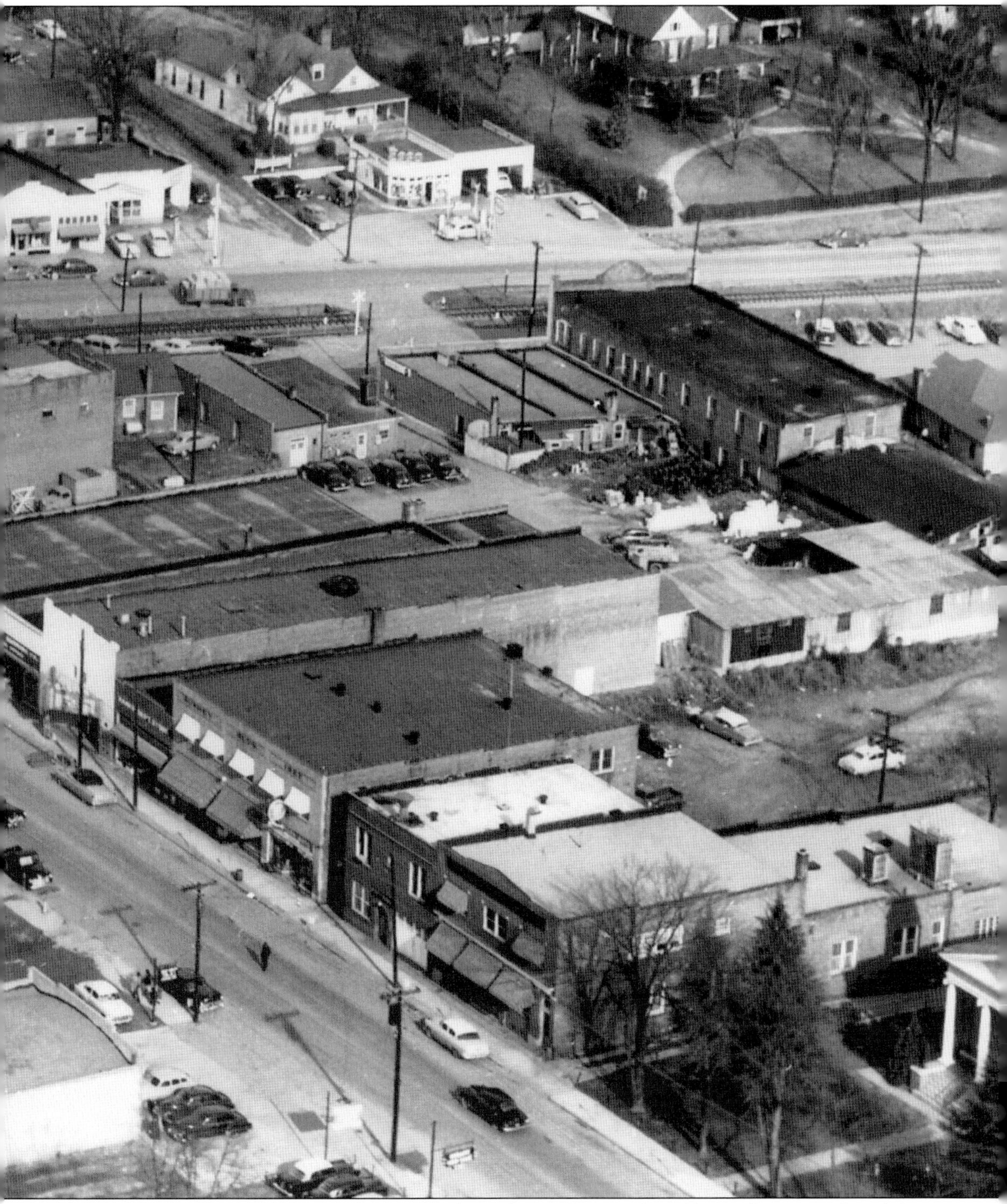

and River Valley Chevrolet (left, just south of the Lutheran church). In the top right of the photograph is the stately Augusta Rhyne Cannon house, located at 137 East Charlotte Avenue. Built in 1894, the house was recently designated as a historic property by the Gaston County Historic Preservation Commission. (Courtesy of Millican Pictorial History Museum.)

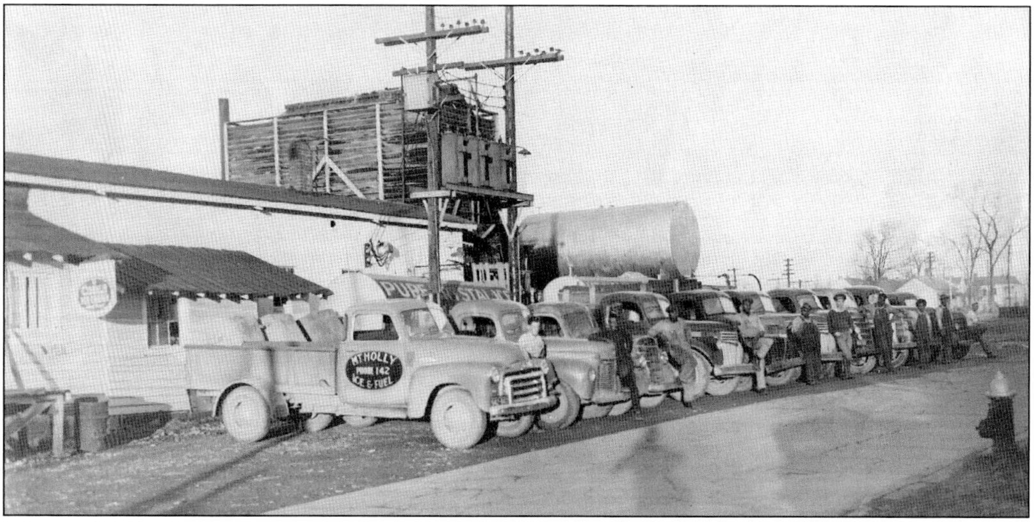


**MOUNT HOLLY ICE AND FUEL.** Customers had only to call 142 for delivery of ice or coal. Trucks hauled ice and coal along regular routes, much like the home milk deliveries of the time. The company, owned and operated by the Thompson family, was located at the top of the hill between East Central Avenue and the railroad tracks. (Courtesy of Linda Thompson Sherrill.)

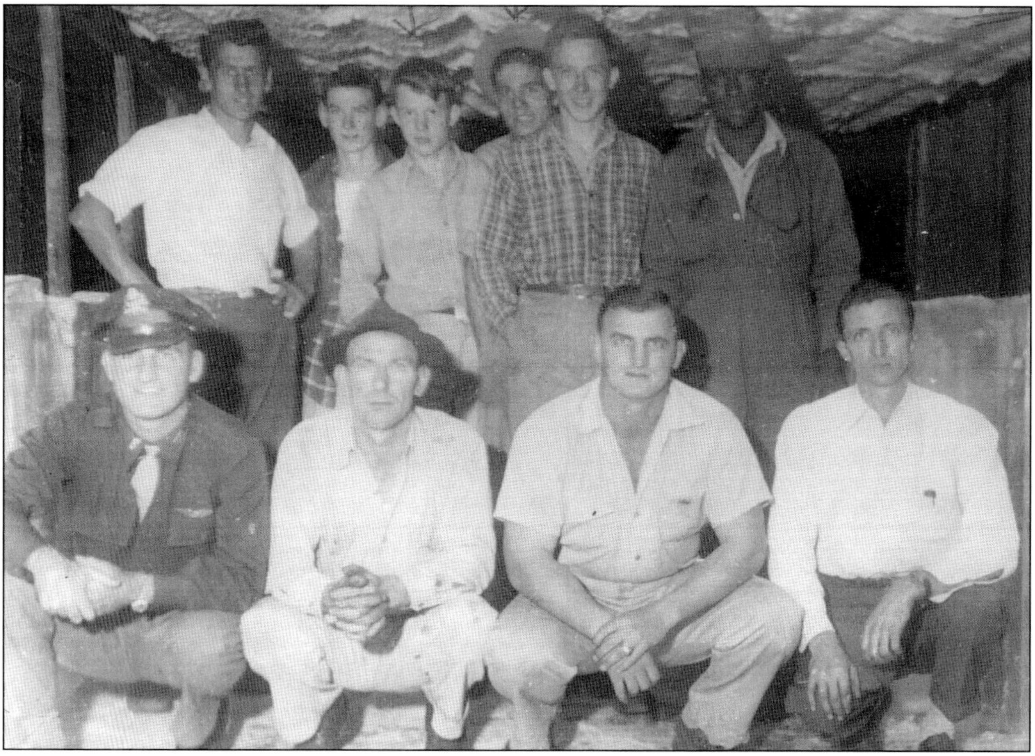

**INSIDE THE ICE HOUSE, 1943.** Lt. J.B. Thompson is home on leave. In this photograph are, from left to right, (first row) J.B. Thompson, Lee Bryant, Dick Thompson, and Oscar Banks; (second row) John Flowers, J. Mannes, J. Putnam, Neb Hollis, Jack Jolly, and Fred Burris. Two of the men, coach Dick Thompson and Neb Hollis, are in the Mount Holly Sports Hall of Fame. (Courtesy of Linda Thompson Sherrill.)

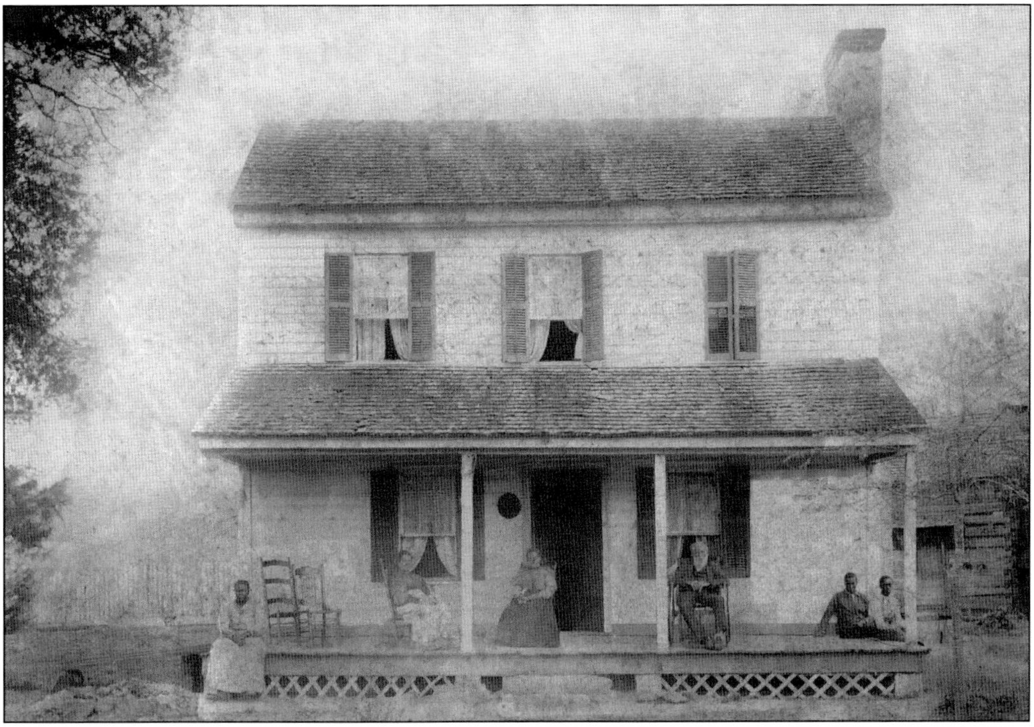

**Willowside, 1800s.** This house was built by William Rankin (1760–1853) and was inherited by his son Richard Rankin (1804–1899). Richard Rankin was at the 1842 Hoffman-Rhyne Store meeting that created Gaston County. Rankin served several terms in the North Carolina Legislature. The Rankin farm held 300 acres on Stanley Creek, northwest of Mount Holly. (Courtesy of Dr. Richard Rankin.)

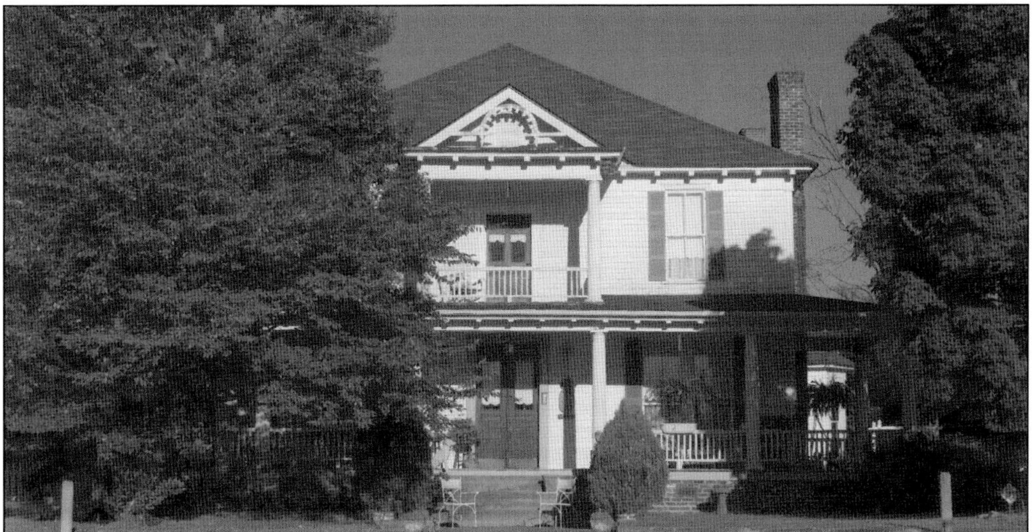

**Anderson Wesley Davenport House, Built around the 1830s.** Davenport was a successful farmer operating north of Woodlawn. His son Richard Kelly Davenport was mayor of Mount Holly in the 1880s. The house still stands at 1505 North Main Street and is designated a Gaston County Historic Property. (Courtesy of Nancy McIntosh.)

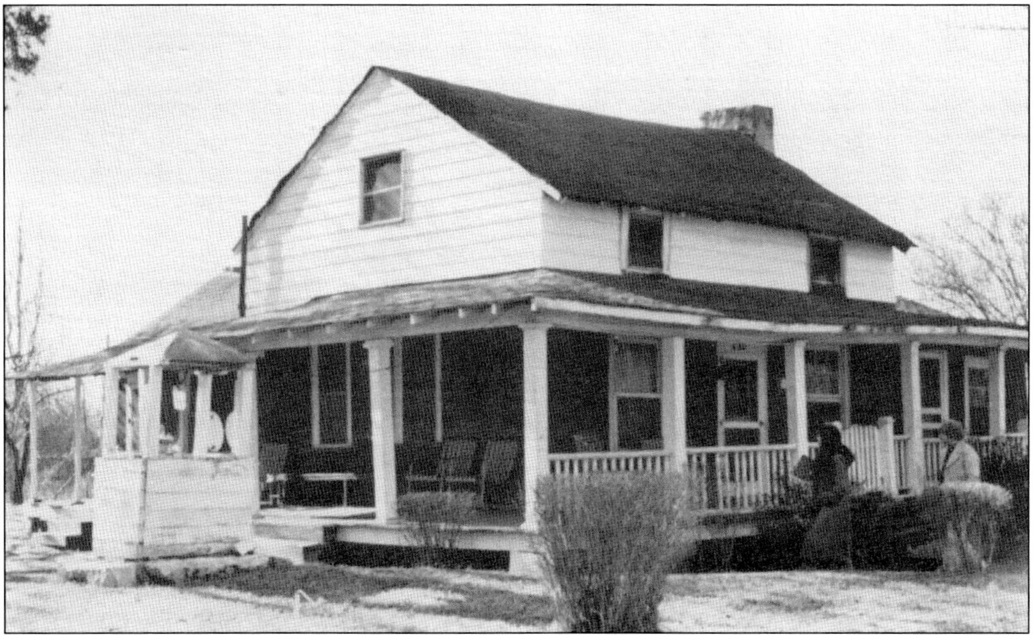

**RAMSES HUNTER HOUSE.** Hunter, a former slave and respected member of the African American community in Mount Holly, built this house soon after the Civil War. It was located at the corner of Glendale Avenue and Hawthorne Street in the Freedom neighborhood. Sadly, it was demolished several years before this publication. (Courtesy of Gaston County, North Carolina.)

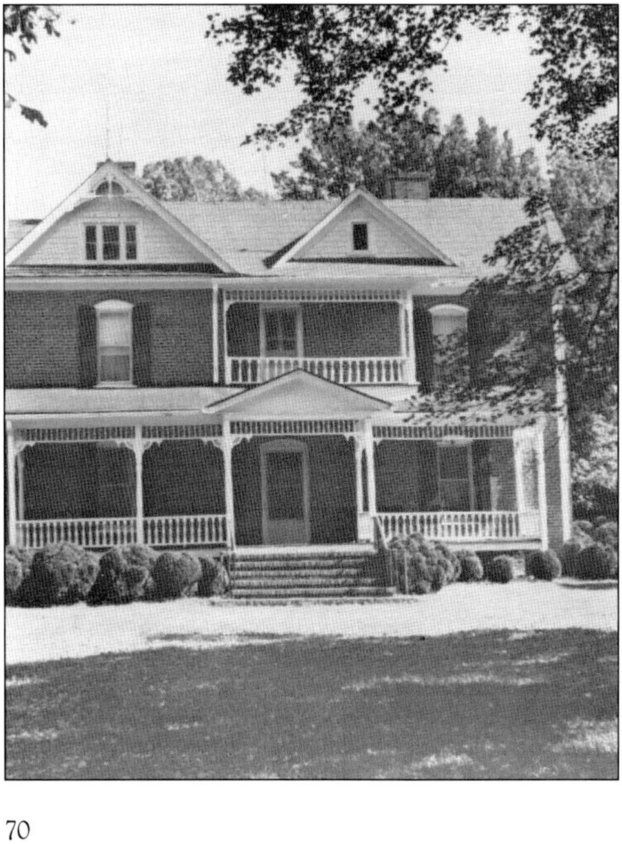

**DELLINGER-NANTZ HOUSE, BUILT AROUND 1899.** Dairy farmer Rome Dellinger built the house, then sold it to George R. Nantz. George's daughter Nanie Nantz married Frank Moore and had eight children: Ken, Bill, Hazeline, Frances, Josephine, Jack, Isabel, and Kitty. The Moore children lived in the home for almost 100 years. It is located at 714 North Main Street. (Courtesy of Gaston County, North Carolina.)

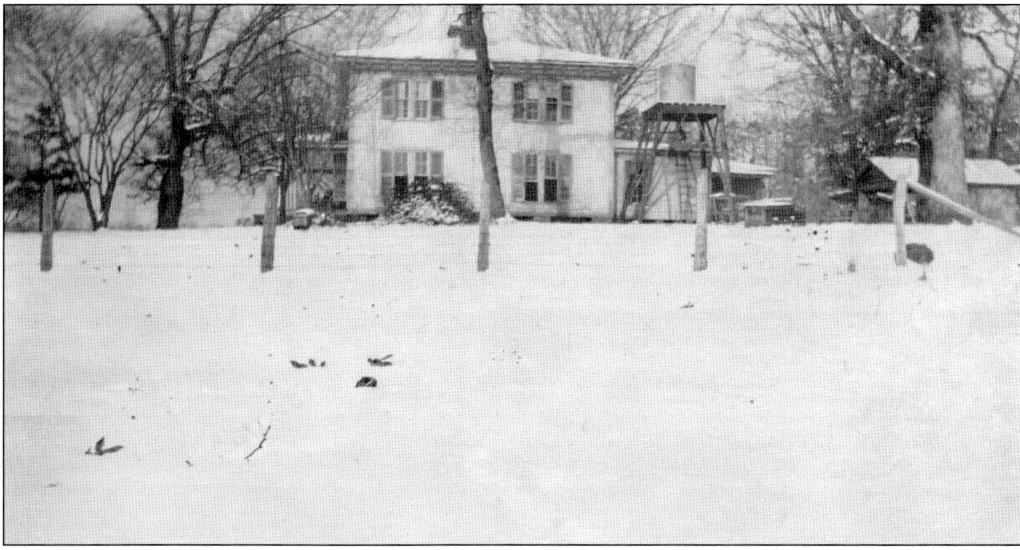

**Johnston-Nims-Spratt House.** Built between 1810 and 1820 by William and Mary Forney Johnston, this is one of the oldest structures in Mount Holly. In 1859, Frederick Nims, a civil engineer for the new Wilmington, Charlotte, and Rutherford Railroad, bought the home and doubled its size. The side of the house is pictured on a snowy day; the porch entrance is on the left, facing Woodlawn Road. (Courtesy of Meg and Jon Barnard.)

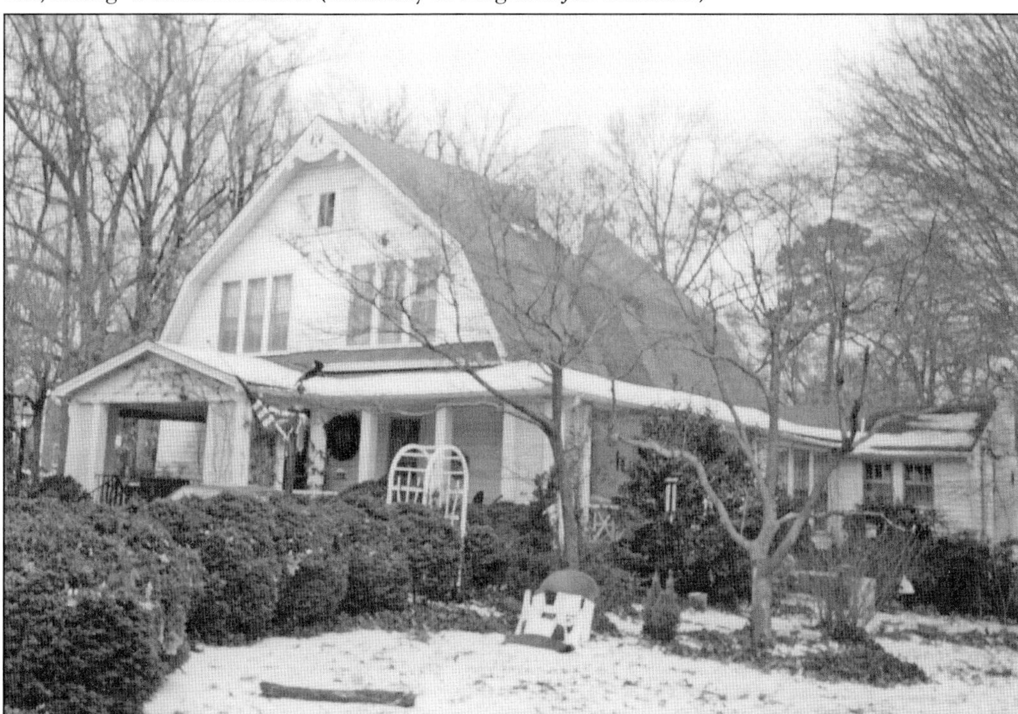

**W.B. Rutledge House.** Very little has changed about this home since it was built in 1878. At the time it was constructed, Rutledge served as a magistrate for Riverbend Township. The house is located on the corner of West Charlotte Avenue and South Hawthrone Street, where it continues to be used as a private residence. (Photograph by C. Alexander.)

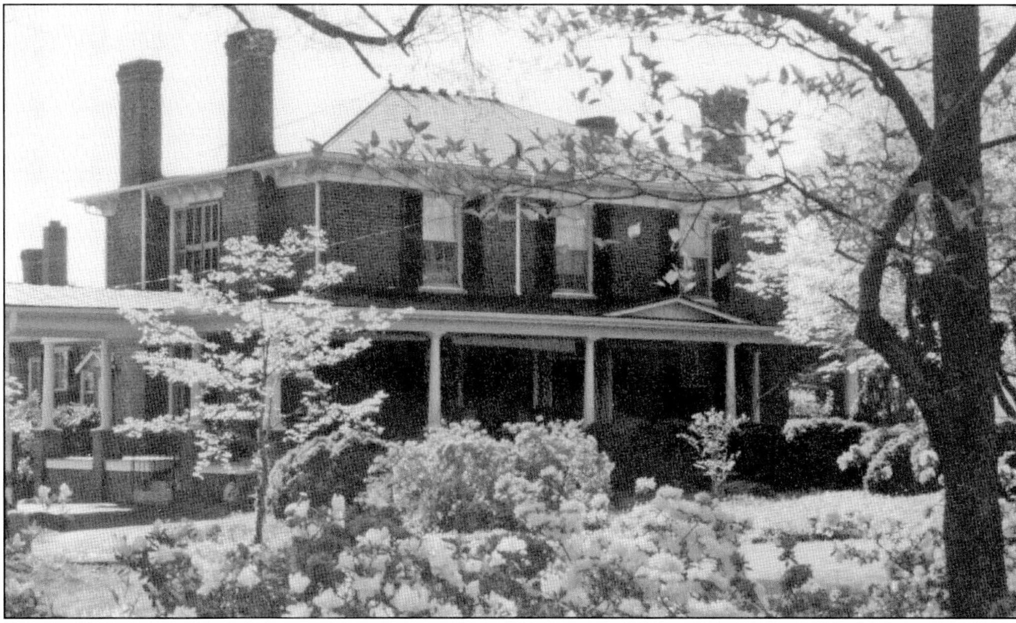

**Moses Hoffman Rhyne Home.** The construction for this stately Greek Revival and Italianate brick home was interrupted by the Civil War, but it was completed in 1865. There are nine fireplaces, each with a distinctive carved mantel. Rhyne, a 52-year-old widower, married 17-year-old Mary Caroline Springs just before moving into the home. The Rhyne home still stands at 1213 West Catawba Avenue. (Photograph by C. Alexander.)

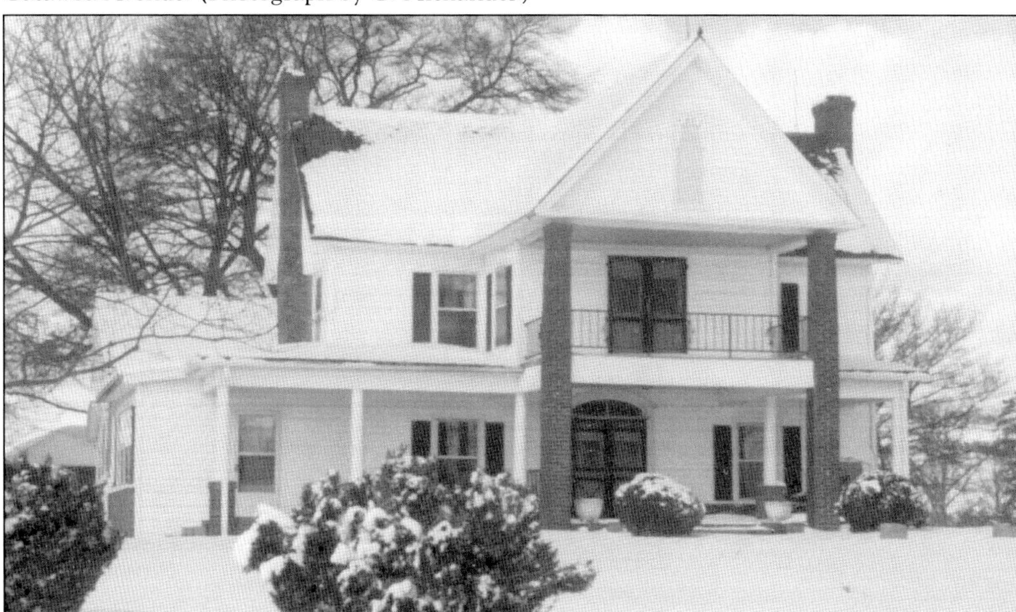

**Thomas Worth Springs Sr. House.** The Sharp family purchased the farmland about 1860, and the original house was built then. In 1903, Thomas W. Springs bought the substantial farm and made major interior and exterior alterations to the house. The house and farm still occupy the prominent elevated area known as Springs' Hill, just above Mount Holly Middle School. (Courtesy of Sarah Springs.)

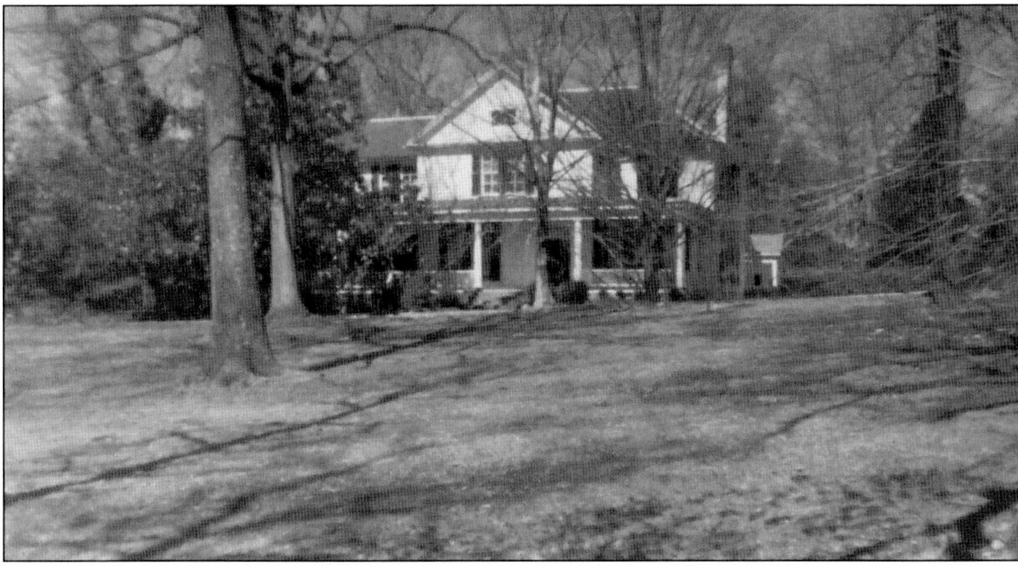

**LUTHER NIMS HOUSE, BUILT AROUND THE 1890S.** Nims built this Colonial Revival–style house at 703 North Main Street. Nims was involved in the Nims Manufacturing Company, located near his property, and was in partnership with Charles Egbert Hutchison in the textile mill business. In the 1990s, the Nims house was removed to make way for a residential development. (Courtesy of Dale Barrow.)

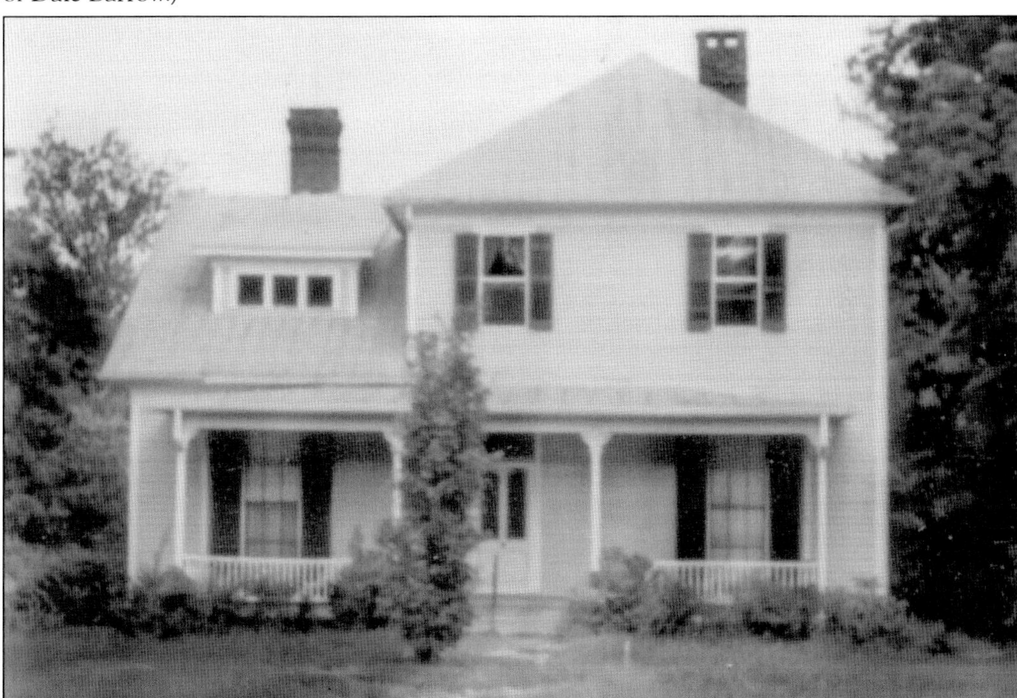

**THOMAS BELK HOUSE.** Built in the 1890s, this frame house originally was only one story high. Located at 233 South Main Street, the structure was enlarged in the early 1900s, when Belk added a second-story section. A gable-roofed well house stood behind the home. The house was razed in the 1990s and replaced by Citizens South Bank. (Courtesy of Sarah Springs.)

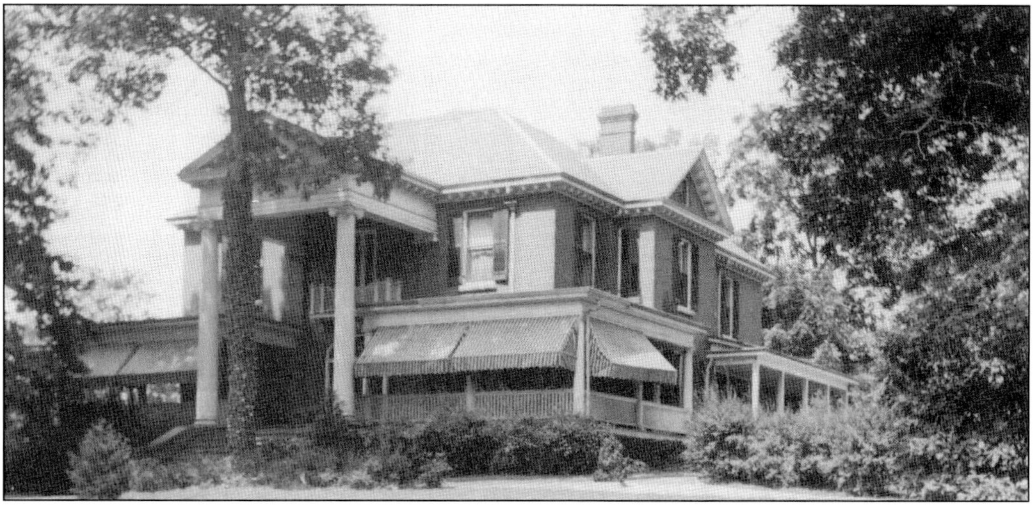

**North Main Street Mansion.** This brick Colonial Revival home was built in 1910 for local textile magnate Charles Egbert Hutchison. Mount Holly contractor R.F. Rankin built the expansive structure, designed by prominent Charlotte architect Louis Ashbury. Today, the house is privately owned. (Reprinted from *American & Efird People: A Century of Quality.*)

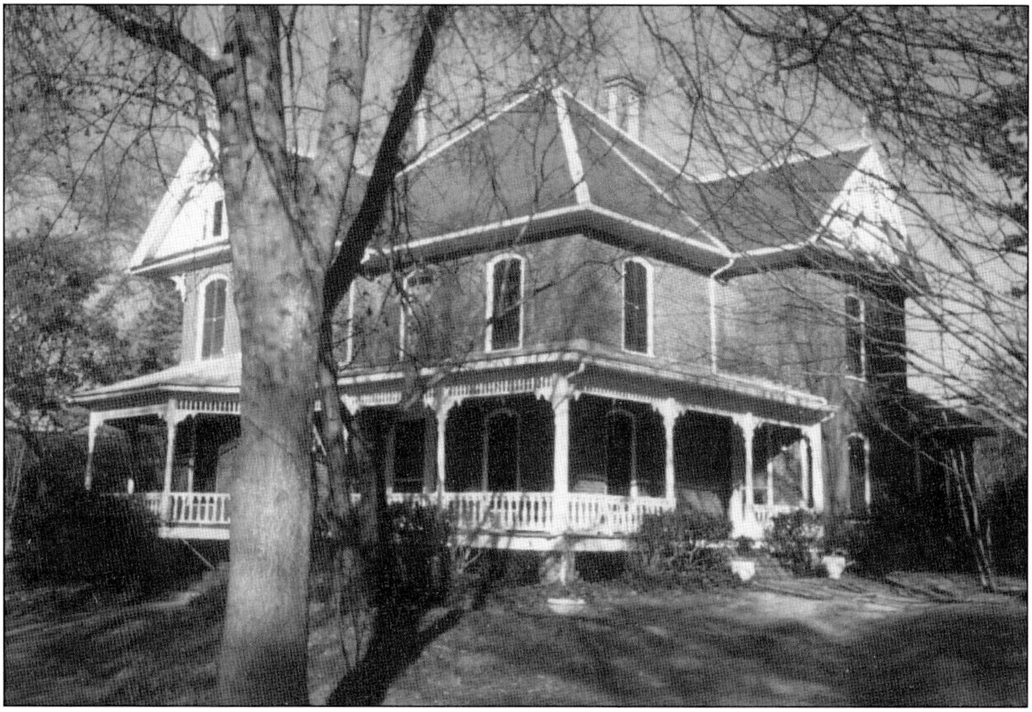

**Augusta Rhyne Cannon House.** This residence was built in 1894 by A.P. Rhyne as a wedding gift to his eldest daughter, Augusta. It is located at 137 East Charlotte Avenue and is considered to be one of the finest Queen Anne homes in Gaston County. Contractor Robert F. Rankin also built this house. (Courtesy of C. Alexander.)

# *Five*

# LIVE, WORK, AND PLAY
## COMMUNITY LIFE

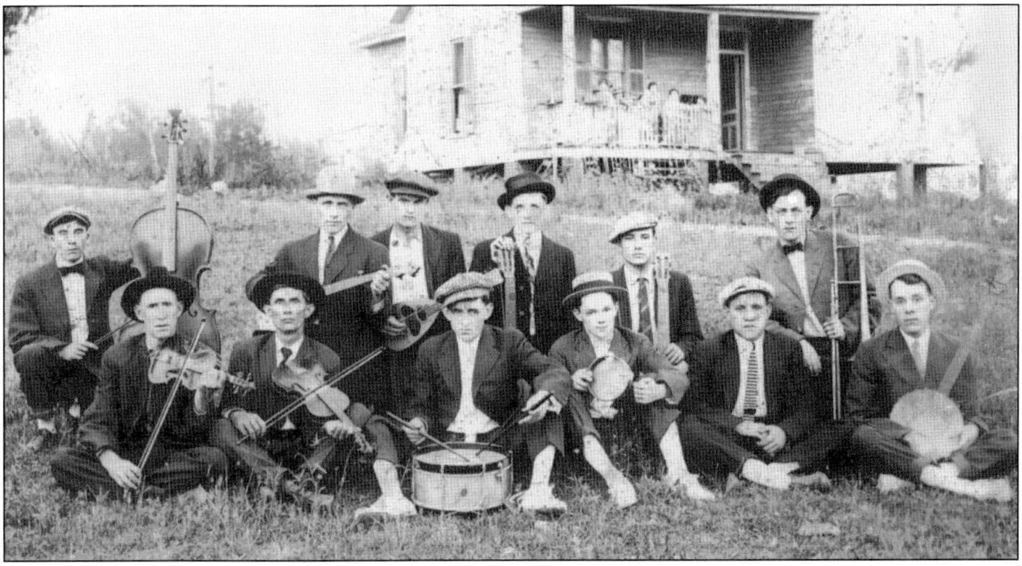

**RIVER TOWN MUSIC.** The young members this Mount Holly band, known as the 1900 String Band, are shown holding their instruments in a front yard. The list of names that are written on the back of the photograph are Watts, Wilkinson, Pool, unidentified, Beam, Nichols, Kirby, Reed, Mauney, Moore, Watts, and Webb. The order in which they are listed was not specified. (Courtesy of the City of Mount Holly Archives.)

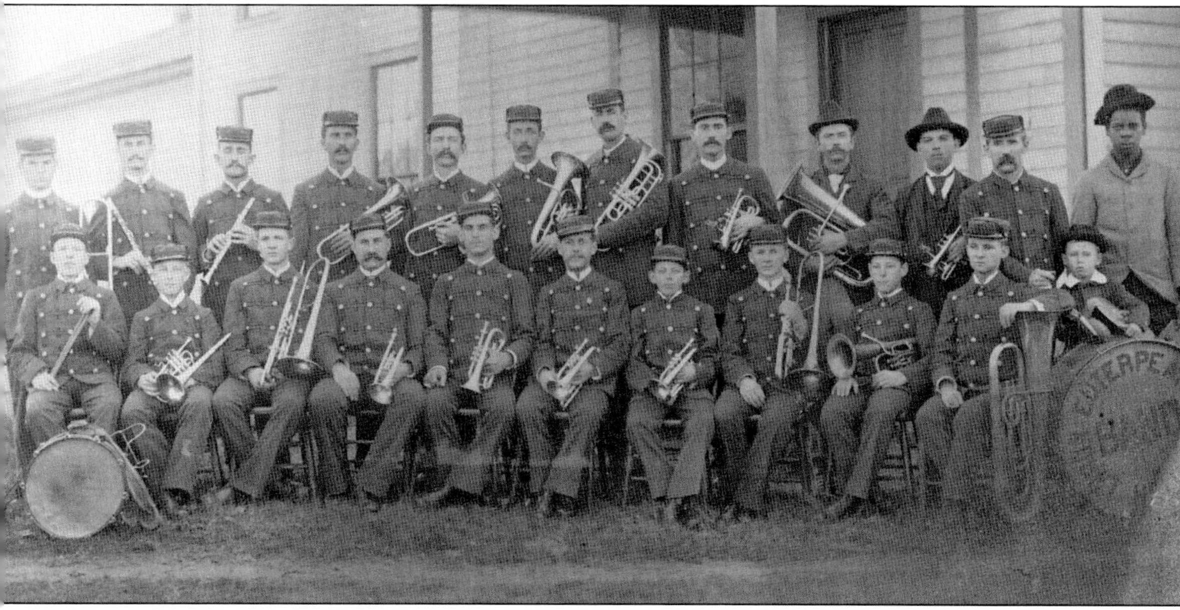

**THE MOUNT HOLLY EUTERPEAN BAND.** In the early 1890s, Capt. Washington Holland formed the Euterpean Band, named after Euterpe, the Greek goddess of music. The band was quite popular in the region. When William McKinley was inaugurated as president in 1897, a private railroad car was sent to Mount Holly for the Euterpean Band, taking them to Washington to perform at the ceremony. After this national event, locals used to say that the Euterpean Band "almost made Mount Holly famous." This photograph was made in front of the Central Hotel. The members are, from left to right, (first row) Buck Wingate, Walter Rhyne, August Peterson, James Costner, John Harris, Capt. "Wash" Holland, Walter Jenkins, Lawrence Holland, Henry A. Rhyne, John Holland, and Willis F. Holland (small boy); (second row) Joe Harris, Ceph Fite, Frank Underwood, John Jones, Turner Johnson, Rome Dellinger, George Jenkins, Leck Harris, unidentified, Terry Fite, Will Cole, and an unidentified gentleman who handled uniforms and instruments. (Courtesy of the National Archives, Washington, DC.)

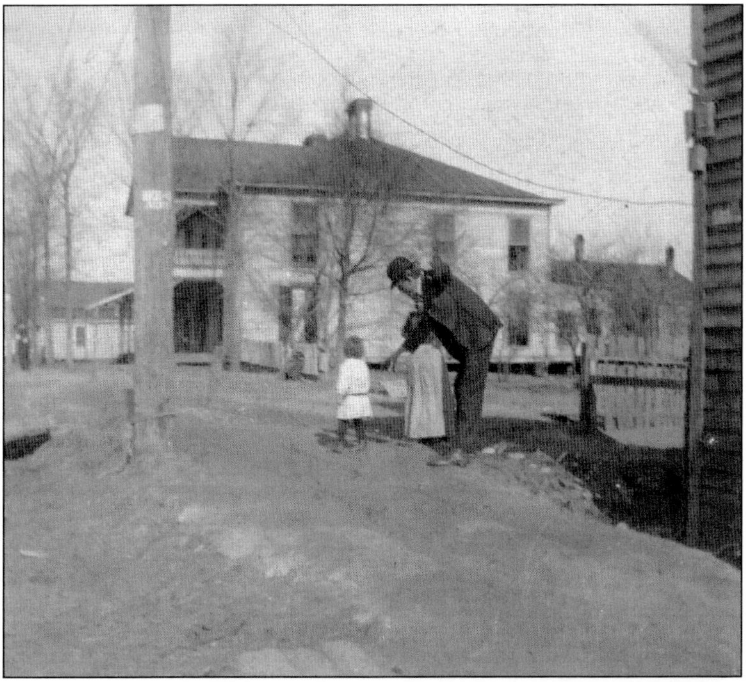

**TENDER STREET SCENE, EARLY 1900S.** The two-story Central Hotel, managed by Mamie Tucker from 1909 to 1918, is in the background behind the people on the sidewalk. Directly across the street was one of two Tucker-Springs stores. The Tuckers lived downtown, and Junius Springs lived south of town, near Tuckaseege Road. (Courtesy of the City of Mount Holly Archives.)

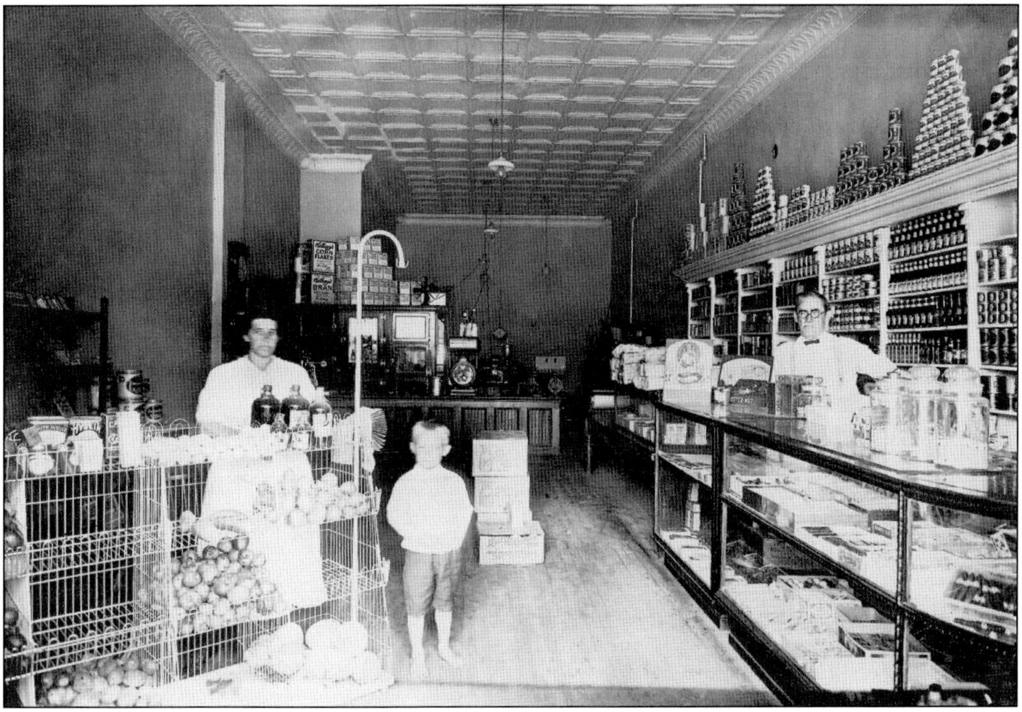

**STORE INTERIOR, C. 1910S.** This photograph is thought to show the interior of the Tucker-Springs store in downtown Mount Holly on South Main Street. Note the child in knickers and the embossed tin ceiling. A careful examination of the items in the back of the store reveals a product common to an entire century of Mount Holly shoppers—Kellogg's Corn Flakes. (Courtesy of Millican Pictorial History Museum.)

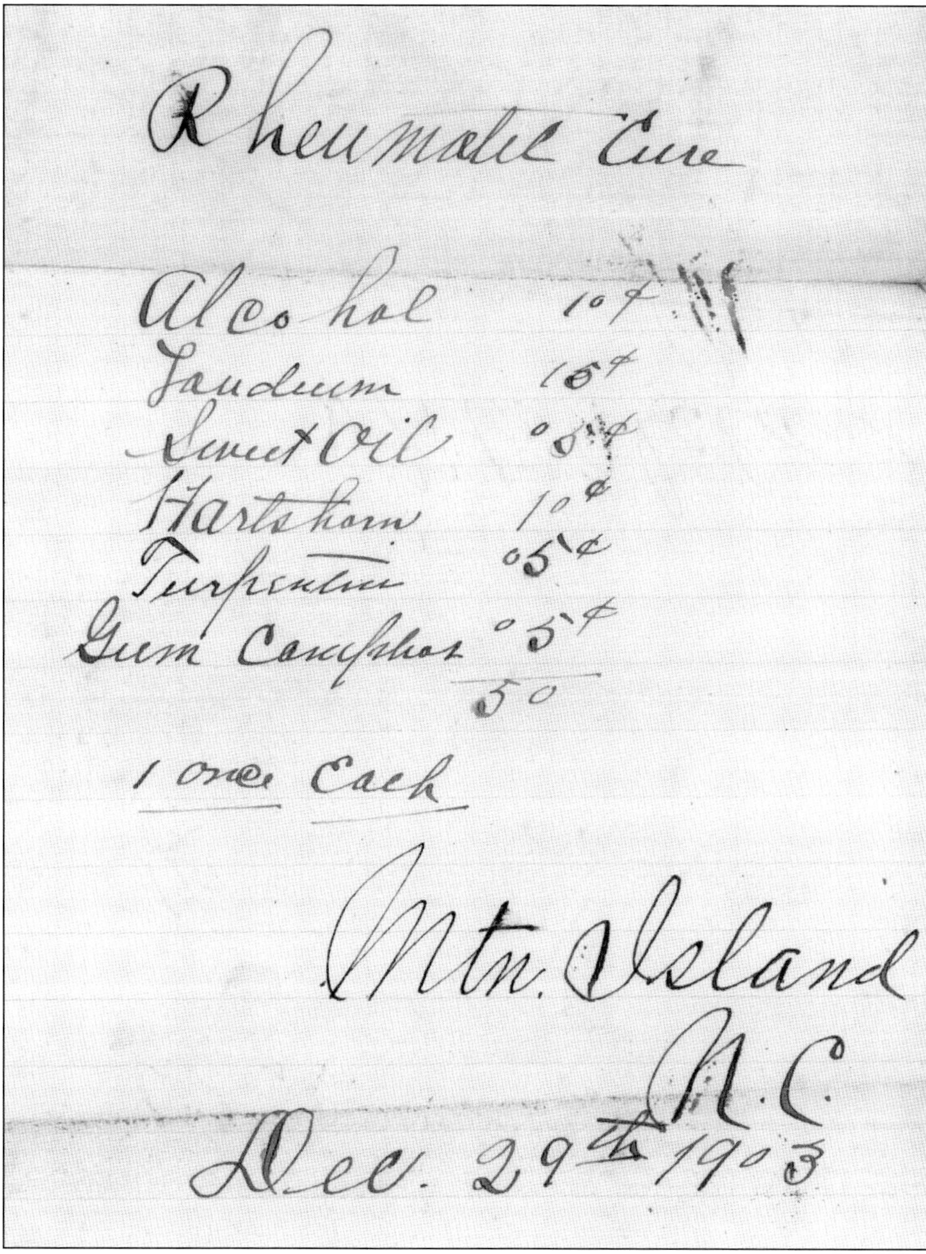

Rheumatic Cure

Alcohol 10¢
Laudum 10¢
Sweet Oil 05¢
Hartshorn 10¢
Turpentine 05¢
Gum Camphor 05¢
50

1 one each

Mtn. Island
N.C.
Dec. 29th 1903

**"Rheumatic Cure," Mountain Island, 1903.** This prescription for the aches and pains of arthritis and rheumatism was either a favorite mixture of a local doctor or pharmacist or a patent medicine formula sold in a general store. The ingredients are alcohol, laudanum (opium), sweet oil, hartshorn (ammonia extract from ground deer antler), turpentine, and camphor. This must have made for a smelly mix. Narcotics like laudanum and even cocaine were sold over the counter nationally until 1914, when the Harrison Narcotics Tax Act banned the sale of these addictive and potentially dangerous substances in patent medicines. Journal entries from Jim Parker, a Mountain Island plant superintendent, indicate that the village had a doctor. At the time, Mountain Island Manufacturing and Mountain Island Village rivaled Mount Holly in population and amenities. (Courtesy of the City of Mount Holly Archives.)

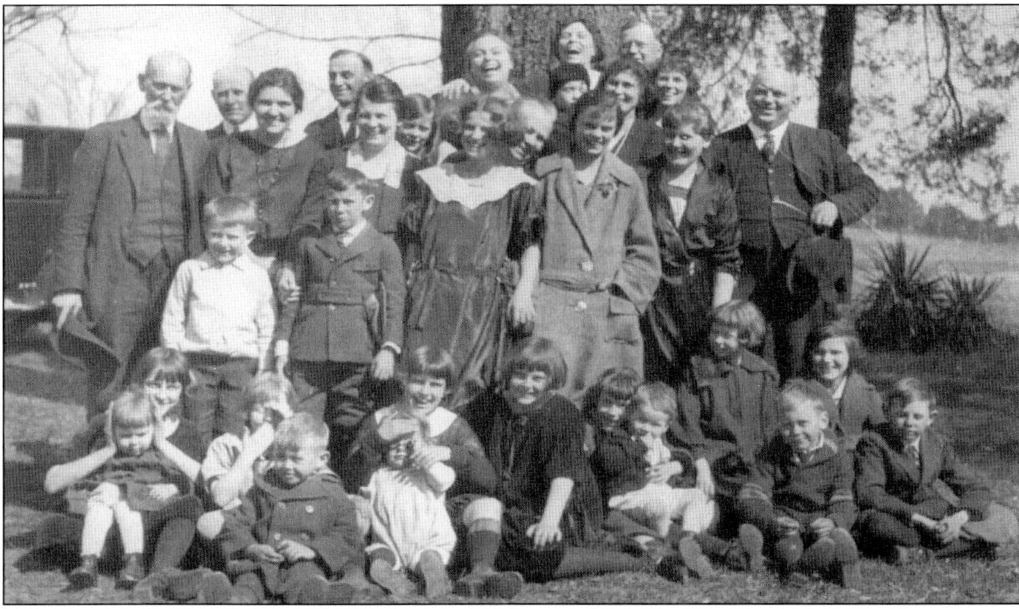

**Families Gather on Easter, 1923.** The photograph includes the families of W.B. Rutledge, A.M. Henderson, James Arthur Rhyne (from left to right, the men standing in back), and Frank and Dick Rankin (the two men standing in the back, second from right and right). Their ancestors, James Rutledge, Thomas Rhyne, and Samuel Rankin, were friends and neighbors in the greater Woodlawn community as early as the 1770s. (Courtesy of C. Alexander.)

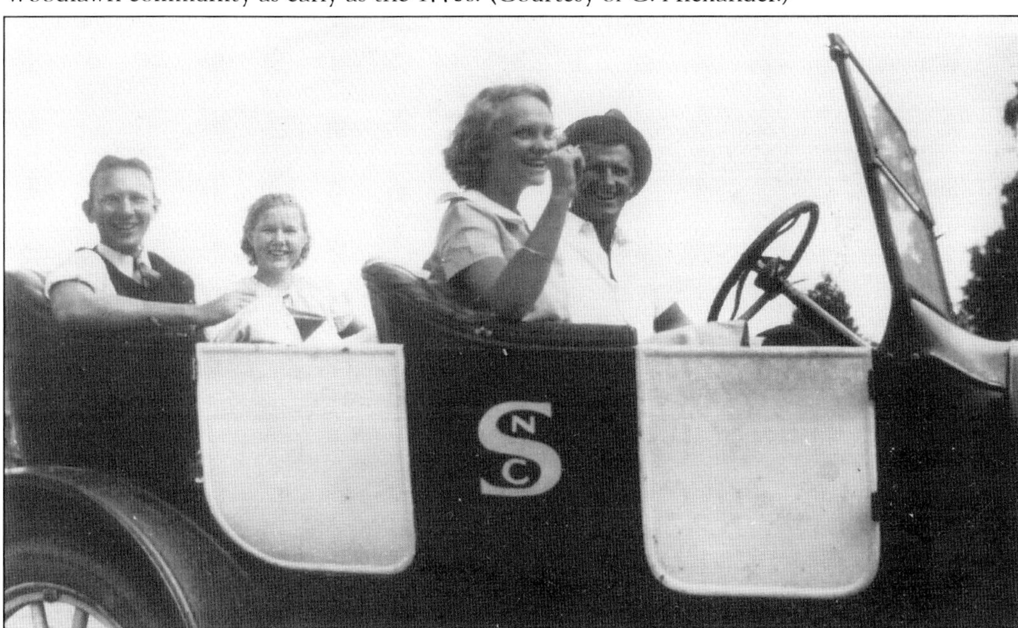


**Wolfpack Automobile, c. 1930s.** Future coach Dick Thompson is driving this grand North Carolina State jalopy. His friend Kemp Shuford Michael is in the back seat. Beside Michael is an unidentified lady friend. Seated beside Thompson is his future bride, Louise Holland, granddaughter of "Wash" Holland, founder of Holland Drug Company and the Euterpean Band. (Courtesy of Linda Thompson Sherrill.)

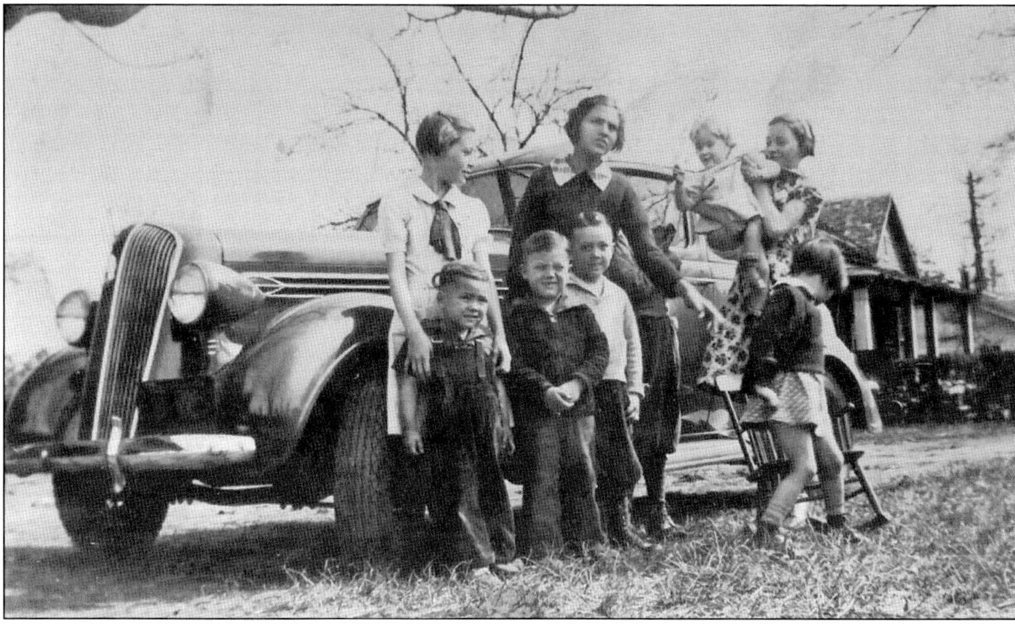

**Children before the War.** Included in this image from the early 1940s of the Carpenter and Fortner families are, from left to right, (first row) Dickie Carpenter, Jack Carpenter, Burmah Carpenter, and June Fortner; (second row) Wrene Benfield, Marie Painter, Nancy Fortner, and Grace Benfield. The scene is on West Charlotte Avenue. (Courtesy of Elizabeth A. Noble.)

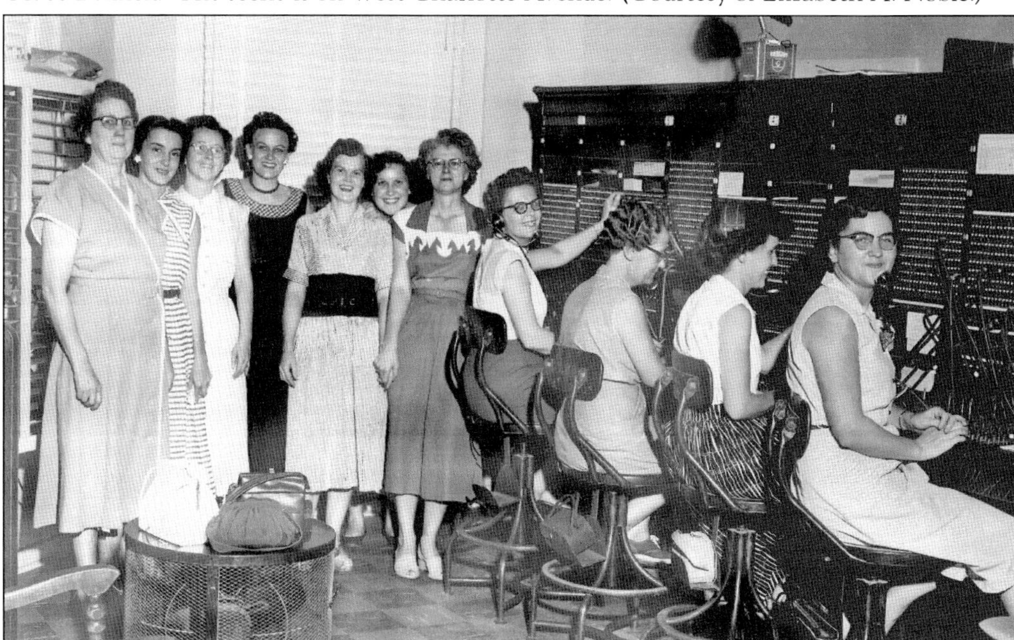

**Southern Bell Telephone Operators.** In the days before automatic telephone exchanges, operators connected calls on large switchboards. Mount Holly's telephone exchange was located on the second floor above the old post office at 109 East Charlotte Avenue. In the 1950s, automatic switching replaced many operators, and the switching equipment was moved to a building on East Glendale Avenue. (Courtesy of Millican Pictorial History Museum.)

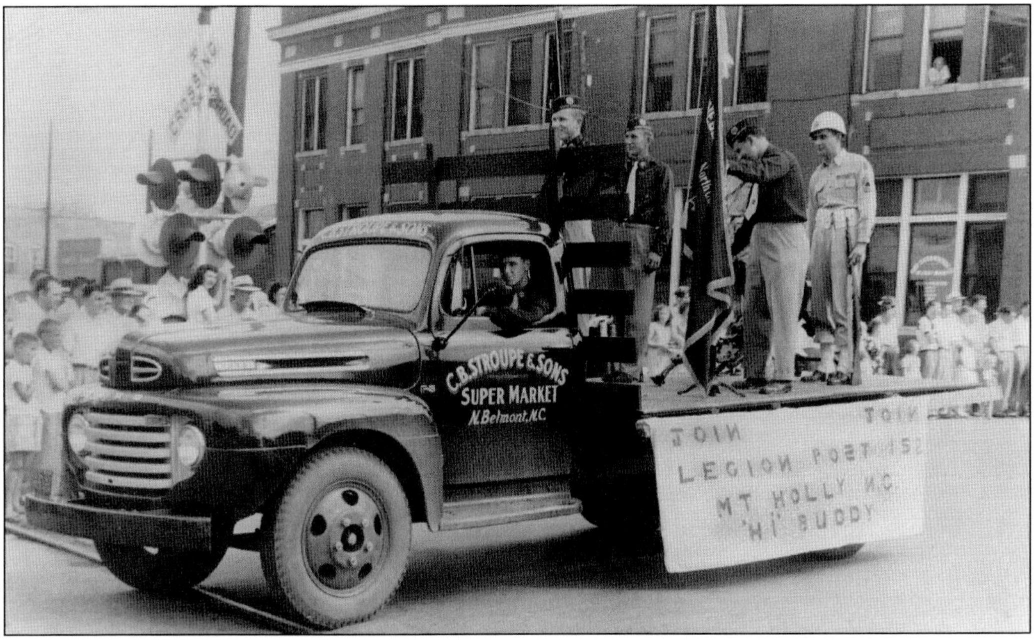


AMERICAN LEGION IN TEXTILE PARADE. The American Legion post float is riding in a C.B. Stroupe and Sons Super Market truck from North Belmont. The First State Bank and Trust Company (formerly Central Bank and Trust Company) was located in the two-story building in the background. (Courtesy of Millican Pictorial History Museum.)

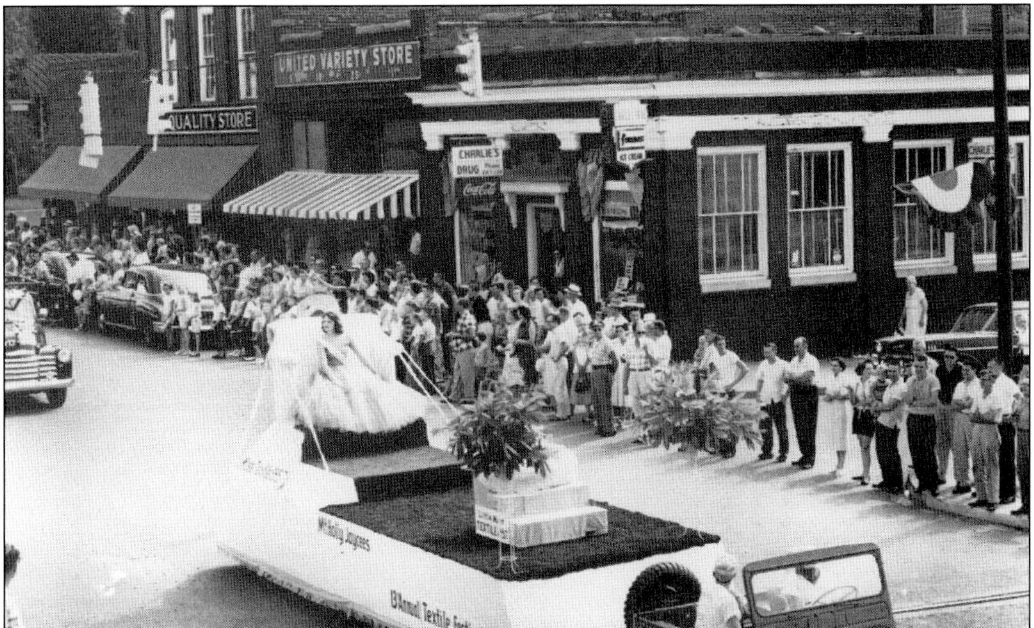


ANNUAL TEXTILE FESTIVAL, 1957. This parade float, pulled by a World War II jeep, is crossing the tracks at the corner of Main Street and Central Avenue. The nearest building, then housing Charlie's Drug Store, was originally the Mount Holly Bank. Note the attractive fabric awnings, which are now making a comeback in downtown Mount Holly. (Courtesy of Millican Pictorial History Museum.)

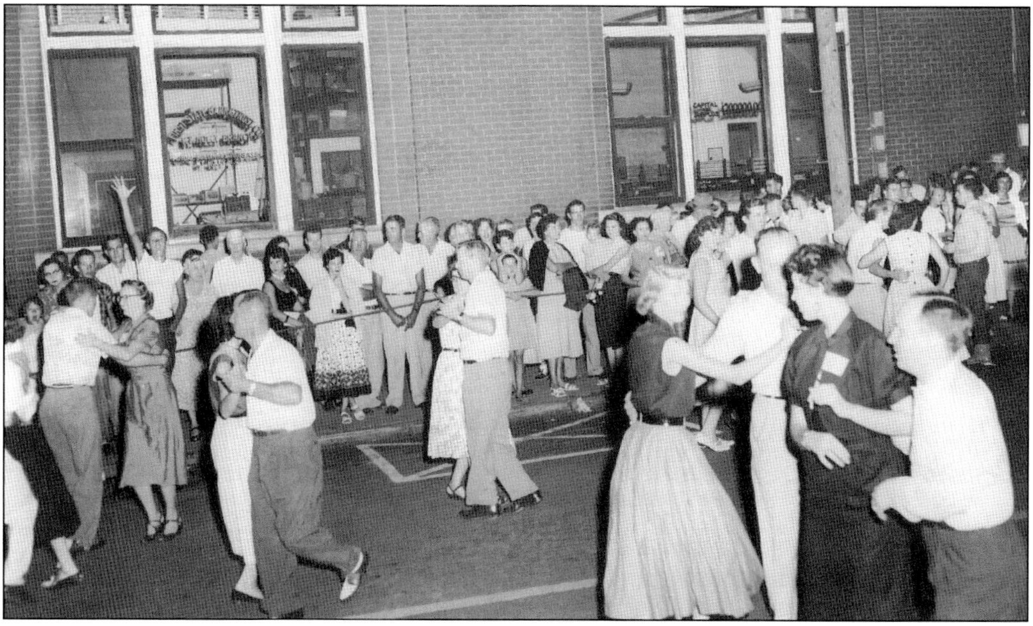

**Mount Holly Street Dance, 1950.** According to the *Mount Holly News* on August 4, 1950, the Durene Street Dance had a huge crowd that danced to the music of Thad Lawing and his band. Tickets cost 50¢ and were on sale from Mount Holly Jaycees and local drugstores. A mob of local residents and visitors from surrounding towns jammed East Central Avenue. The Durene doubleheader baseball game was also on tap, with a number of prizes being given away. The Durene Golf Tournament, Durene Banquet, Durene Parade, boxing matches, and a beauty contest were all part of the Durene Festival Week, which was sponsored by American Yarn and Processing Company. Note the fashions of the day—long pleated swing skirts that accentuated the waistline. (Both, courtesy of the City of Mount Holly Archives.)

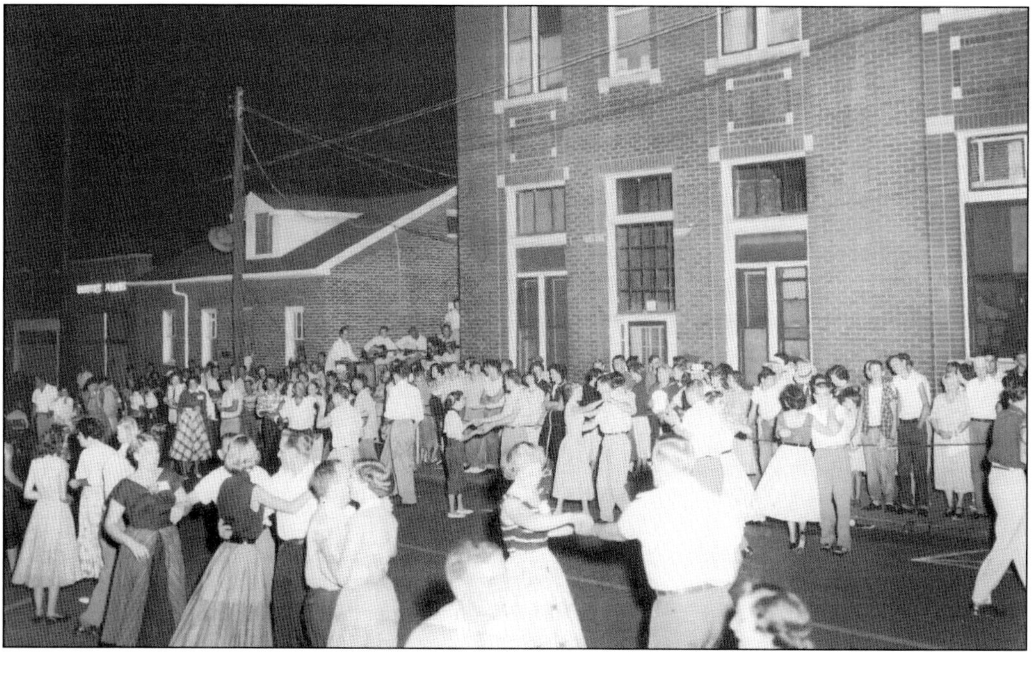

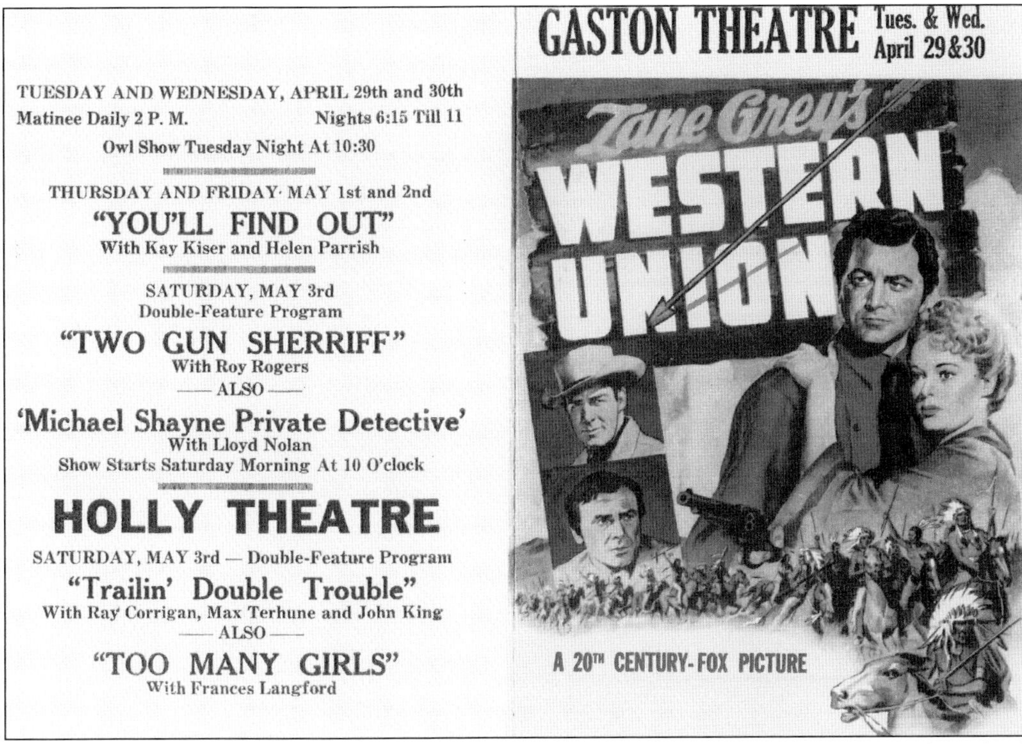
TUESDAY AND WEDNESDAY, APRIL 29th and 30th
Matinee Daily 2 P. M. Nights 6:15 Till 11
Owl Show Tuesday Night At 10:30

THURSDAY AND FRIDAY· MAY 1st and 2nd
"YOU'LL FIND OUT"
With Kay Kiser and Helen Parrish

SATURDAY, MAY 3rd
Double-Feature Program
"TWO GUN SHERRIFF"
With Roy Rogers
— ALSO —
'Michael Shayne Private Detective'
With Lloyd Nolan
Show Starts Saturday Morning At 10 O'clock

HOLLY THEATRE
SATURDAY, MAY 3rd — Double-Feature Program
"Trailin' Double Trouble"
With Ray Corrigan, Max Terhune and John King
— ALSO —
"TOO MANY GIRLS"
With Frances Langford



**THEATER PLAYBILLS, 1941.** The Holly Theater was at 111 East Charlotte Avenue and was built about 1920. The Gaston Theater, at 119 South Main Street, was built a little later and presented movies until the mid-1960s, when it was remodeled into the Paul Derr Clothing Store. (Courtesy of Millican Pictorial History Museum.)

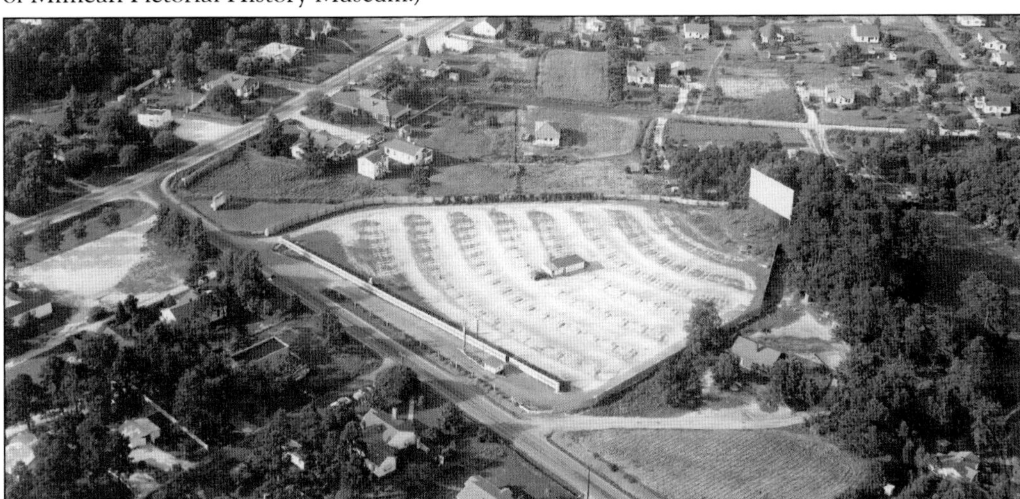

**MOONLIGHT DRIVE-IN THEATER.** The Mount Holly area's only drive-in theater was located near the corner of Belmont–Mount Holly Road and Beaty Road in the Catawba Heights neighborhood. Drive-ins were quite popular nationally after World War II and until the 1960s, when television and higher real estate prices put pressure on many open-air theaters to close. (Courtesy of Millican Pictorial History Museum.)

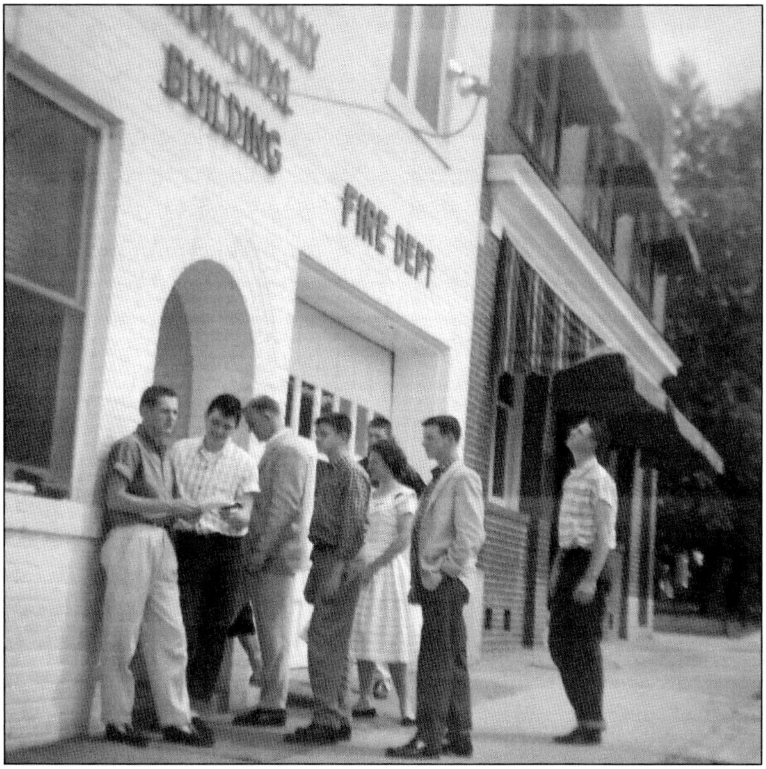


**THE MOUNT HOLLY MUNICIPAL BUILDING, C. 1960.** This photograph was taken looking south along South Main Street. Note the arched entrance and garage door (page 60). The young men sport the era's classic look—crew cuts, penny loafer shoes, and white socks. The building in the background was American and Efird's headquarters until its offices moved to American Street in 1967. (Courtesy of Millican Pictorial History Museum.)

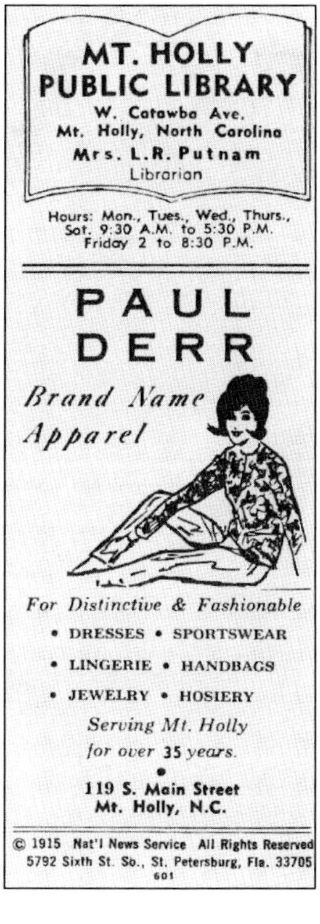


**PAUL DERR CLOTHING STORE.** This is an advertising bookmark from the Mount Holly Public Library. Paul Derr was known for high-quality, fashionable merchandise and great service. Originally located in the Summey building on South Main Street, the clothier moved to the site of the Gaston Theater when it closed in the late 1960s. (Courtesy of the City of Mount Holly Archives.)

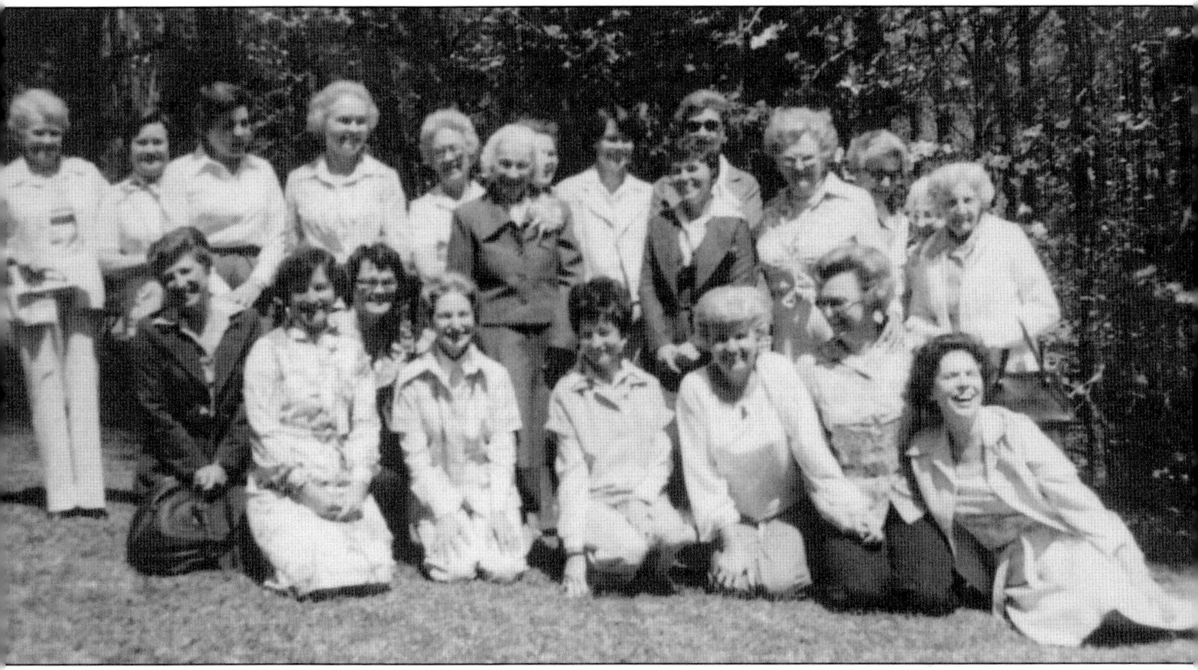

**MOUNT HOLLY GARDEN CLUB, C. 1970S.** The Mount Holly Garden Club meeting was held to honor Lollie Rankin Kendrick (center, with corsage). Kendrick's two daughters, Anne K. Brinkley (left of Kendrick) and Frances K. Springs, are kneeling in front of her. The picture was taken in the backyard at the home of Mackie Keeter Love (second row, fourth from left). Love's mother, Georgia Keeter, was also in attendance (second from the right in the second row). The organization was made up of leading women in the community who had a focus on education and service. Members learned about plants, gardening, and the community. They purchased books and donated them to the library and planted trees and flowers, often in memory of local people. The group maintained plantings as a way of beautifying the city of Mount Holly. (Courtesy of Frances K. Springs.)

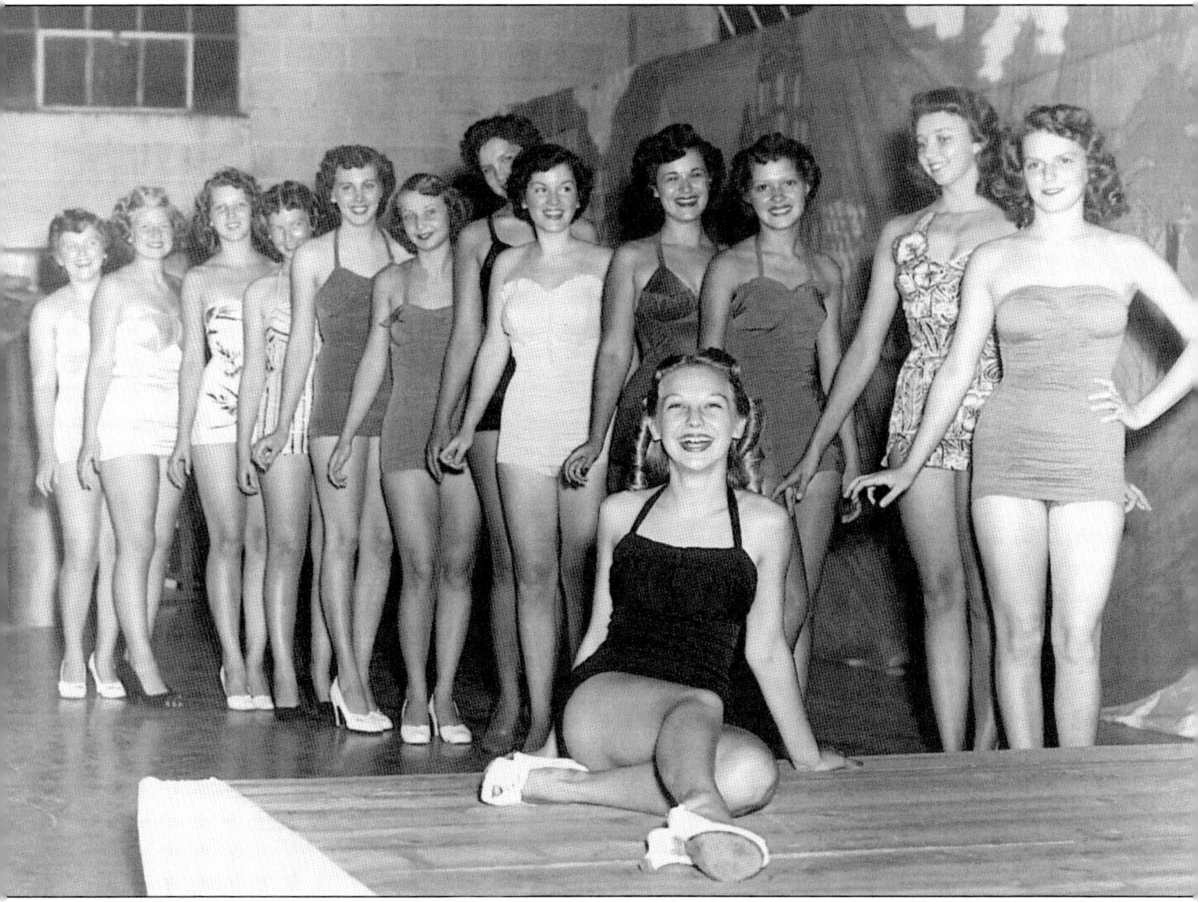

**MISS DURENE CONTEST, 1951.** American Yarn and Processing Company staged an annual Durene Festival in Mount Holly, complete with a dance, beauty pageant, and downtown parade. The company motto in the 1940s and 1950s was "We are proud of Durene." The Durene Association of America was composed of American Yarn and Processing and eight other leading mercerizers in the United States. The company boasted about the quality of their yarns, establishing a high standard for their Durene products. To emphasize the local pride-building potential of a quality label, American Yarn and Processing sponsored a spring festival and a company-wide beauty pageant. Each plant of the American Yarn and Processing Company group nominated a Durene contestant. The winner, Miss Durene, was selected at the pageant and reigned over the rest of the festival. This photograph was taken in the Mount Holly High School gymnasium. (Courtesy of Millican Pictorial History Museum.)

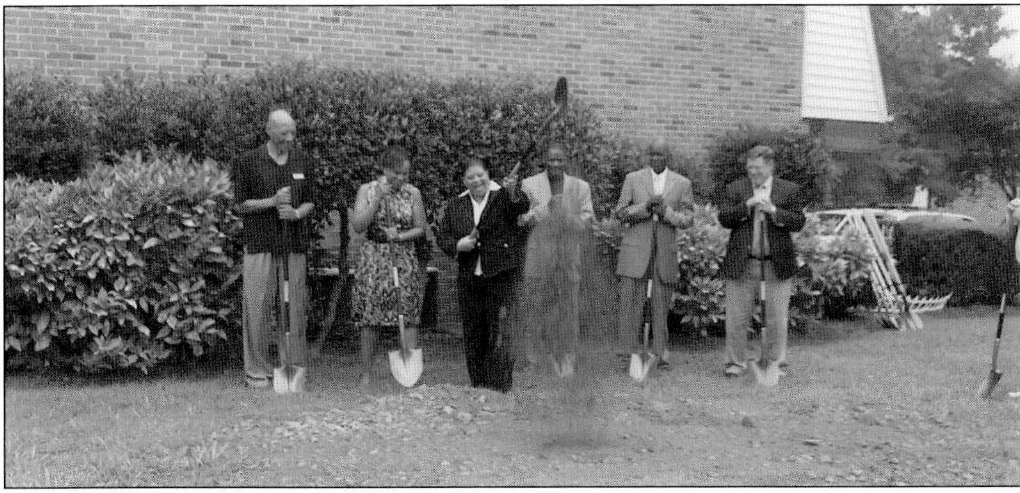

**Rollins School Memorial Ground-Breaking.** On August 15, 2009, the Mount Holly Black History Forum and the City of Mount Holly held a ground-breaking ceremony for the A.M. Rollins School Memorial on South Hawthorne Street. Dignitaries assembled included, from left to right, David Meachem, Kisha McLain, Caroline Reid, Danny Jackson, John Hope, and Mayor Robert Whitt. The memorial is 150 feet from the site of Ramses Hunter's house (page 70). (Courtesy of the City of Mount Holly.)

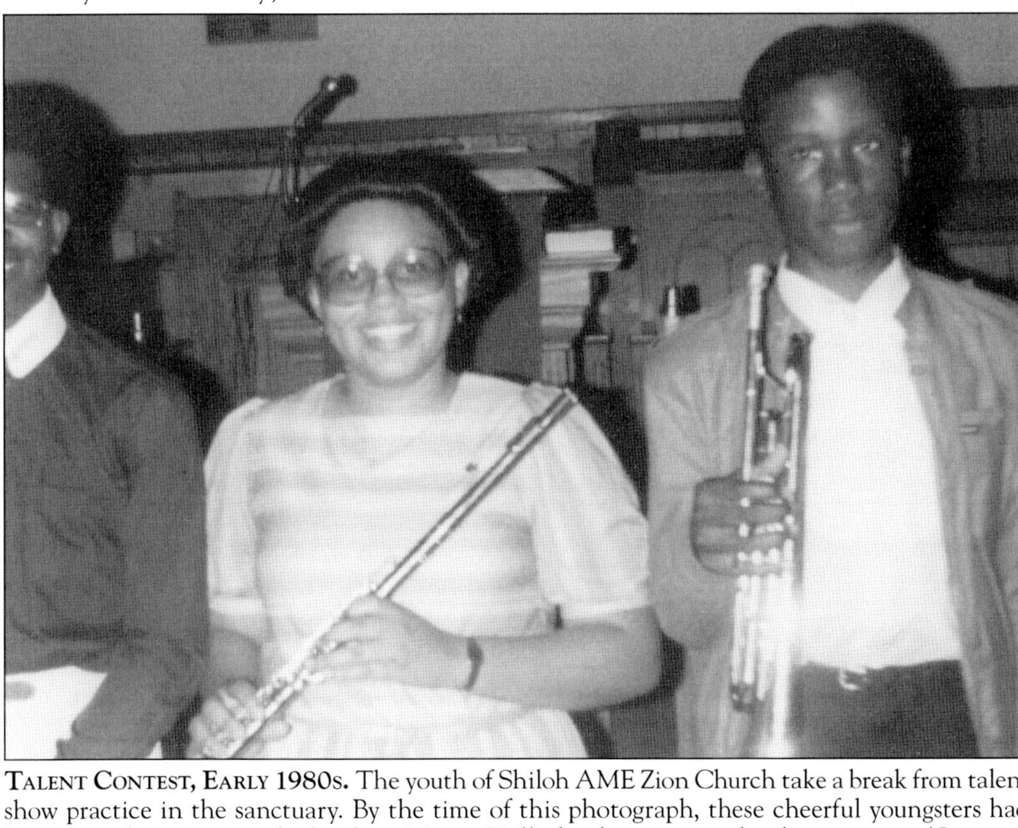

**Talent Contest, Early 1980s.** The youth of Shiloh AME Zion Church take a break from talent show practice in the sanctuary. By the time of this photograph, these cheerful youngsters had been attending integrated schools in Mount Holly for their entire school experience. (Courtesy of Essie Mae McGill.)

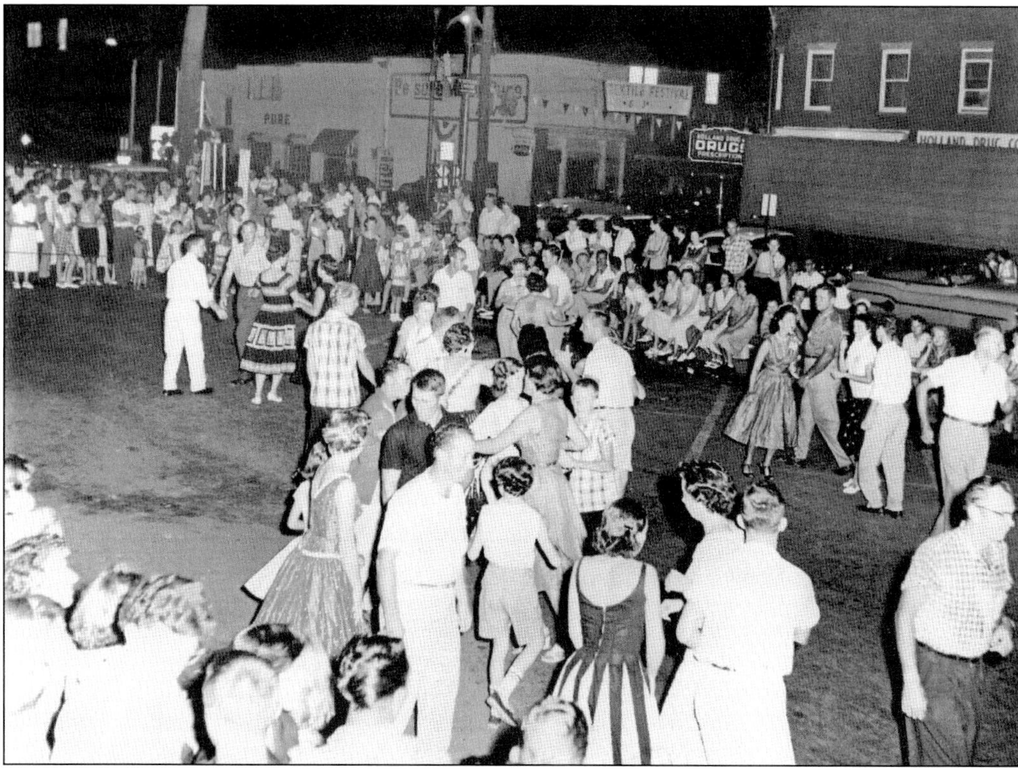


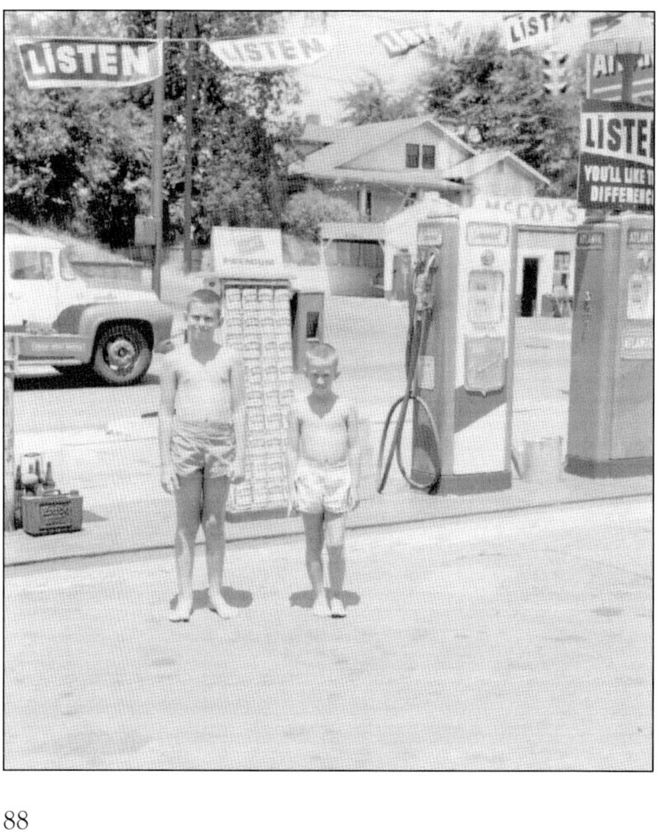


**Street Dance, Looking North.** This 1950 photograph pictures dancers on East Central Avenue, with Charlotte Avenue and North Main Street in the background. Holland's Drug Store is on the right in the background and the Pure gasoline station on the other corner. The gas station is located in the remnant of the old Rhyne building. (Courtesy of Millican Pictorial History Museum.)

**Atlantic Service Station, 1958.** The father of these two boys took this photograph at the southeast corner of Main Street and Catawba Avenue. Atlantic was a popular fuel brand along the East Coast until the early 1970s. Note the rival McKoy's service station on the other corner, below the Tucker house. (Courtesy of Adrian and Mina Beatty.)

# *Six*

# Icons and Characters
## Notable People

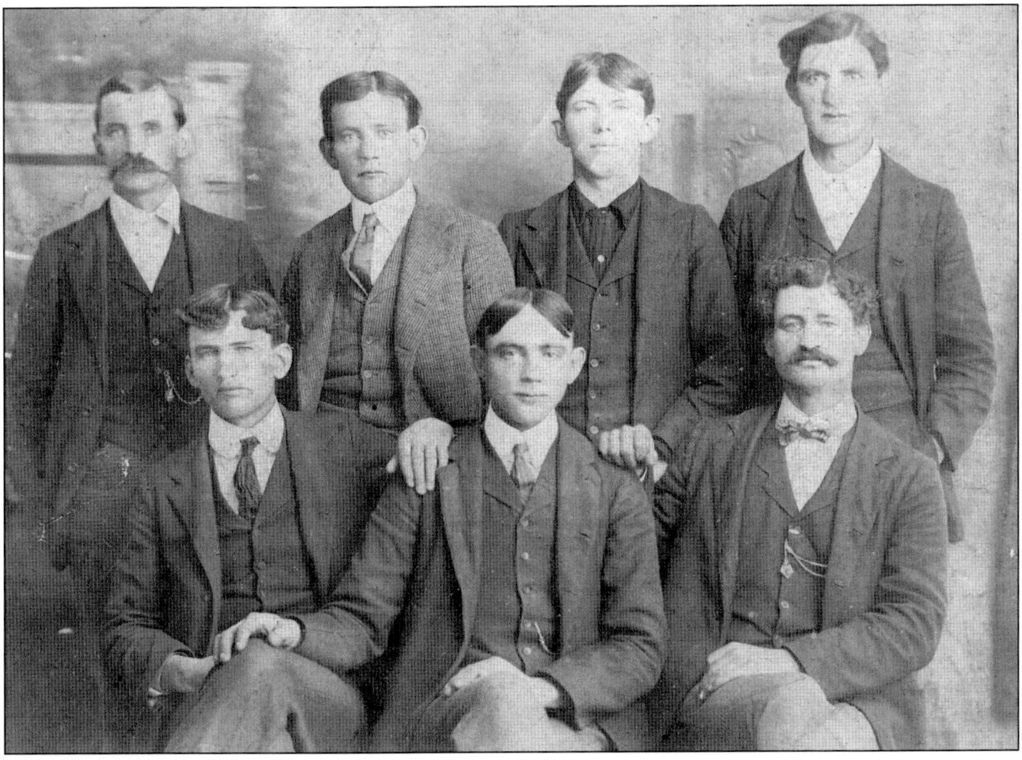

**The Young Lions.** This photograph of Mount Holly gentlemen is from the early 1900s. All are wearing their coats open to display their fashionable waistcoats. In this photograph are, from left to right, (first row) Ed Thompson, Tom Dunn, and T.H. Thompson; (second row) Jup Stowe, Bob Dixon, Lee Monk, and Lee ?. Ed Thompson was chief of police in Mount Holly from 1913 until 1928. (Courtesy of Linda Thompson Sherrill.)

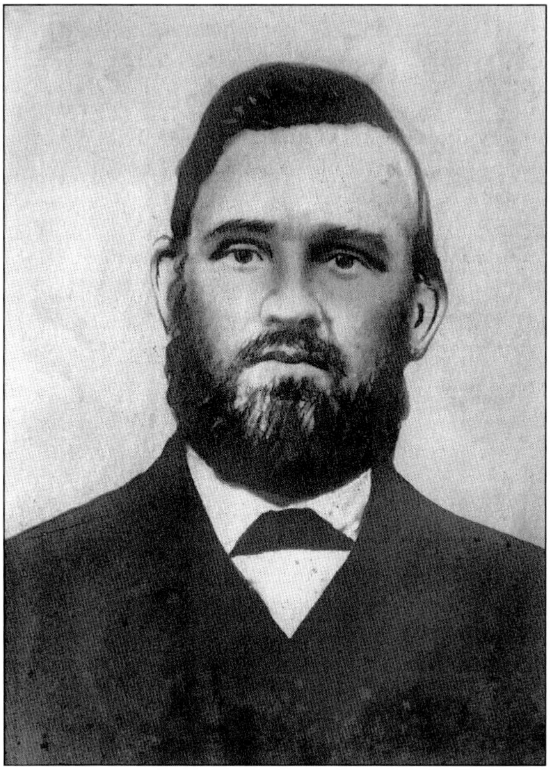

**Moses Hoffman Rhyne.** Rhyne (1812–1888) was one of the original partners in the Woodlawn Cotton Factory. His Hoffman-Rhyne General Store was the location for the 1842 meeting held to establish Gaston County. Rhyne had 11 children, including A.P. and D.E. Rhyne, the two brothers who launched the Mount Holly textile revolution. (Courtesy of C. Alexander.)

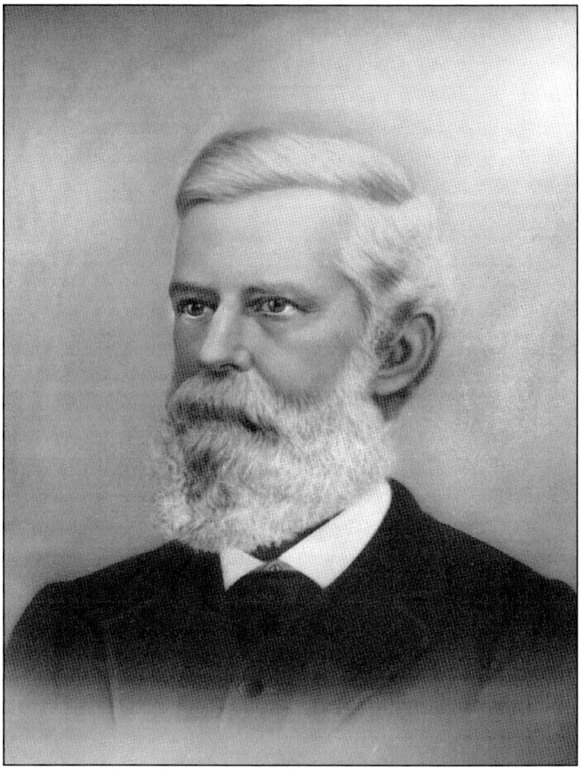

**Charles Lafayette Hutchison.** Hutchison (1824–1893) started his general store on Main Street shortly after the Civil War. It was there that his two clerks, son C. Egbert Hutchison (founder of American and Efird Mills) and R.L. Stowe (founder of Stowe Mills) honed their business skills. Hutchison's grandfather, Capt. William Hutchison, was a member of the Mecklenburg County Hornet's Nest militia during the American Revolution. (Courtesy of C. Alexander.)

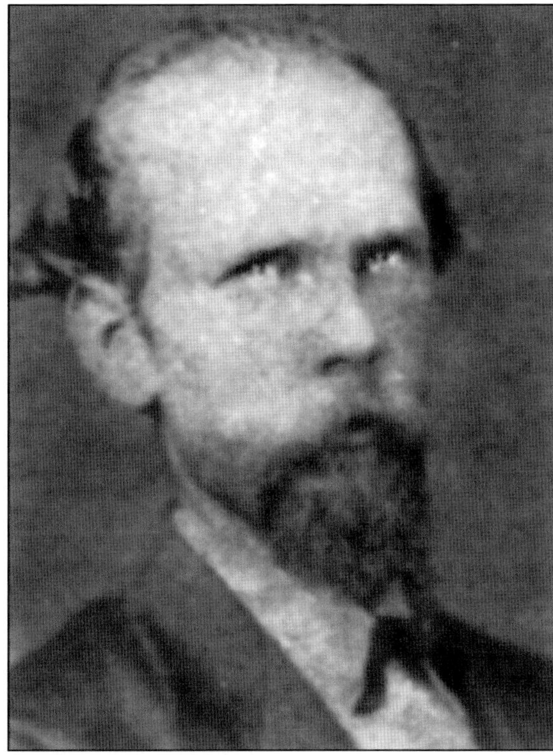

**WILLIAM B. RUTLEDGE.** W.B. Rutledge (1849–1933) was the local tax collector in the 1880s. He was also a farmer, educator, magistrate, and early mayor of Mount Holly, serving from 1896 to 1902, 1907 to 1908, and 1914 to 1917. The Rutledge family was among the first property owners in this section of the county. The oldest of the land grants to George Rutledge dates back to King George II in 1753. The land was on property located beside that of James Kuykendall, who was the first to obtain a grant in the Mount Holly area. A second Rutledge grant, for 320 acres on what is now Dutchman's Creek, was dated May 20, 1754. The home he built in 1878 still stands at the corner of West Charlotte Avenue and South Hawthorne Street. The document pictured below announces Rutledge's schedule for collecting local taxes in 1880. (Photographs by Rick Hauser.)

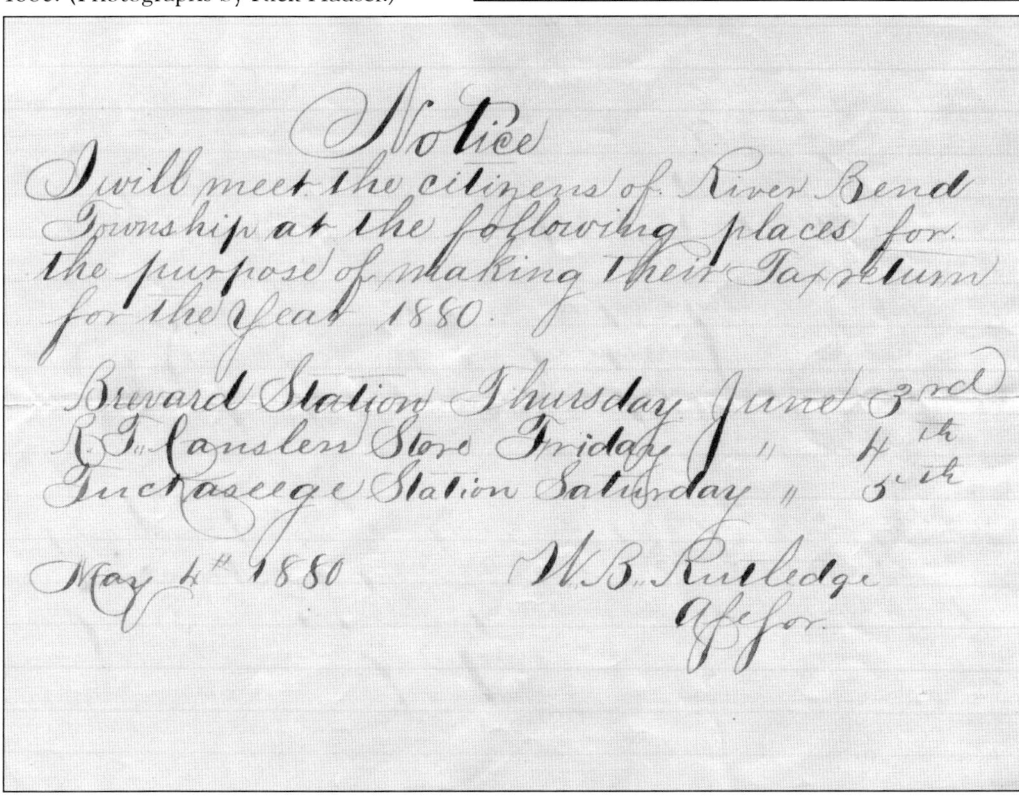

Notice

I will meet the citizens of River Bend Township at the following places for the purpose of making their Tax return for the year 1880.

Brevard Station Thursday June 3rd
R.F. Causler Store Friday " 4th
Tuckaseege Station Saturday " 5th

May 4th 1880

W.B. Rutledge
Assessor

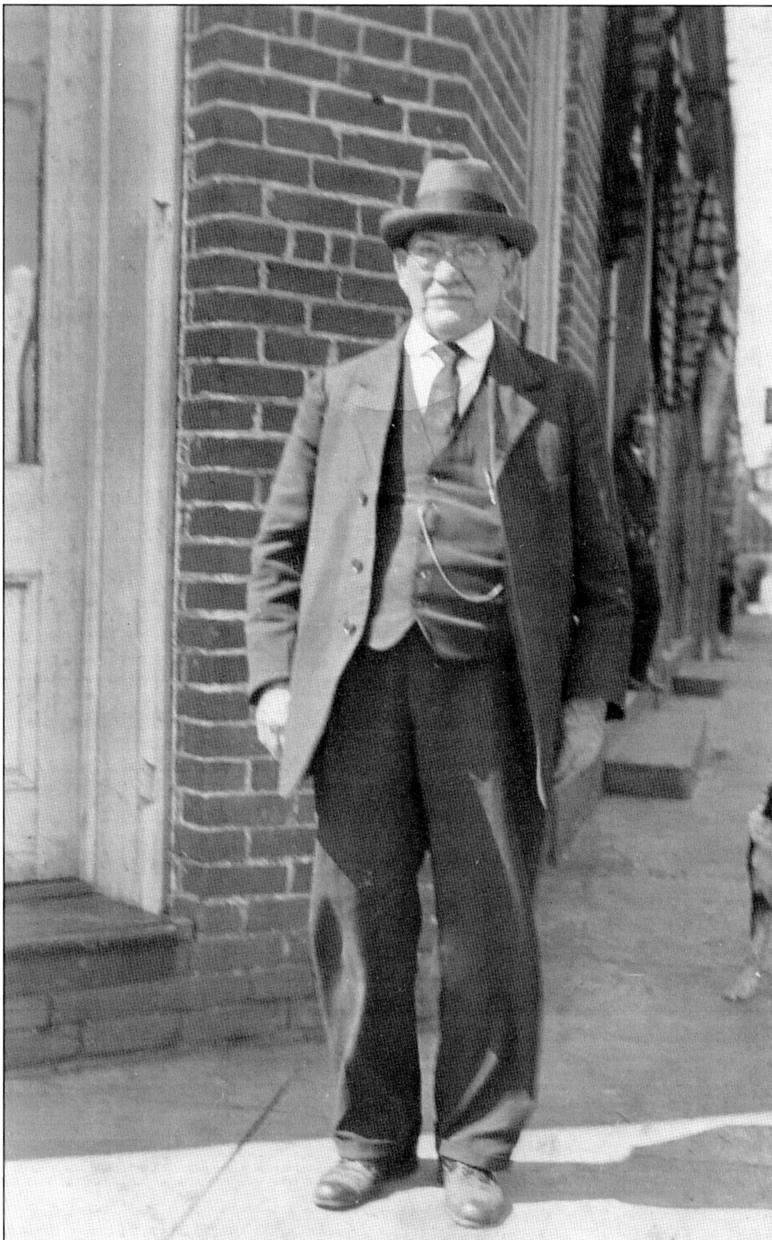

**Abel Peterson Rhyne.** A.P. Rhyne weighted only 88 pounds when he mustered out of the Confederate army in 1865. In 1874, he joined his brother Dan and father-in-law Ambrose Costner in planning the Mount Holly Cotton Mill, which opened in 1875. It was the first textile mill built in Gaston County after the Civil War. This small factory represented the start of a new economy; other mills soon followed. Rhyne built four more mills in Mount Holly. According to family legend, Thomas Edison installed a generator in the Mount Holly Mill in the 1890s, supplying electrical power to other businesses in the town. Thus, the small town of Mount Holly had electric streetlights—although there were only three—in the 1890s, while the big city of Charlotte still used gaslights. (Courtesy of C. Alexander.)

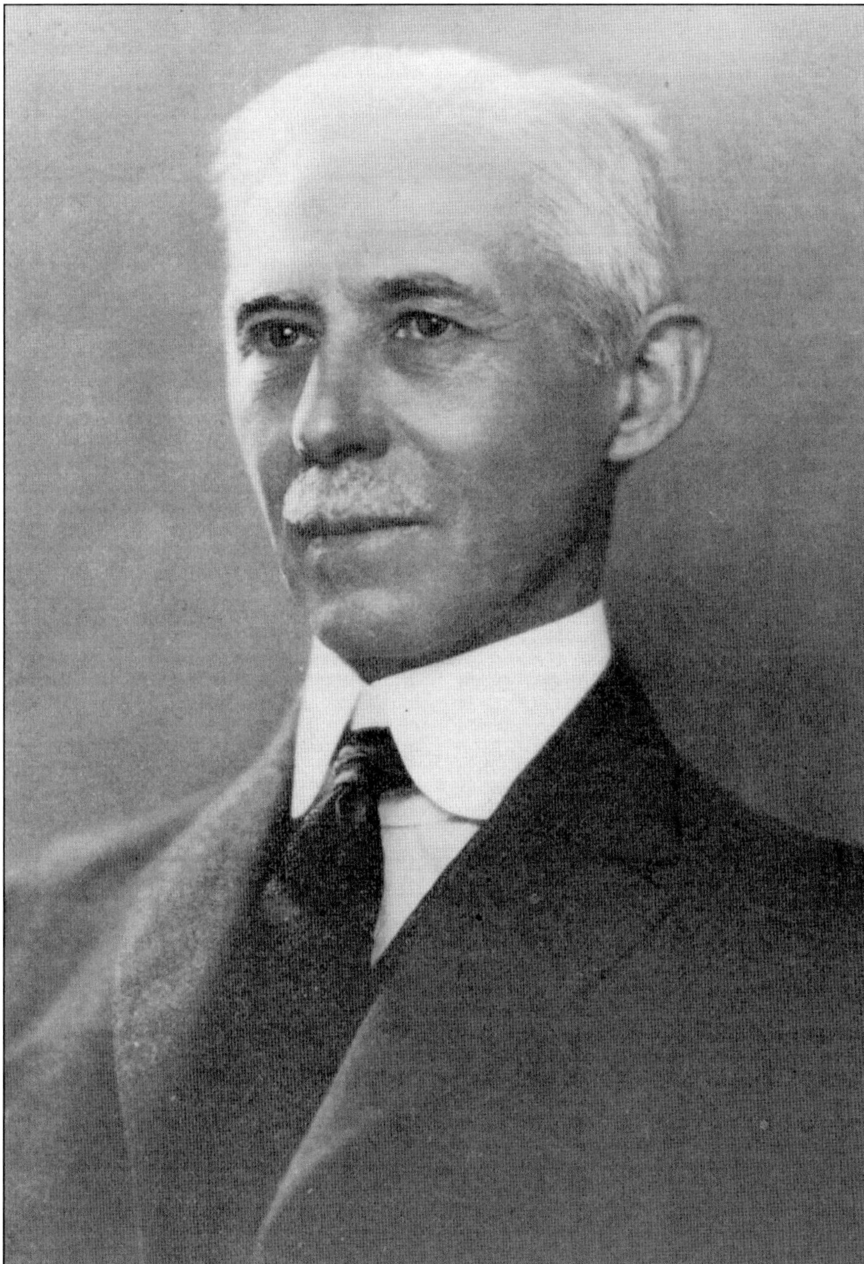

**HARDWORKING MAGNATE.** Charles Egbert Hutchison (1860–1942), a native of Mount Holly, was one of the earliest and most successful of the textile entrepreneurs in Gaston County. He received his early training as a store clerk at his father's South Main Street store. Hutchison's first venture into textiles was as an investor in the Albion (Mount Holly Knitting) Mill along with A.P. Rhyne. He then became a principal in a number of the early Mount Holly mills (Nims, Woodlawn, and Adrian) and was the first mill owner in Gaston County to consolidate all of the holdings into one corporation. This company became the forerunner of today's American and Efird, Inc. In addition to his many business interests, C.E. Hutchison served as chairman of the Mount Holly School Board for 20 years. (Courtesy of Robert A. Ragan.)

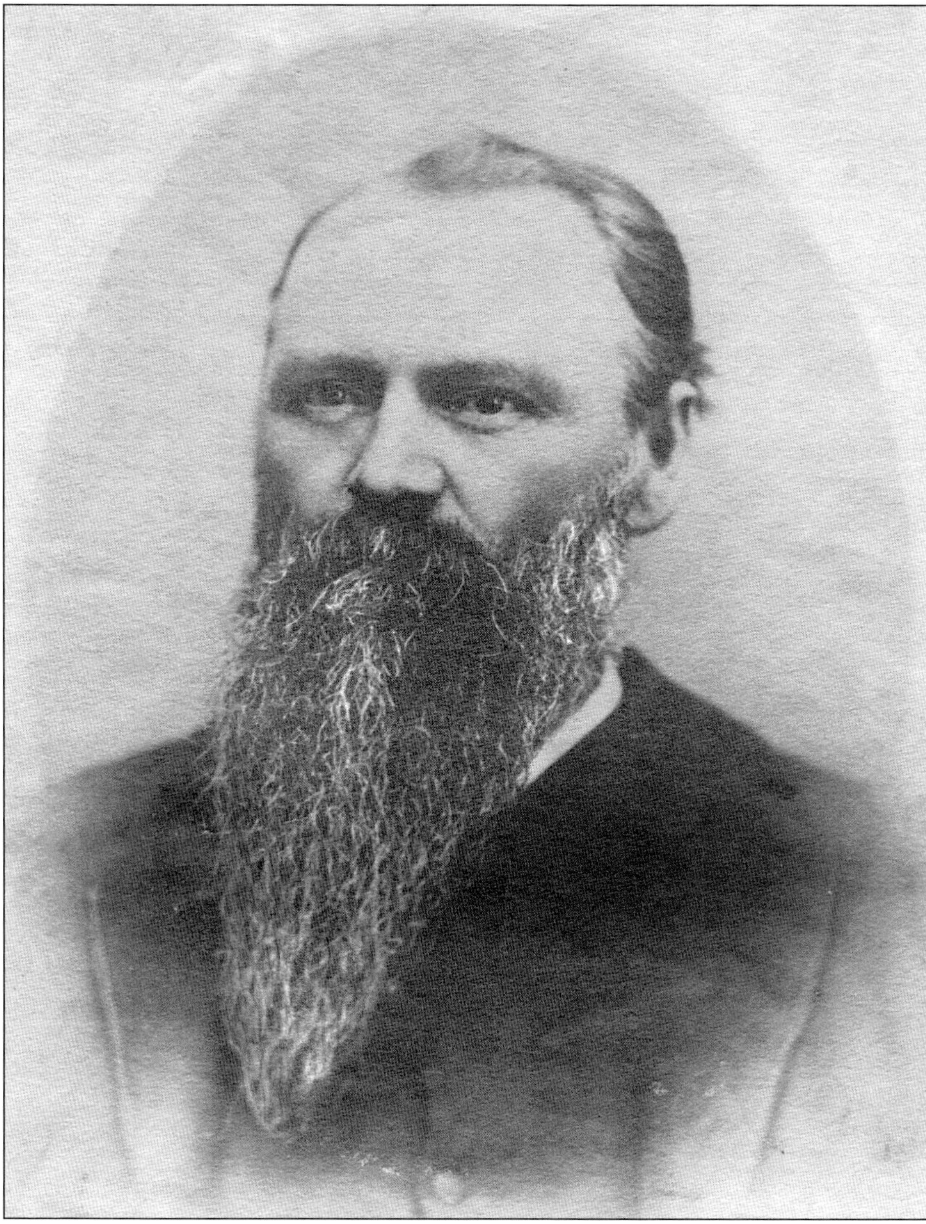

**Robert Calvin Grier Love.** In 1871, R.C.G. Love purchased the former Fredrick Hoffman house and farm. He also purchased the interest of his brother-in-law A.P. Rhyne in the Hoffman-Rhyne Store on Tuckaseege Road. Love had a farm, a cotton gin, and a mercantile store in Woodlawn. He later bought full interest in the store from his father-in-law, Moses H. Rhyne. He also conducted a banking business with small loans from farmers and a personal savings bank in the thrifty farming community. He was postmaster of Woodlawn in 1874, just before the name was changed to Mount Holly. Love later moved to Gastonia, and along with local investors, he built the first steam-powered textile mill, Gastonia Cotton Manufacturing Company. His sons were pioneers in textiles throughout Piedmont region of North Carolina. Love's grandson J. Spencer Love founded Burlington Industries, at one time the largest textile company in the world. (Courtesy of James F. Love III.)

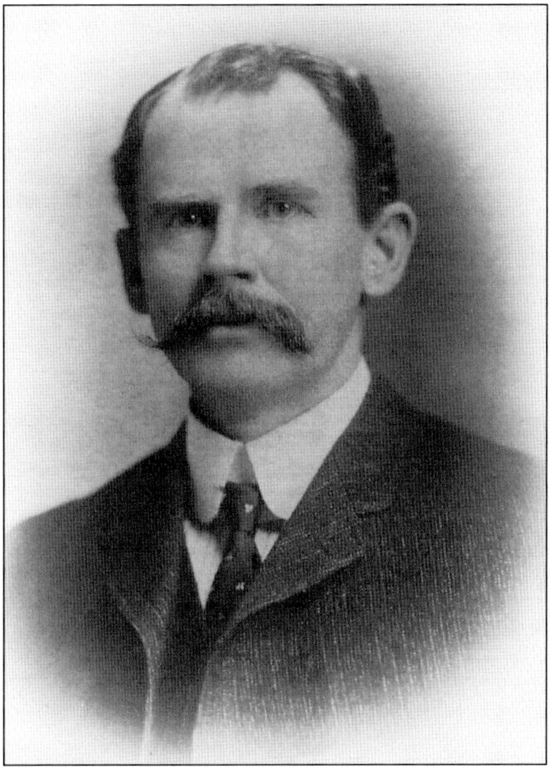

**William Thomas Love.** Love was the first appointed mayor of Mount Holly in 1879. He worked in the Woodlawn store in his youth and later exported his talents to other parts of Gaston County. The town of Ranlo's name is a combination of "Ran" for partner John Rankin and "lo" for Love. Love was elected mayor of Gastonia, serving for two terms, and he also served in the state legislature. (Courtesy of James F. Love III.)

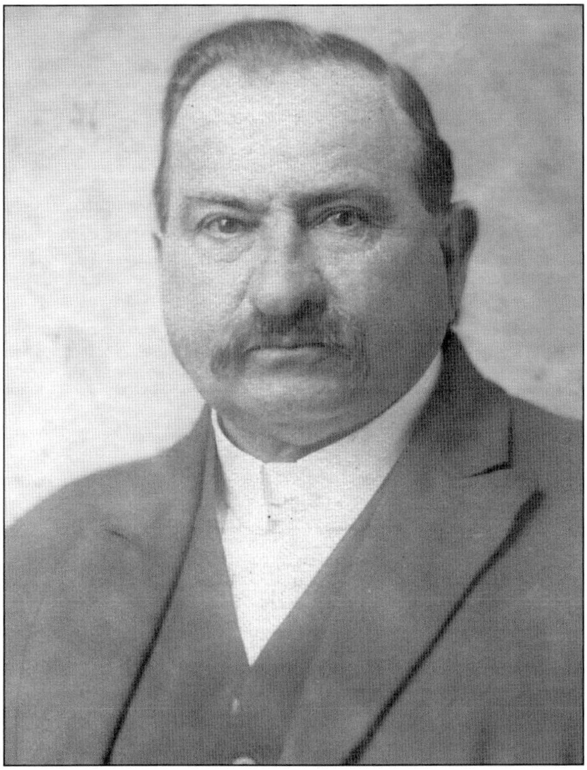

**Daniel Efird Rhyne.** Rhyne (1852–1933), along with his brother A.P. Rhyne and Ambrose Costner, built the Mount Holly Cotton Mill. He went on to own 20 textile mills and was president of four banks. Called "Uncle Dan" by everyone, he was known for his humility and generosity. Lenoir-Rhyne University was named in his honor. (Courtesy of C. Alexander.)

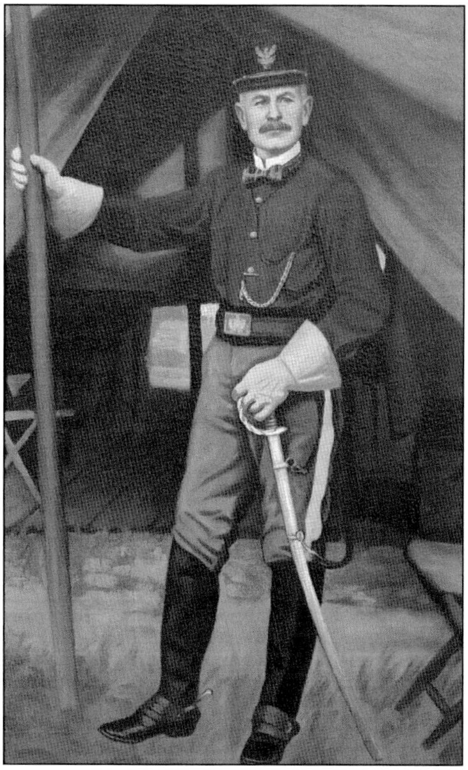

**Capt. Washington Holland.** In the 1880s, Holland (1851–1926) formed a ceremonial militia company. Soon after, Captain Holland settled in Mount Holly. In 1893, he opened Holland's Drug Store. He opened the first telephone exchange and the first launderette and sold the first ice cream in Mount Holly. He also started a great band (page 76). (Courtesy of the Gaston County American Military Museum; photograph by Rick Hauser.)

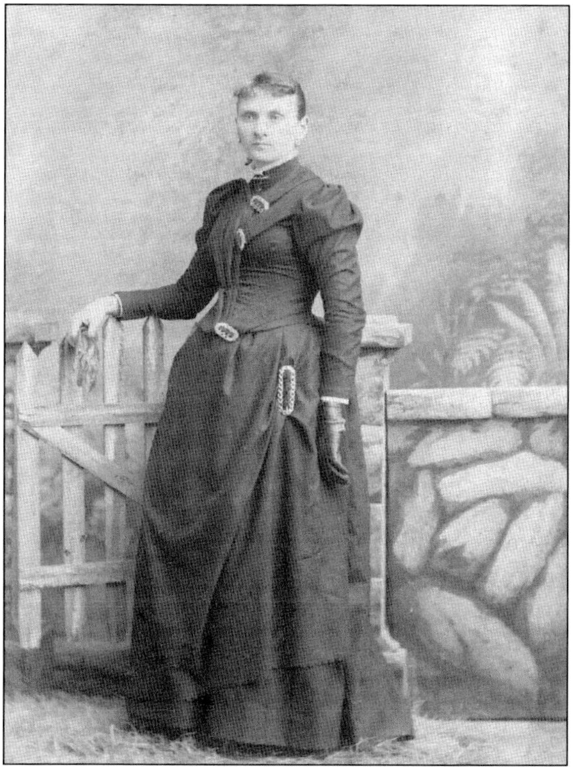

**Margaret Shufford Rhyne Holland.** Margaret Rhyne (1867–1904) was the wife of Capt. Washington Holland. This photograph, by Belk's Studio in Charlotte, was made in the mid-1880s. Note the fashionable rider's glove. Maggie Holland was the daughter of Moses Rhyne and Mary Caroline Springs. (Courtesy of C. Alexander.)

**MYLDRED LIPSCOMB.** Lipscomb is very much in fashion with her fur coat and cloche hat that would be fitting for any flapper in the 1920s. Lipscomb was a senior class sponsor at Mount Holly High School, class of 1930. In 1957, she was still at Mount Holly High, teaching Latin and English. (Courtesy of the *Holly Hawk* yearbook, 1930.)

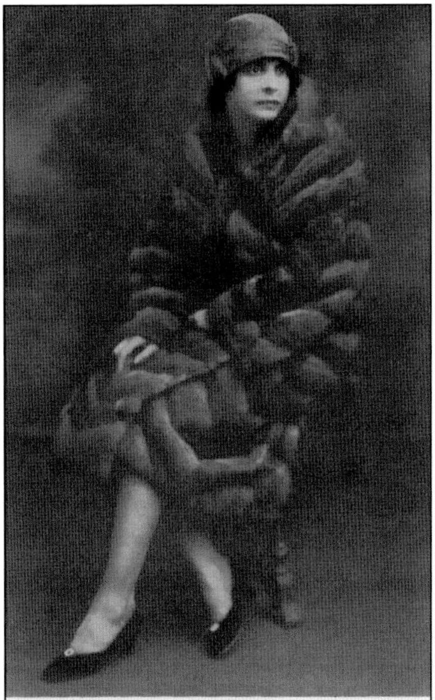

MISS MYLDRED LIPSCOMB
*Sponsor Senior Class*

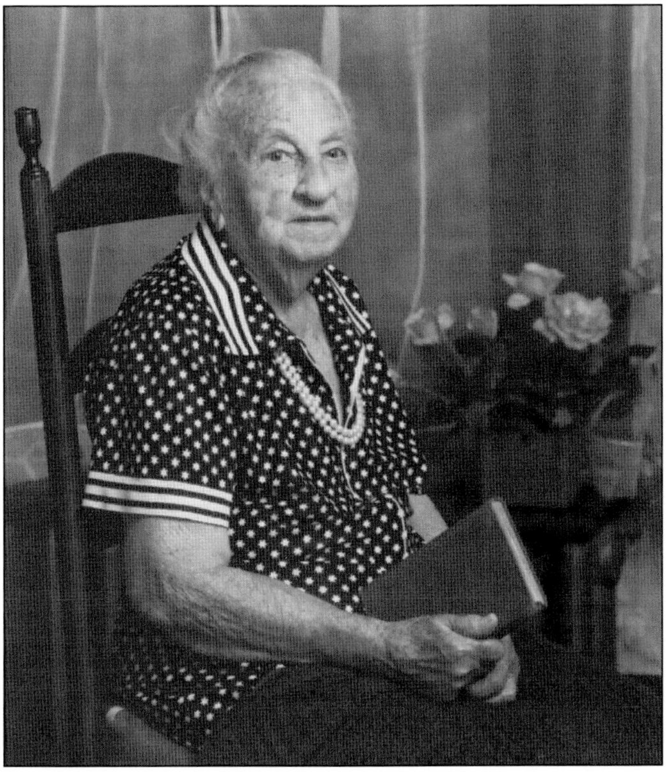

**GERTRUDE COSTNER.** She was the wife of James Ambrose Costner, who was a partner in the Mount Holly Cotton Mill with the Rhyne brothers. "Aunt Gertie," as she was called by generations of adoring children, lived in an ornate late-Victorian house on a hill overlooking South Main Street and the P&N railroad. (Courtesy of Betty M. Belk.)

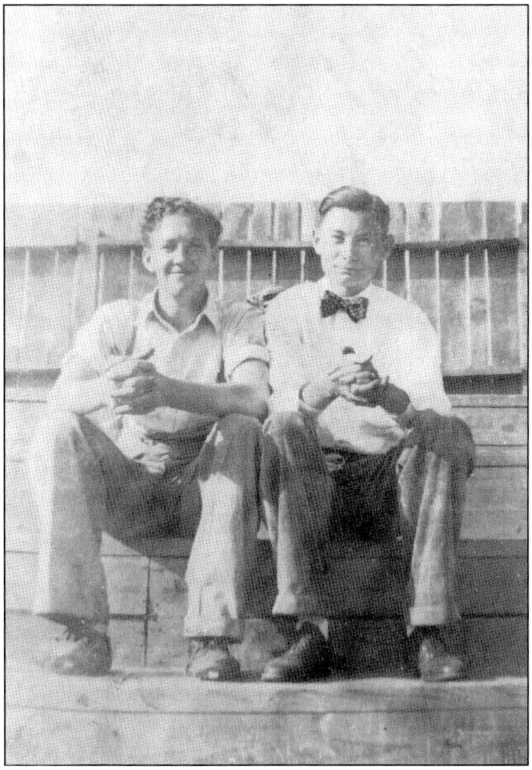

**HIGH SCHOOL STUDENTS, C. 1938.** Frank Craig (left) and John Benfield are sitting in the wooden field bleachers located across from the Mount Holly High School. The athletic facilities were across Hawthorne Street from the high school and other classroom buildings. (Courtesy of Wrene Benfield.)

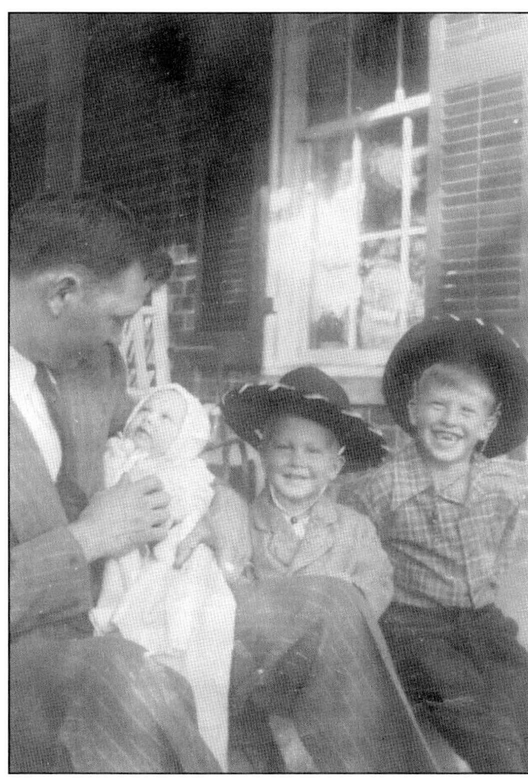

**CHAPPIE AND THE COWBOYS.** Charles "Chappie" A. Rhyne is pictured with his sons Joe, Steve, and Charles Jr. (Charlie) at the West Catawba Avenue home place in 1949. Chappie Rhyne is best remembered for serving as the county commissioner representing the Riverbend Township in the 1970s and 1980s. (Courtesy of C. Alexander.)

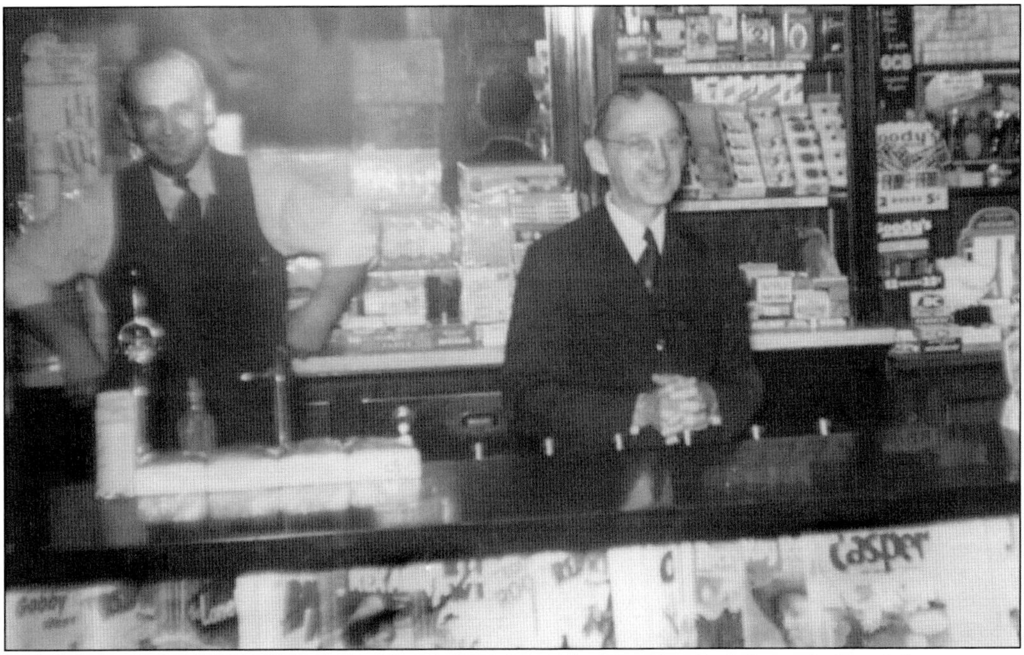


**WILLIS "POP" HOLLAND.** Willis Holland (right) and his brother Ralph are behind the counter at Holland Drug Store. Holland's filled prescriptions and provided various sundries, including fountain drinks and comic books, to several generations of Mount Holly families. Holland Drug Store closed its doors in 1988. (Courtesy of Linda Thompson Sherrill.)

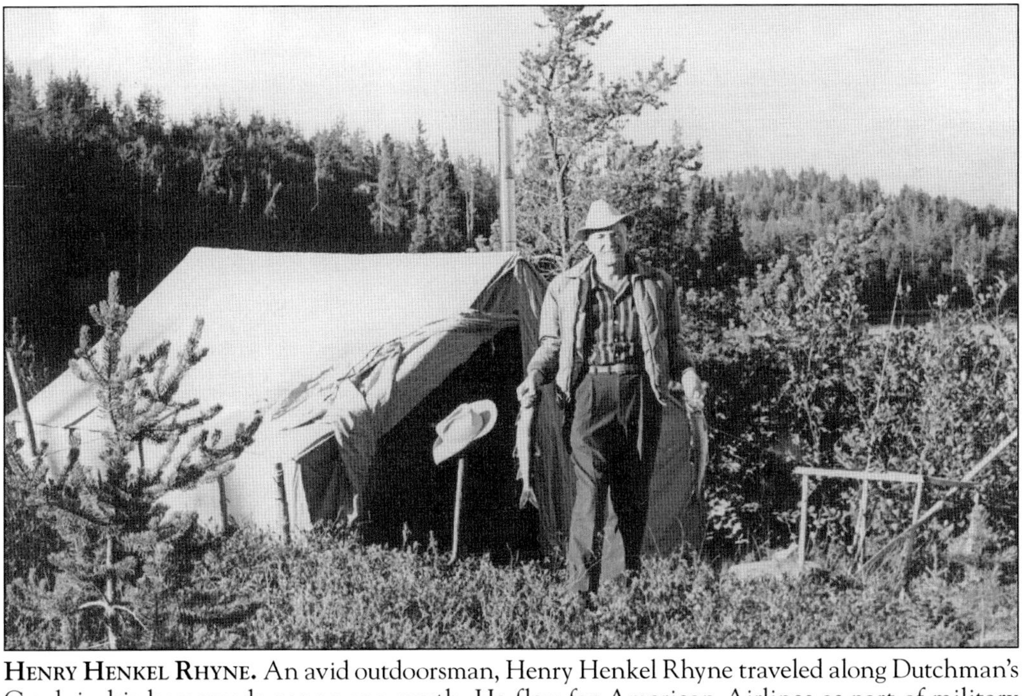

**HENRY HENKEL RHYNE.** An avid outdoorsman, Henry Henkel Rhyne traveled along Dutchman's Creek in his homemade canoe as a youth. He flew for American Airlines as part of military transportation during World War II. The home where he was born and raised is now the Robin's Nest Bed and Breakfast on North Main Street. (Courtesy of C. Alexander.)

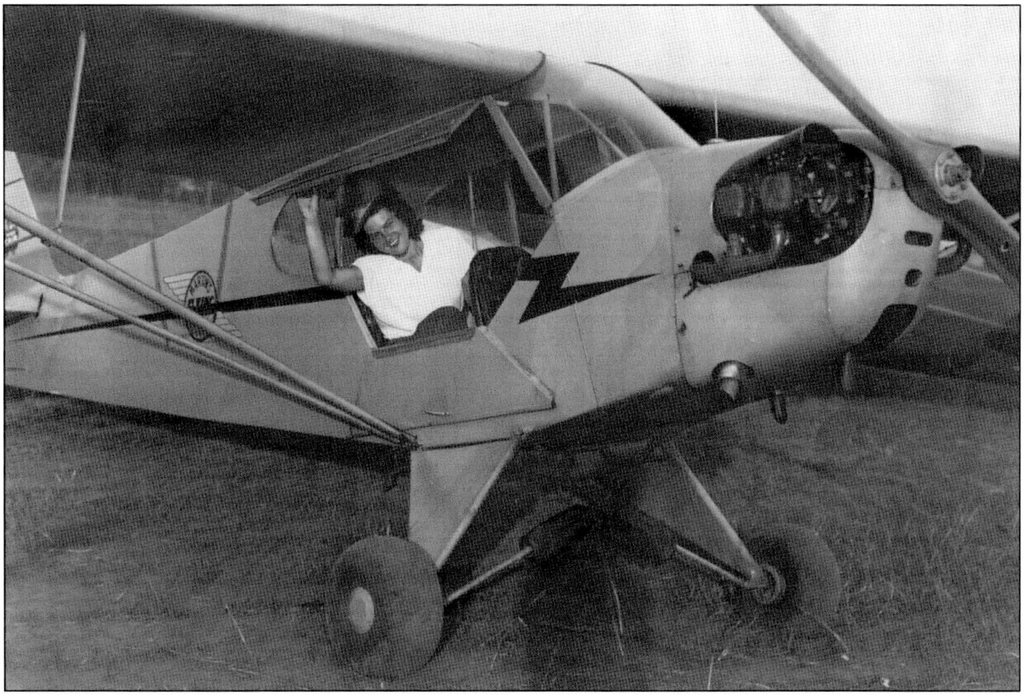

**LIB NICHOLS, FIRST WOMAN PILOT.** Born in 1921, Mary Elizabeth Cash Nichols was Mount Holly's first woman pilot. Richard Mauney started the Mount Holly Airport about 1946, and Lib Nichols flew there during the years 1948 to 1952. The airport had a 2,000-foot grass and gravel runway near present-day Westland Farm Road. (Courtesy of Daphne E. Barton.)

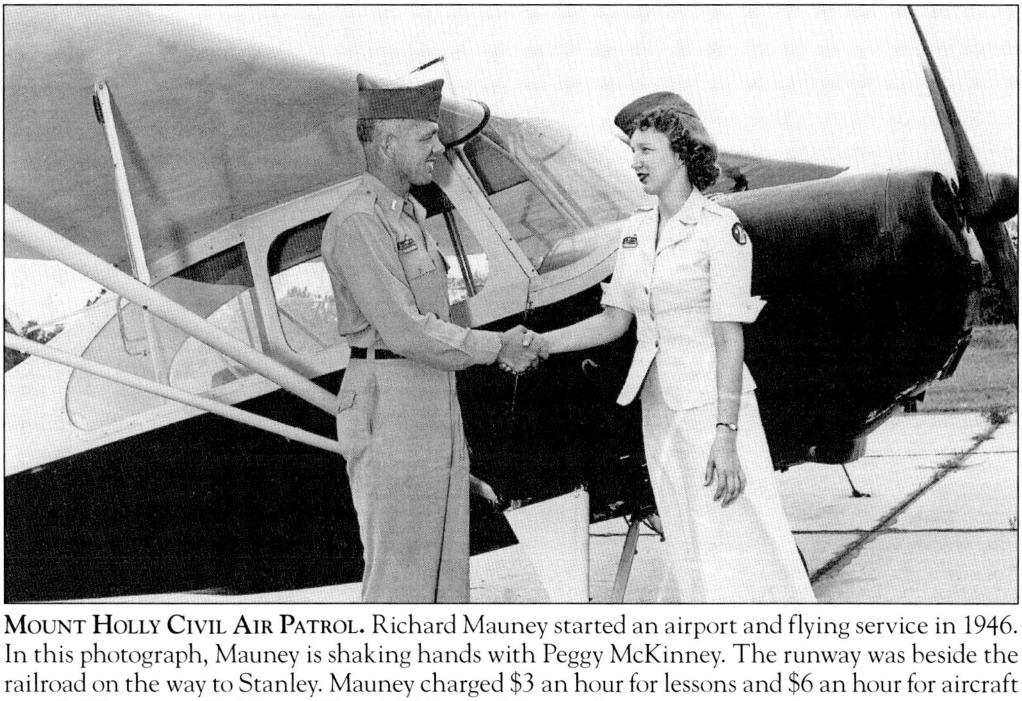

**MOUNT HOLLY CIVIL AIR PATROL.** Richard Mauney started an airport and flying service in 1946. In this photograph, Mauney is shaking hands with Peggy McKinney. The runway was beside the railroad on the way to Stanley. Mauney charged $3 an hour for lessons and $6 an hour for aircraft rental. (Courtesy of Millican Pictorial History Museum.)

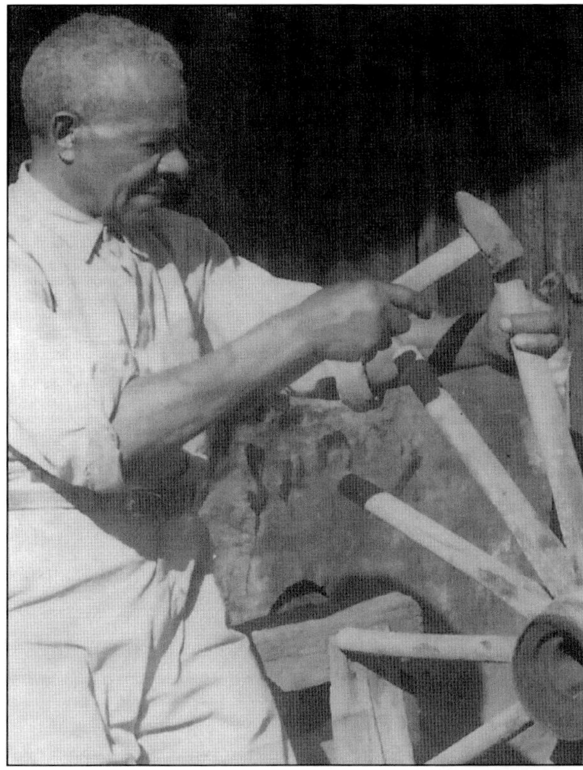

**Local Blacksmith, c. 1950s.** Andrew Bailey was a local blacksmith who worked in his building on West Catawba Avenue, just west of the Mount Holly Library. He repaired farm implements and wagon wheels, shoed horses and mules, and made various iron products. (Courtesy of the City of Mount Holly Archives.)

**Kemp Ervin Michael in the Boiler Plant.** This photograph of Kemp Ervin Michael was taken in 1935 in the boiler room of the American plant. Michael was foreman of American's steam plant. He was the first of four generations in Mount Holly. Sons Kemp Shuford Michael and Forney Michael became FBI special agents. (Courtesy of Kemp A. Michael.)

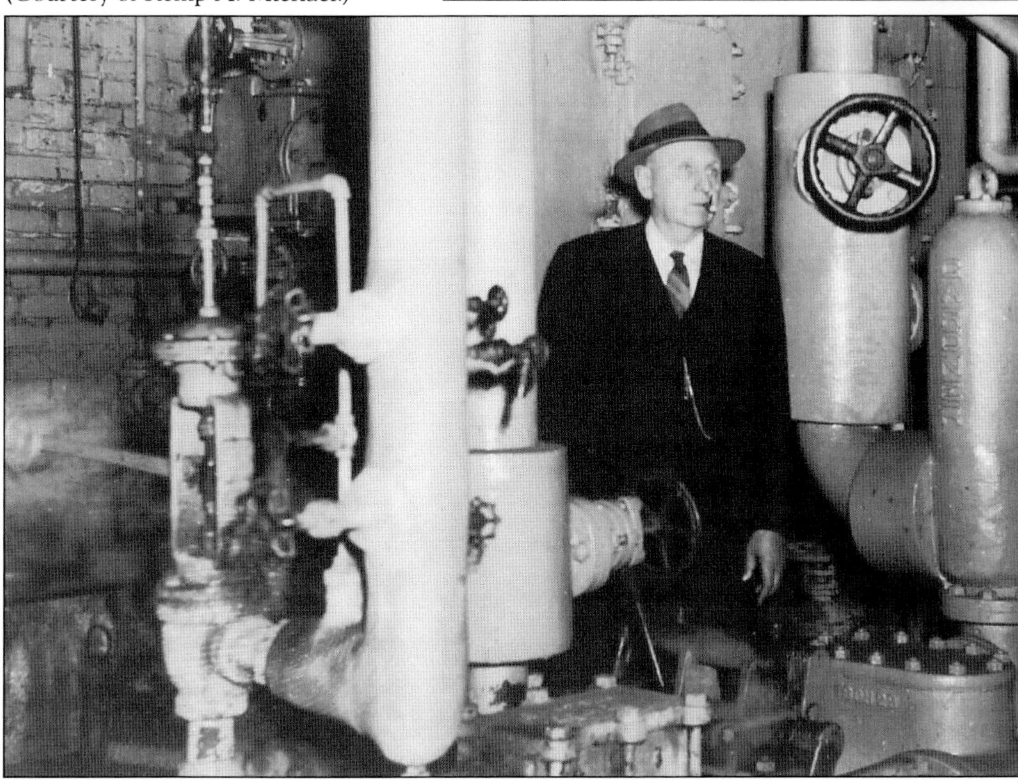

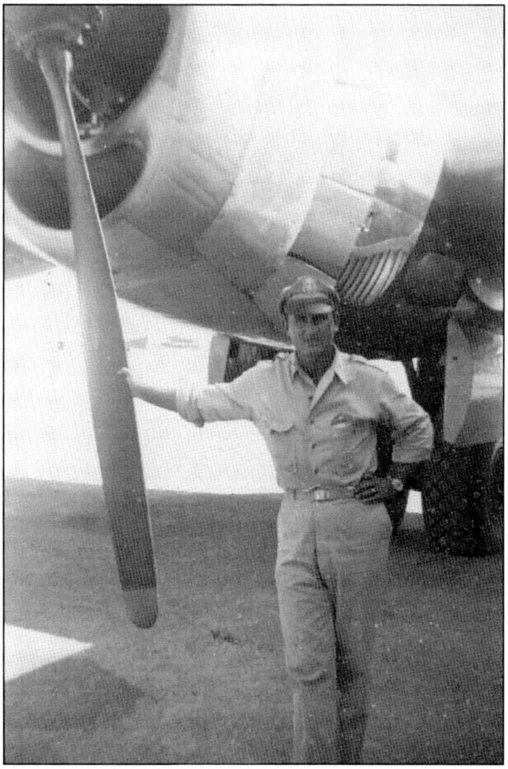

**J.B. THOMPSON IN THE WAR.** Lieutenant Thompson, later owner of Mount Holly Ice and Fuel, flew B-29 bombers in the Pacific during World War II. Thompson was a big man, so the photograph conveys the sheer size of this gigantic aircraft. Thompson's brother Dick was a respected high school coach in both Mount Holly and Stanley. (Courtesy of Linda Thompson Sherrill.)

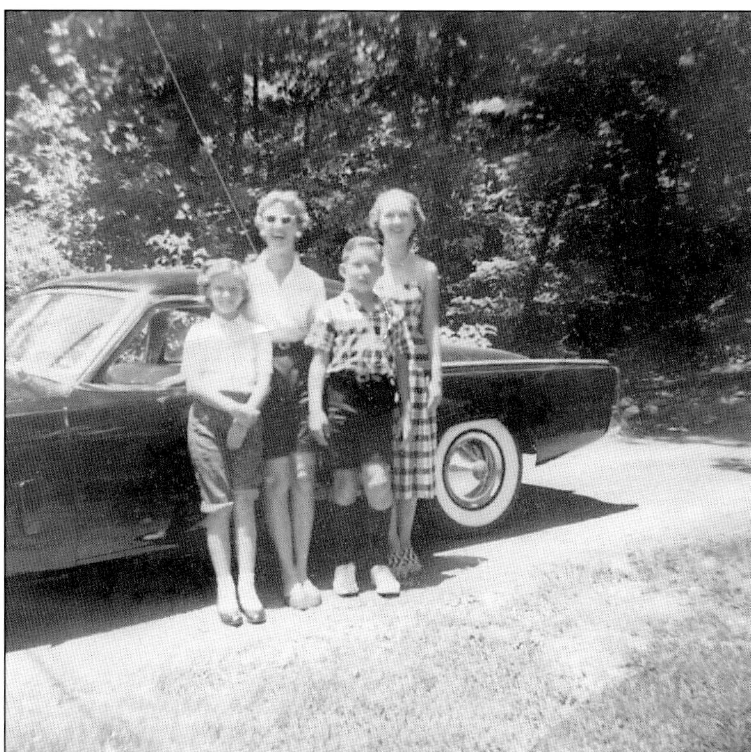

**WOODLAND PARK, 1957.** Aunt Ann Keeter Fowler (adult on left) visits her sister Mackie Love (adult on right) on Dogwood Drive in her 1953 Studebaker. Jimmy and Mimi Love (Guin) stand by the car. Jimmy asked aunt Ann to save the car for him, and it became Jim's first car. He still occasionally drives his prized Studebaker Commander, 50 years later. (Courtesy of James F. Love III.)

*Seven*

# Apple of My Eye
## Mount Holly Schools

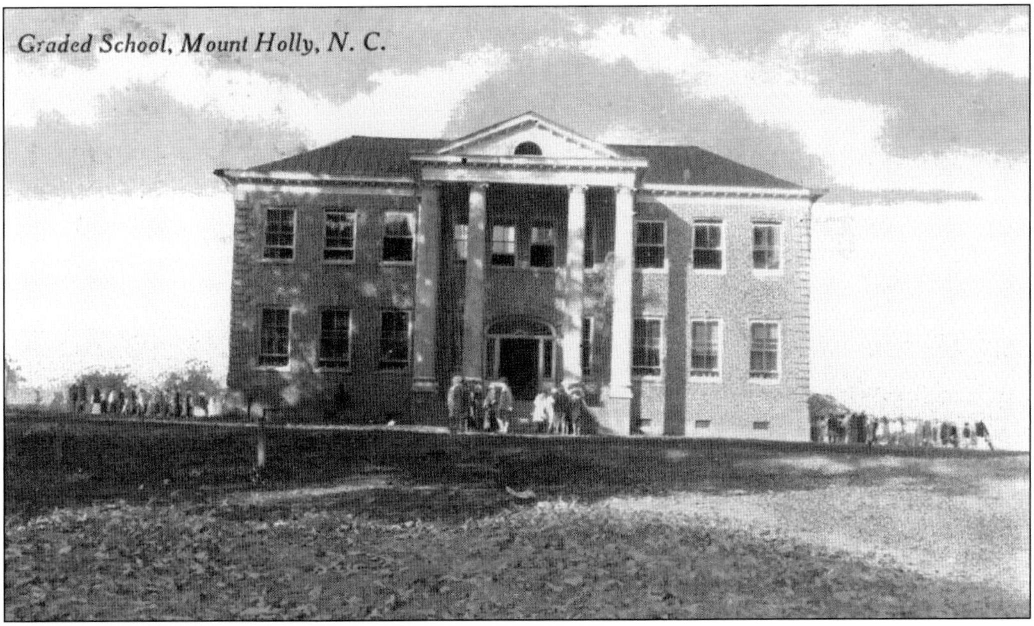


**Central Avenue Schoolhouse.** The first brick school building was erected here in 1910. Citizens thought this building would be adequate for 25 years. However, by 1914, there was not enough room to house the rapidly expanding student body. Therefore, two rooms were rented downtown over the Holland Drug Store—one for the first grade and the other for home economics classes. (Courtesy of C. Alexander.)

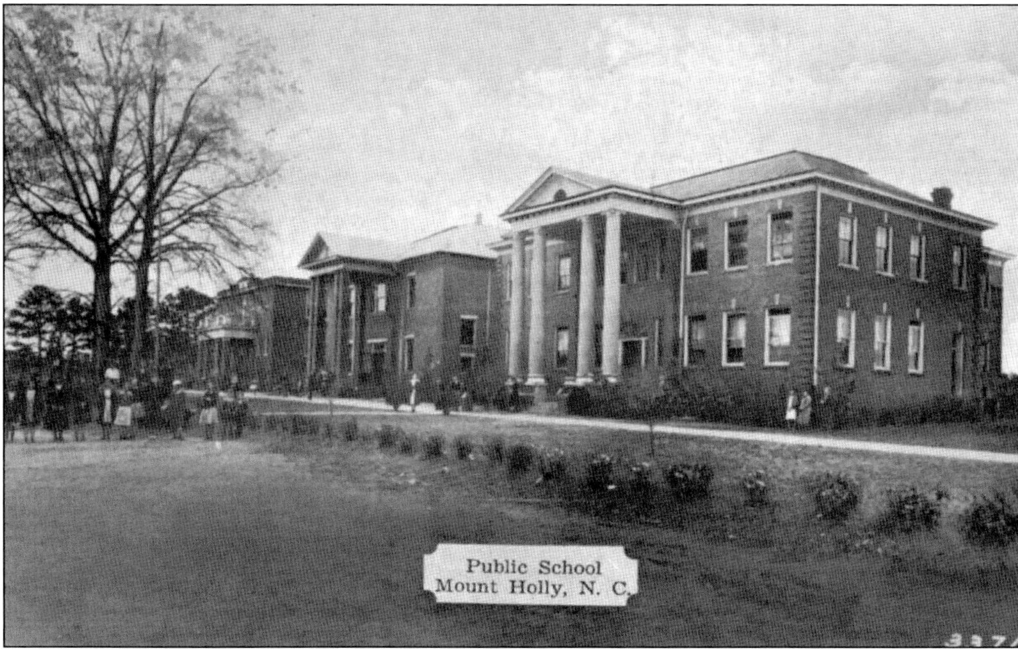


**Public School Complex.** By 1916, a second school building was constructed beside the first, and a third was added in 1923. The children of James Arthur Rhyne lived about two miles away and drove a pony cart to school. Rhyne built a small barn for the rig just south of this third building. Oddly, the schoolchildren never bothered the ponies. (Courtesy of C. Alexander.)

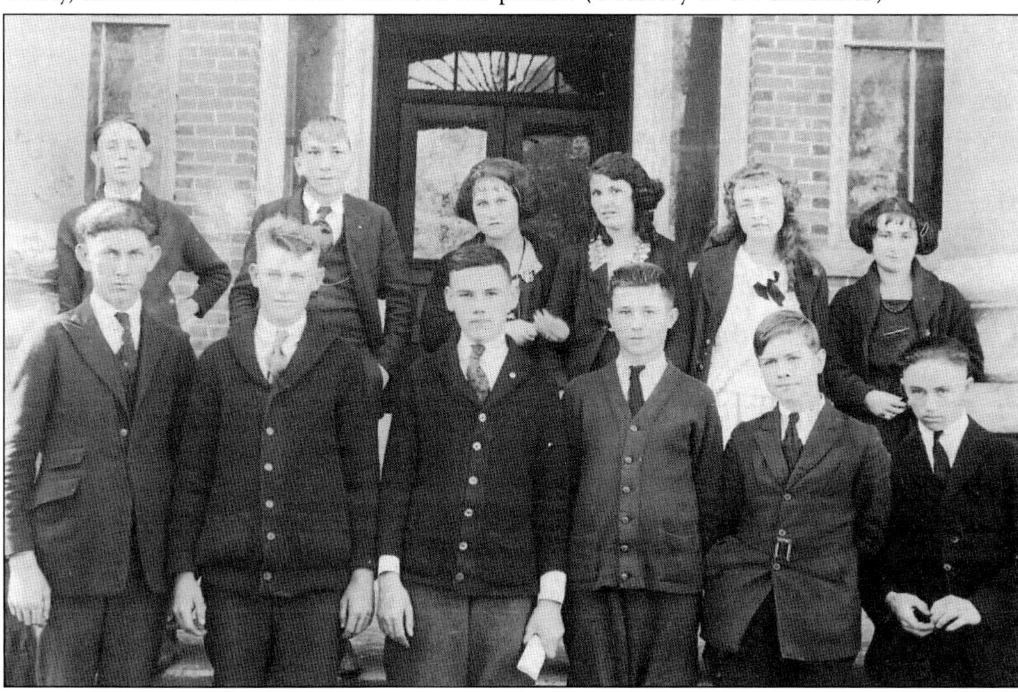

**Class of 1922.** Members of the 1922 class of Mount Holly High are dressed for success and ready to take on a world full of changes. In 1922, the Soviet Union was formed, and the tomb of King Tutankhamen was discovered in Egypt. (Courtesy of Millican Pictorial History Museum.)

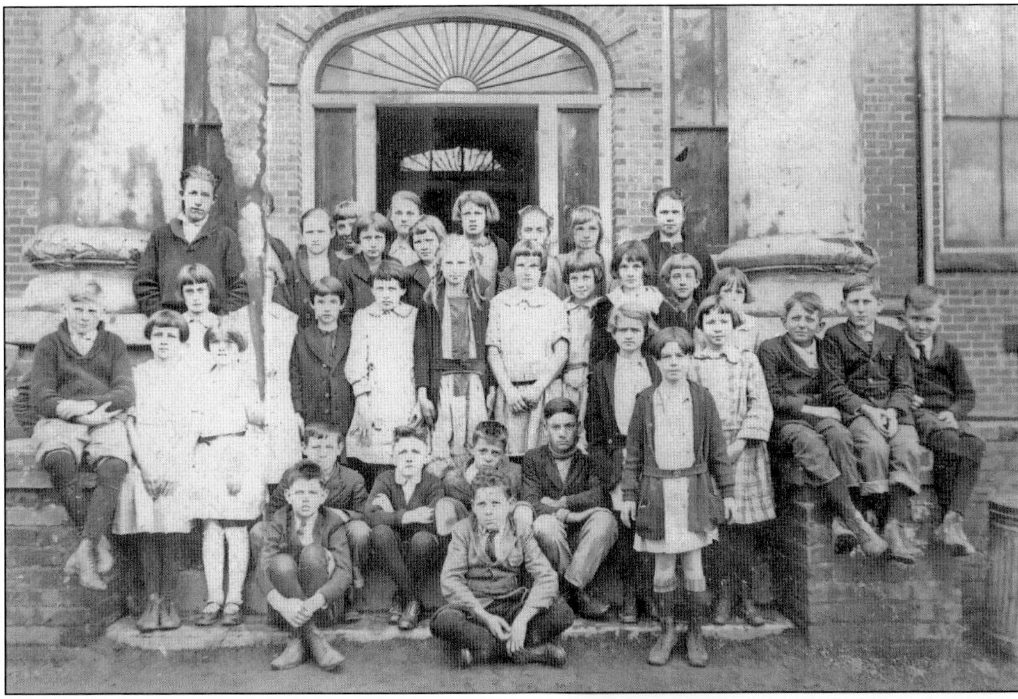

**SCHOOLCHILDREN, C. 1920S.** This brick school building was constructed in 1910. This building and its two sister buildings that were built soon after served Mount Holly children until around 1970. Notice the period clothing and brogans worn by the young students. (Courtesy of the City of Mount Holly Archives.)

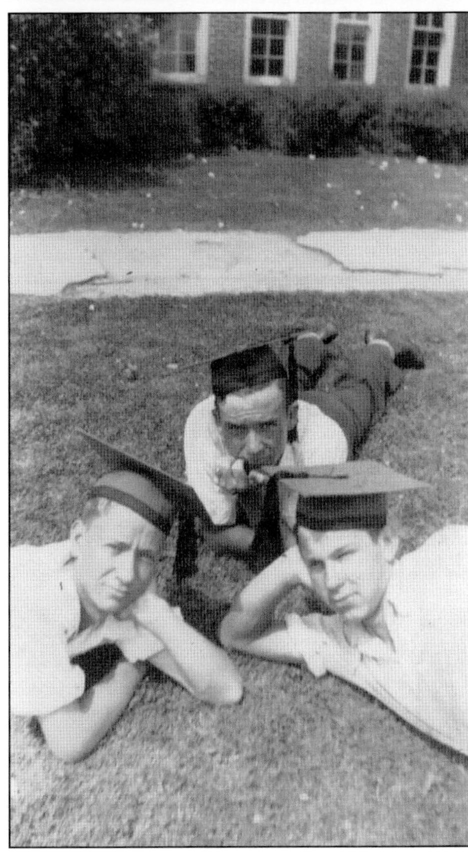

**MOUNT HOLLY HIGH SCHOOL GRADUATION.** From left to right, Baxter McIntosh, Bufford Price, and Carl Broome gather on the front lawn in front of the Mount Holly High School building on Hawthorne Street in this c. 1930s photograph. (Courtesy of Wrene Benfield.)

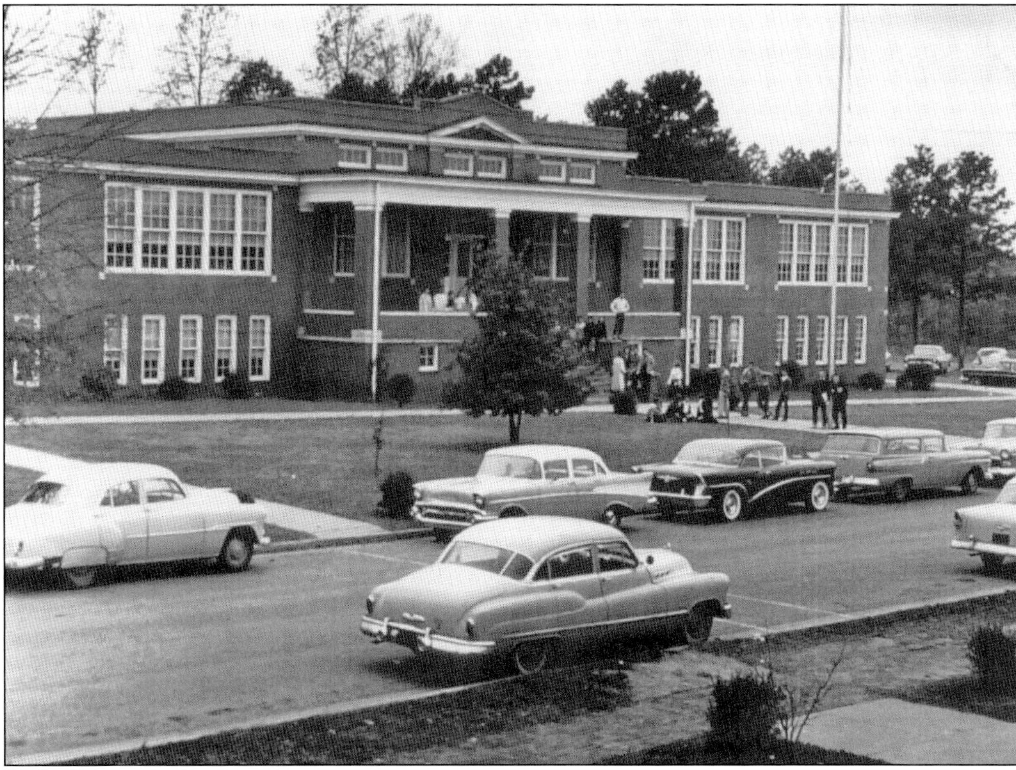

**Mount Holly High School in the 1950s.** This photograph was taken from the band room and gymnasium. Notice the steps and portico in the main entrance—a splendid place for socializing and flirting before the bell rang. Students recall the subtle trampoline effect of the old pine floors in the hallways. (Courtesy of Betty Black.)

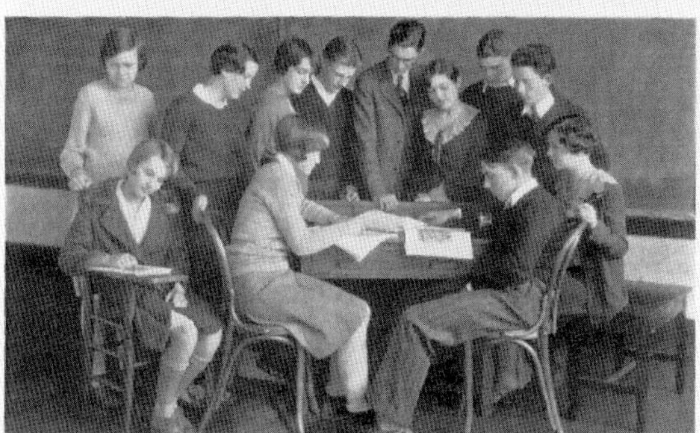

The Staff

S. M. Askins, Jr., *Faculty Advisor*

| | |
|---|---|
| Mary Dunn | *Editor-in-Chief* |
| Rudd Cline | *Assistant Editor-in-Chief* |
| Kitty Rankin | *Advertising Manager* |
| Alonzo Reep | *Photographic Editor* |
| Donald Rhodes | *Sports Editor* |
| Amy Holland | *Sophomore Representative* |
| Wilson Moore | *Business Manager* |
| Eleanor Spratt | *Assistant Business Manager* |
| Mildred Cornette | *Senior Editor* |
| Ethel Pratt | *Joke Editor* |
| Weir Grice | *Junior Representative* |
| Virginia Vass | *Freshman Representative* |

**First *Holly Hawk* Staff.** In 1930, despite the Depression, the senior class sponsored the first Mount Holly High School annual, the *Holly Hawk*. Mary Dunn (Warren) was editor-in-chief, assisted by Rudd Cline; Wilson Moore was business manager, assisted by Eleanor Spratt. (Courtesy of the *Holly Hawk*, 1930.)

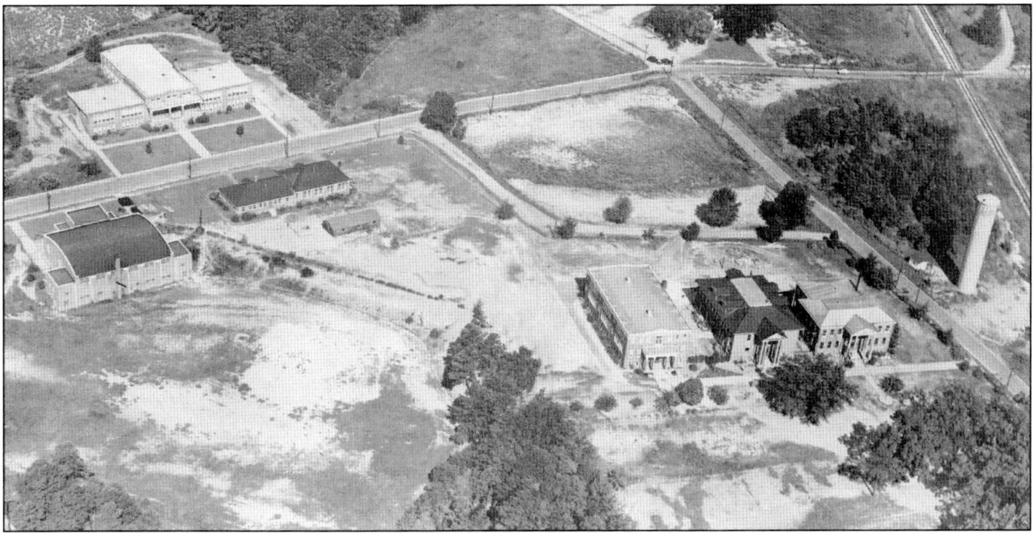

**Aerial View of School Complex, c. 1940s.** Notice the town water tower on the right, beside the three elementary school buildings. The high school is in the top left of the photograph. The practice fields in the left foreground do not have gridiron lines. Robert Alexander's old mulberry tree is at the top right. (Photograph from 1951 *Holly Hawk*, courtesy of Bobby John Rhyne.)

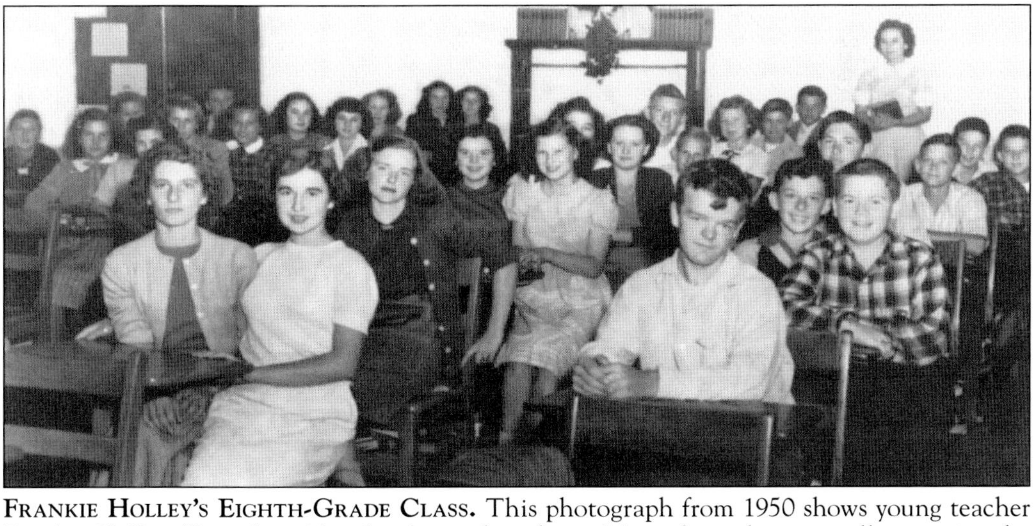

**Frankie Holley's Eighth-Grade Class.** This photograph from 1950 shows young teacher Frankie Holley (Stowe) and her bright-eyed students. Many from that era will recognize the school desks. Bold students carved their initials on the wood, forming a hodgepodge tattoo over the years. (Courtesy of Millican Pictorial History Museum.)

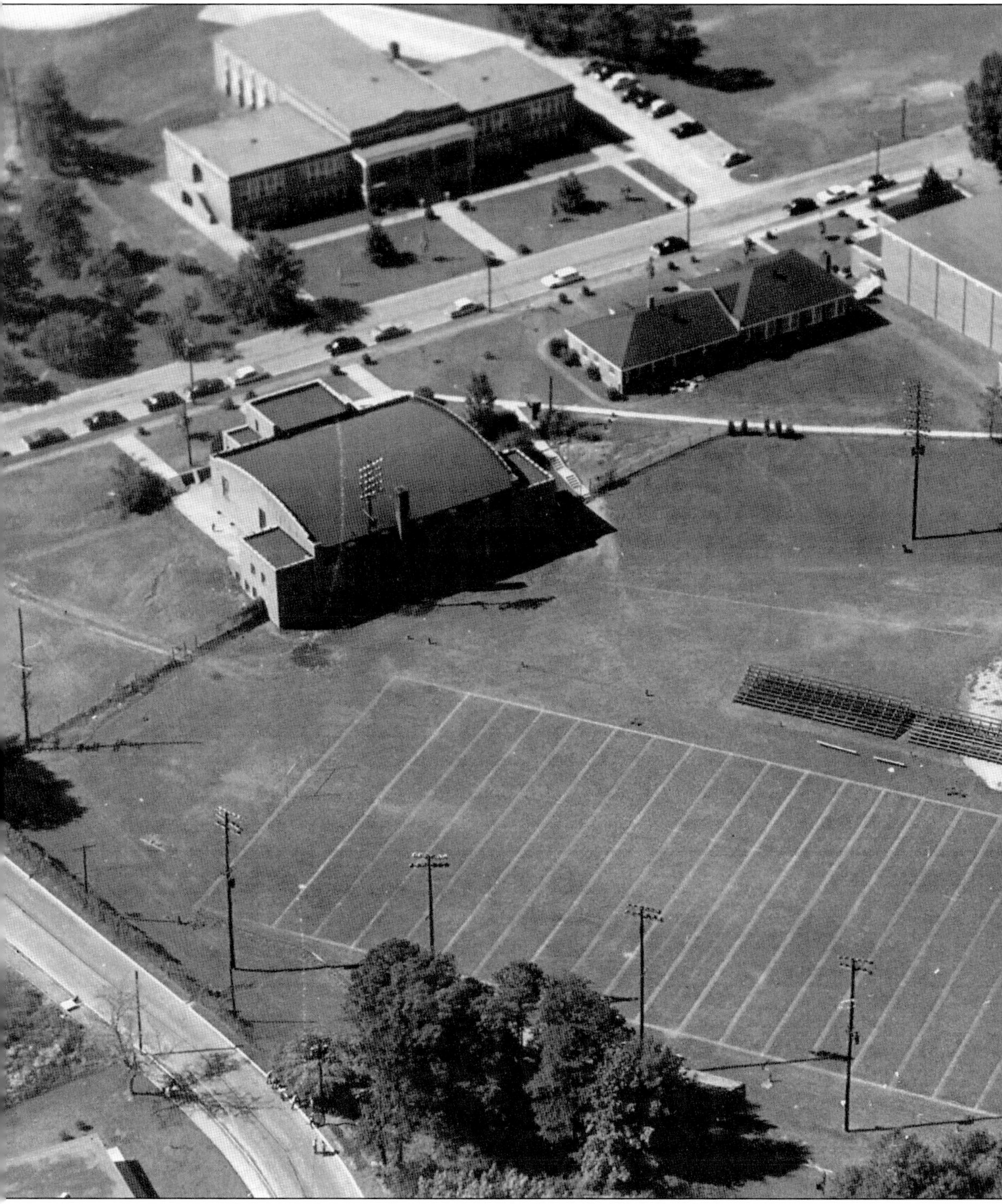

**Aerial View of School Complex, c. 1950s.** The large field in the foreground has been striped, and light poles have been erected, indicating that Costner Field, dedicated in 1953, is now being used for football and baseball games. A one-story first-grade structure has been added behind the tall elementary buildings. Notice the public library to the bottom left, strategically positioned

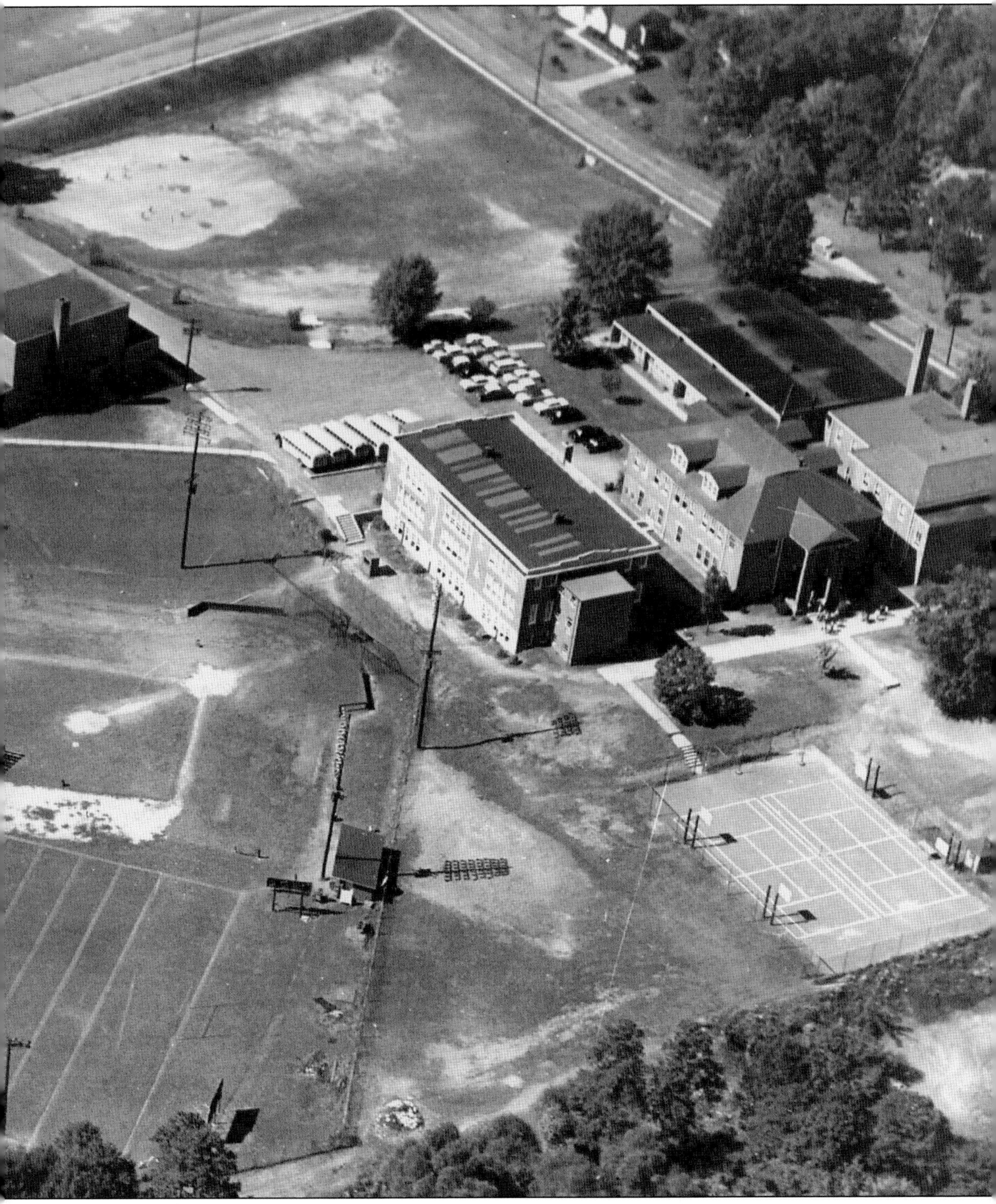

to entice children walking home from school. The Mount Holly School, just two blocks from Main Street, was the center of life for much of the town and a large part of the town's identity. (Courtesy of Millican Pictorial History Museum.)

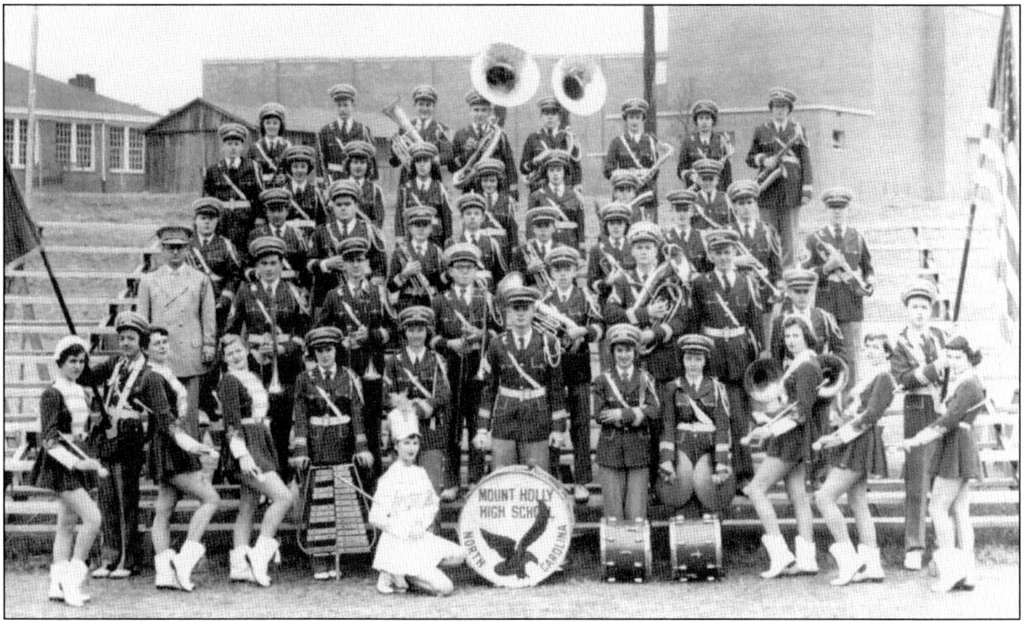


**MOUNT HOLLY HIGH SCHOOL BAND, 1954.** Standing on the bleachers of the home side at Costner Field, the marching band displays their post–World War II military-style uniforms. Robert Black, on the left in the light-colored uniform, came to Mount Holly in 1950 and was director there until the high school moved to East Gaston High in 1972. Note the Hawk bass drum. (Courtesy of Millican Pictorial History Museum.)

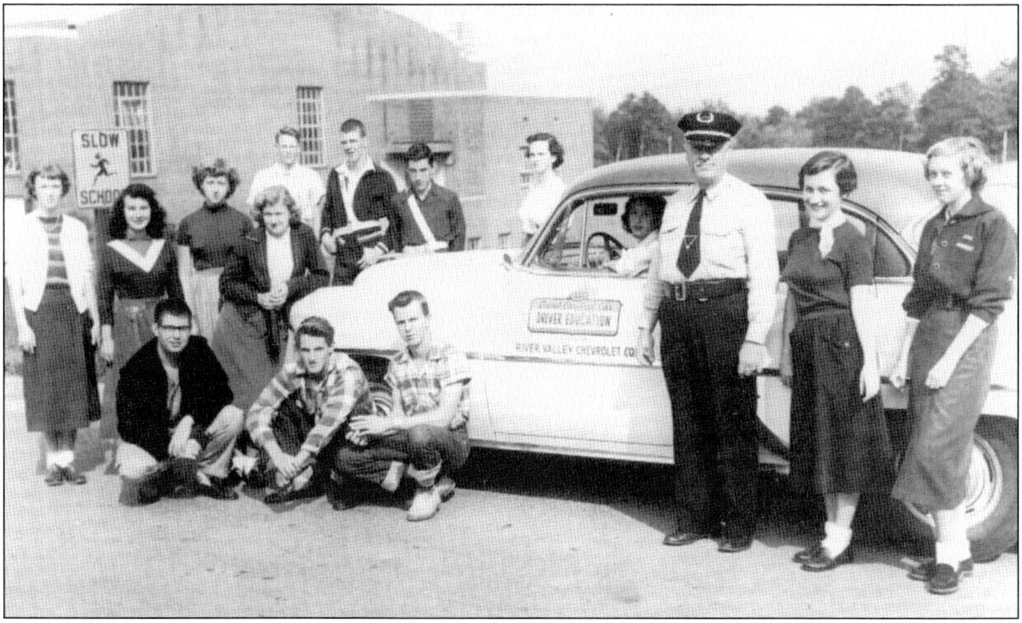


**DRIVER'S EDUCATION, 1954.** The students and their mobile classroom are on Hawthorne Street. The gymnasium and Costner Field are in the background. The brand-new automobile was supplied by River Valley Chevrolet, which was on South Main Street beside Good Shepherd Lutheran Church. Note the bobby socks on the young ladies. (Courtesy of Millican Pictorial History Museum.)

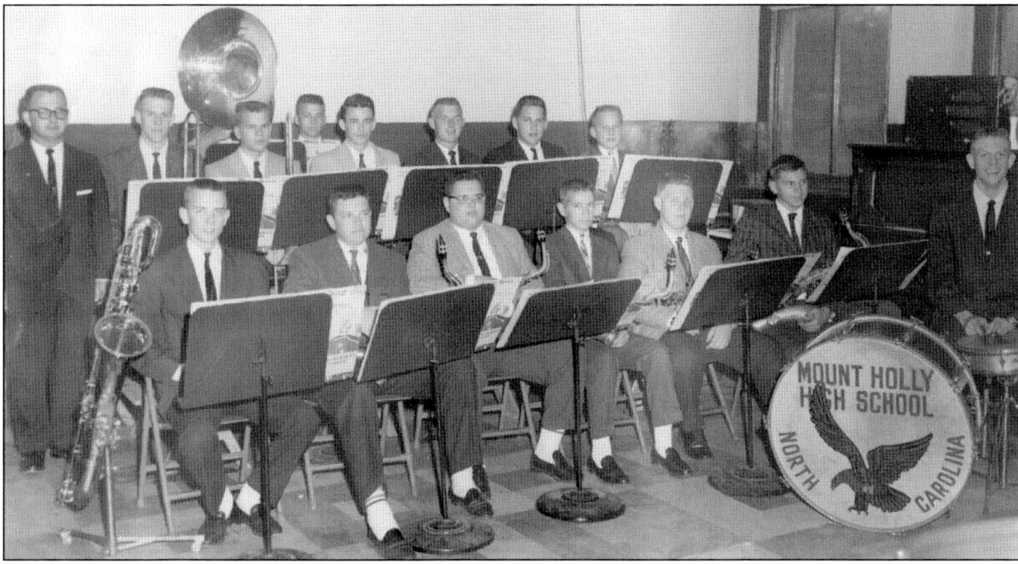


**DANCE BAND, C. 1950S.** The Mount Holly High School Band had a dance band that played evening performances and other events, such as the community dinner. The band members are, from left to right, (first row) Jim Fuller, David Hager, Doug Stowe, Ernie Kelly, Pat Hardesty, Julian Hall, and Eddie Blackwood; (second row) director Robert Black, Ray Blackwood, Jim Ware, Jimmy Lee, Roy Andrews, Wesley Ashe, Tommy Stowe, and Jimmy Love. (Courtesy of Betty Black.)

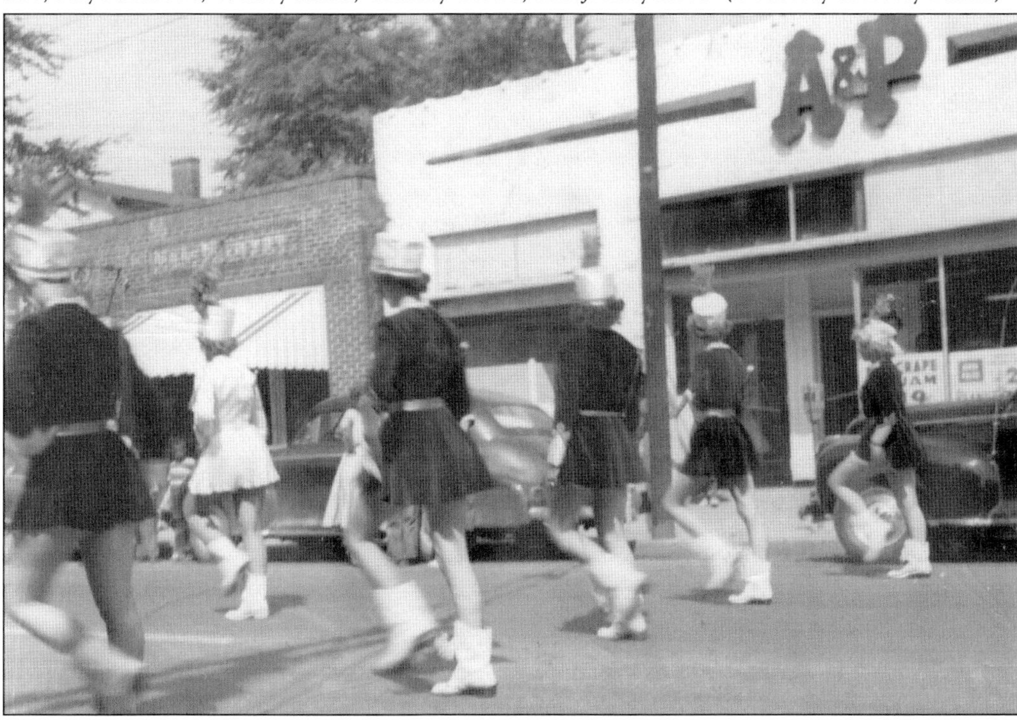


**MARCHING PAST THE A&P.** The majorettes of the Mount Holly Hawks march past the old A&P grocery store on North Main Street. The marching band was famous for its fast cadence and "lights out" programs at Friday night football games. In 1960, the A&P moved to South Main Street. (Courtesy of Betty Black.)

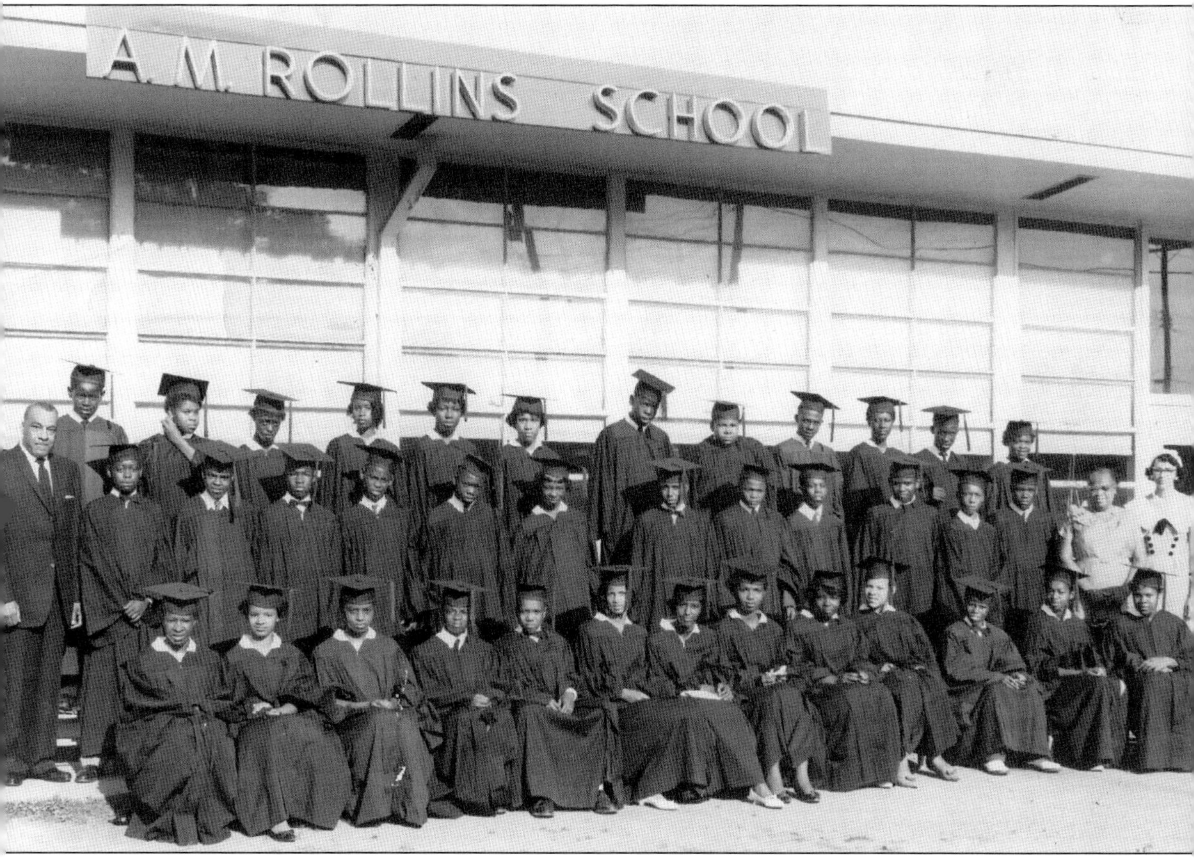


**EIGHTH-GRADE CLASS, ROLLINS SCHOOL, 1960.** A.M. Rollins School closed in the late 1960s when the public schools were integrated. Former students have fond memories of the school, located on Hawthorne Street in the Freedom neighborhood. Gathered for this photograph are, from left to right, (first row) Geraldine Johnson, Joyce Ross, Joyce Sifford, Ronnie Gardner, Daniel Moore, Patricia Currance, Dianne Gaston, Alma Henderson, Callie S. Graham, Linda Starr, Gary McArkle, Margie Graham, and Doris Shipp; (second row) Mr. Rollins (principal), Abraham Burris, James Lindsay, Leon Morrison, Charles Scott, Gary Grier, Gloria Robinson, Terry Tate, James Cornelius, William Sherrill, Hiawatha Rankin, Rayfield Reid, Velvin Lewis, Miss Kress (supervisor), and Mrs. Reid (supervisor); (third row) Randolph Anderson, Joyce Shipp, Barbara Glade, Frankie Pope, Betty Black, Lillian Sherrill, James Burris, James Blalock, Marcus Smith, Mary Bradley, Wayne Gardner, and Eva Hill. (Courtesy of Geraldine Johnson, May Johnson, and Gloria Mack.)

*Eight*

# Glory Days
## Our Sports Heritage

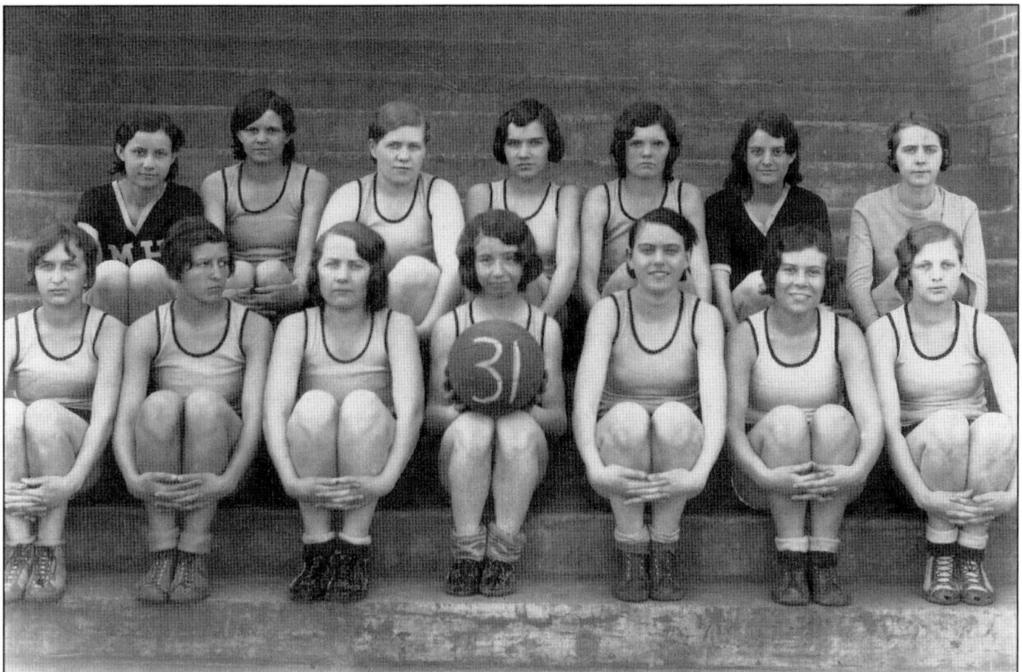

**Depression-Era Hoopsters.** The 1931 Mount Holly High School girls' basketball team was photographed on the high school steps. The team has more members than the entire high school class of 1917, which had 13 graduates. High school enrollment grew quickly in the 1920s because of Mount Holly's population boom (the town's census reports a population that doubled from 1,160 in 1920 to 2,254 in 1930). (Courtesy of Millican Pictorial History Museum.)

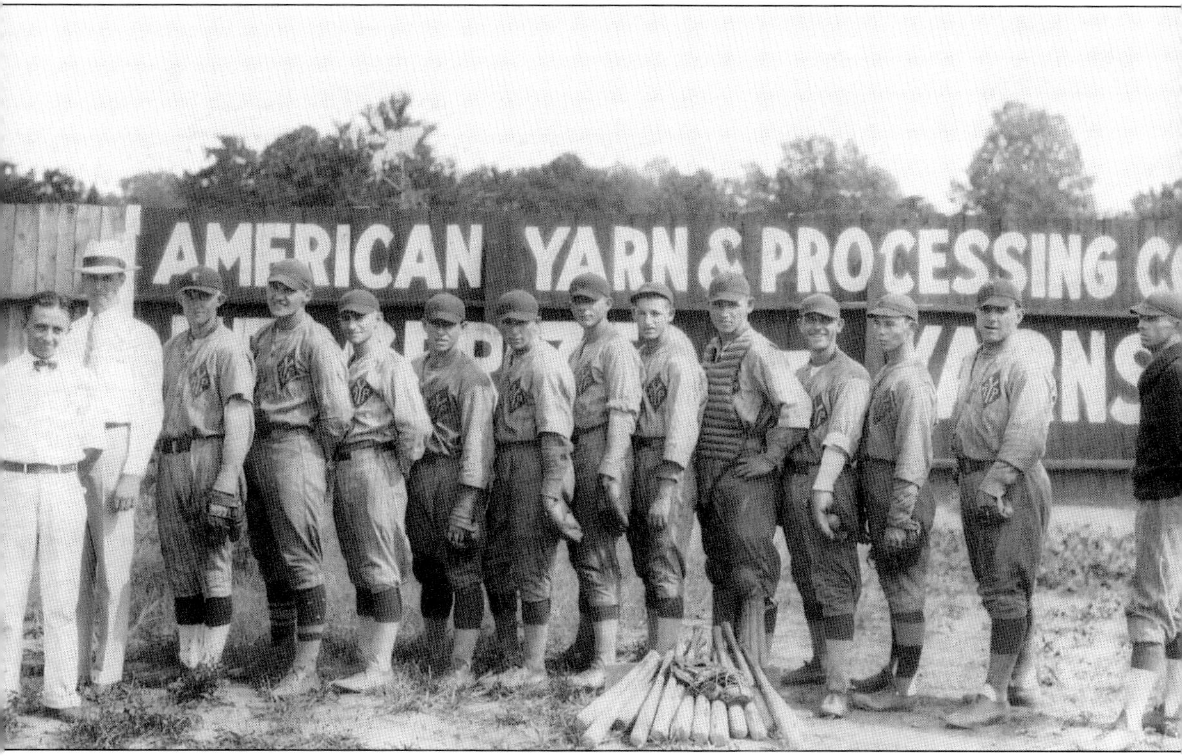


**AMERICAN YARN AND PROCESSING BASEBALL TEAM, C. 1920S.** Baseball was America's pastime before World War II. Company teams were the pride of the community. American Yarn and Processing and Superior Yarns in the Tuckaseege area had many teams through the years, both for men and women. Many descendants of the players in this photograph still live in Mount Holly. The little man in the bow tie is the father of one of the authors. In this photograph are, from left to right, Adrian Beatty, Charles Edwin Hutchison (C.E. Hutchison's son), Doug Nims, Henry Kistler, Clarence Abernathy, Tate Hicks, Don Causby, "Kack" Huffstetler, Gus Hartsoe, Austin Auten, Ed Cross, Adam Hoard, Ed Williams, and Andy Ferguson. (Courtesy of Millican Pictorial History Museum.)

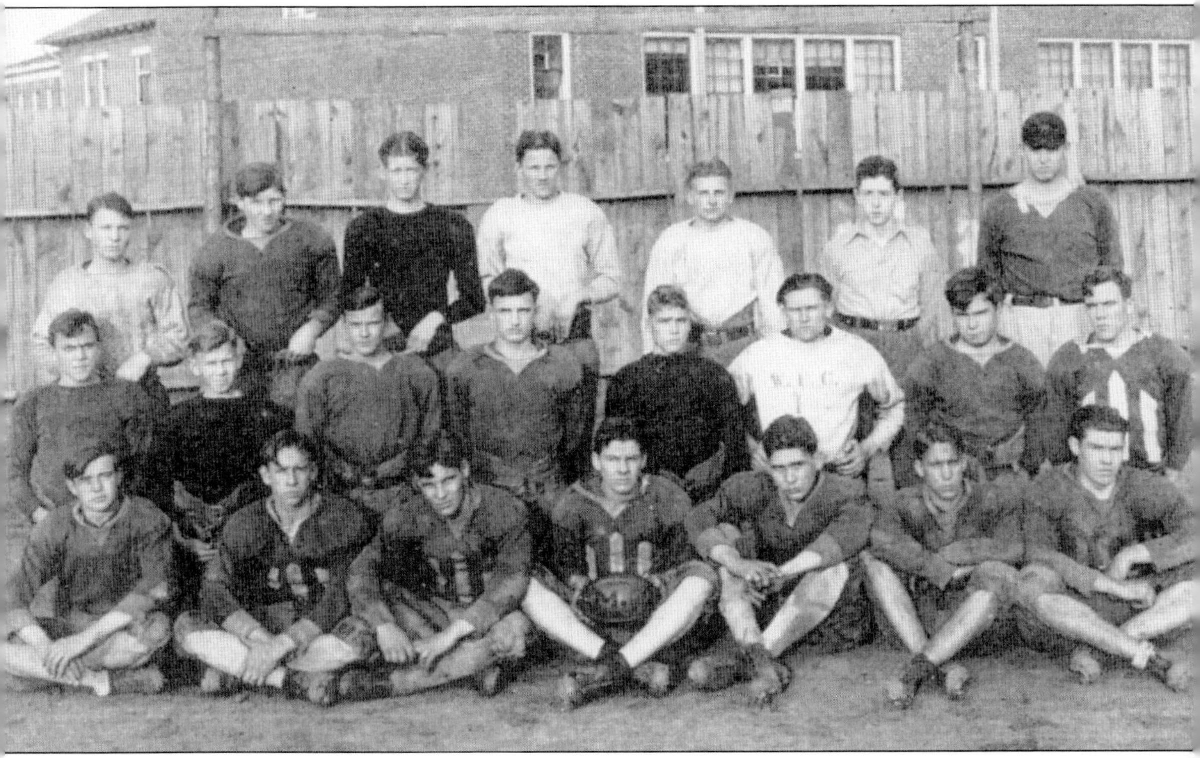

**1930 MOUNT HOLLY FOOTBALL TEAM.** This rugged team was undefeated. Only Shelby scored against the team's mighty defense. In this era, there was no state championship system. The yearbook caption identifies players by their playing position, but not their position in the photograph. The team manager was David Albright, and A. Seaton Holt coached the team. The players, listed by position, are as follows: Hollis Dunn, left end; Sydney Pryor, left tackle; B.C. Taylor Jr., left guard; Fred Hoover, center; Richard Thompson, right guard; Yates Stroupe, right tackle; Frank Tucker, right end; T.L. Ware Jr., captain and quarterback; Coley Woodham, left halfback; Wilson Moore, right halfback; and Donald Rhodes, fullback. Substitutes were Alonzo Reep, John Davenport, Weir Grice, Marshall Rhyne, Woodrow Kendall, Franklin Johnson, Jack Dunn, Kenneth Moore, Claude Lowe, Russell Jones, Ward Rhyne, Henry Clark, and James Cole. (Courtesy of the *Holly Hawk*, 1930.)

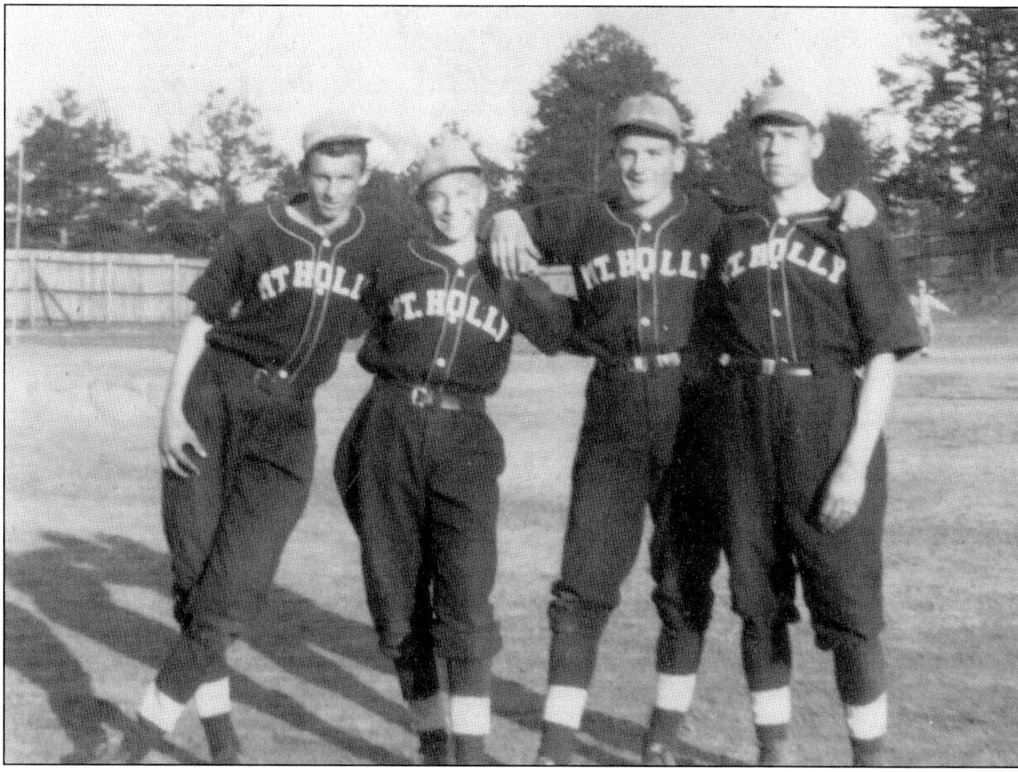


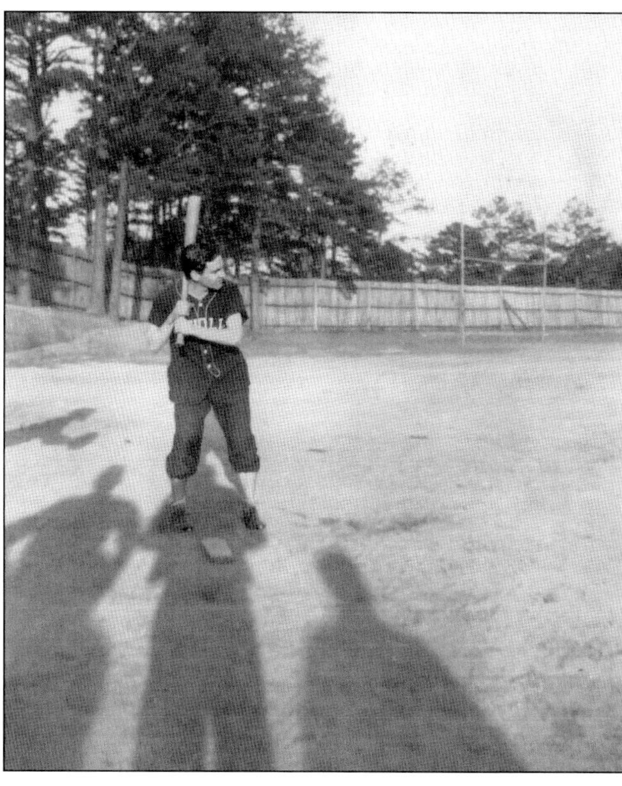

**Mount Holly High School Baseball Team.** Members of the school baseball team are pictured in the 1930s wearing their uniforms and standing on the athletic field across from the high school building. The fields were multipurpose, used for football as well as baseball. (Courtesy of Wrene Benfield.)

**Noah Huffstetler at Bat, Late 1930s.** By the look of the deep shadows, Noah is facing Catawba Avenue, ready to knock one over the wooden fence. A few years after this photograph was taken, Huffstetler was in a very different sort of image, shown safely emerging from a shell crater on a battlefield of Europe after having been buried alive. (Courtesy of Wrene Benfield.)

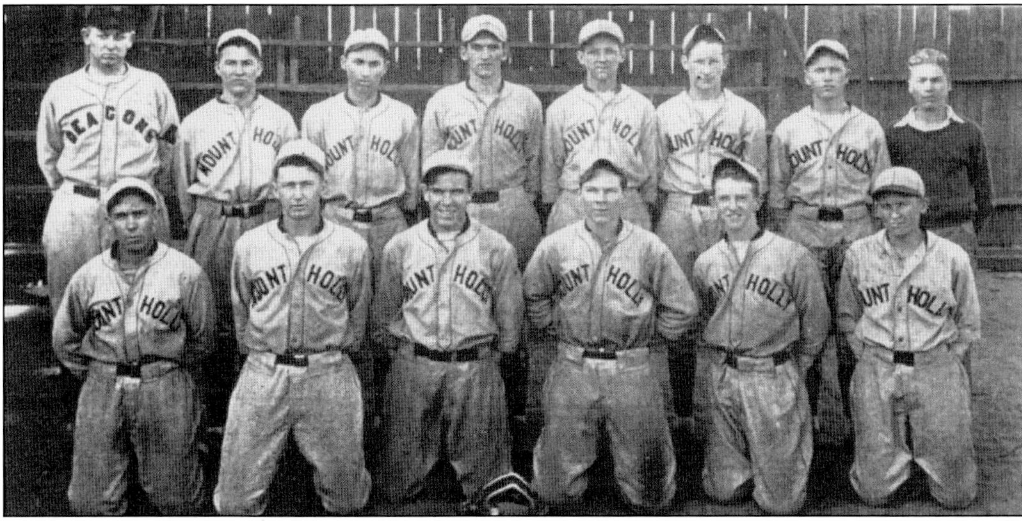


**MOUNT HOLLY HAWKS, 1930.** The 1930 Mount Holly High School baseball team finished with a winning record of 6-4-1. In this photograph are, in no particular order, Cletis Lineberger, Clyde Hunt, Fred Hoover, J.P. Warren, Sam Smith, Wilson Moore, coach A.S. Holt, William McElduff, Hollis Dunn, T.L. Ware, Jack Stewart, Franklin Johnson, Thomas Jenkins, and manager Weir Grice. (Courtesy of Millican Pictorial History Museum.)

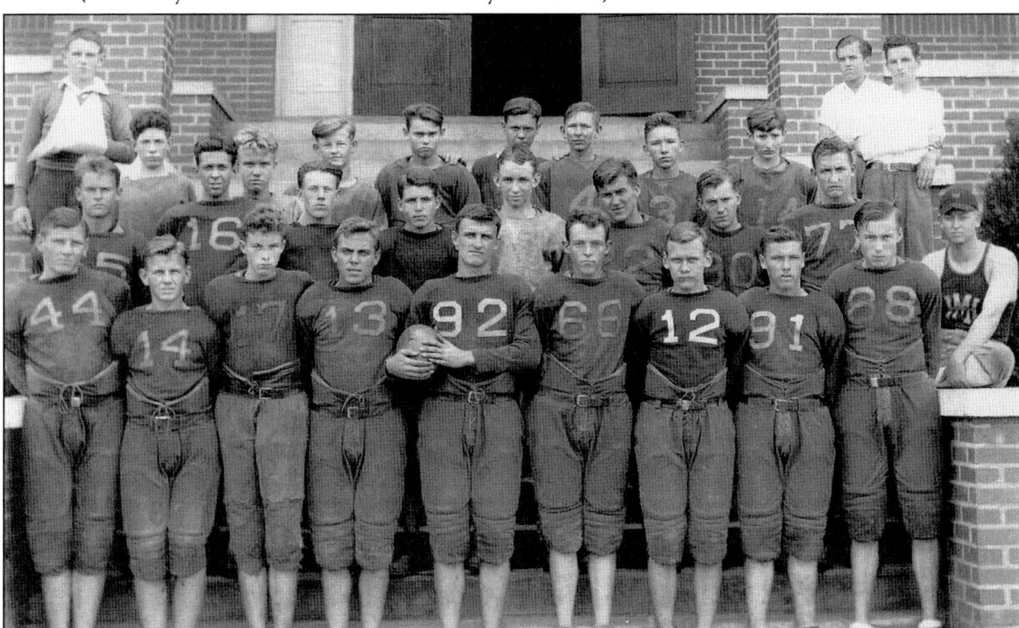

**THE 1931 HAWK FOOTBALL TEAM.** The Hawks lost only one game; the score was 7-6. Included in this team photograph are, from left to right, (first row) Russell Jones, Ken Moore, Gilbert Hart, Jack Dunn, Dick Thompson, Dwight Johnson, Rutledge Rhyne, George Smith, "Burr Head" Stroupe, and coach Seaton Holt; (second row) Bill Spray, Tom Warren, Randy Crump, Ed Stowe, Hill Welch, Cletis Lineberger, Lynn Beatty, and J.B. Thompson; (third row) Frank Rankin, Red Howie, Bo Bo Stabler, Shorty Helton, Reid Hollis, G. Patterson, Shuford Michael, Raymond Outen, Allen Smith, Jay Noles, and manager Charles Stroupe. (Courtesy of Millican Pictorial History Museum.)

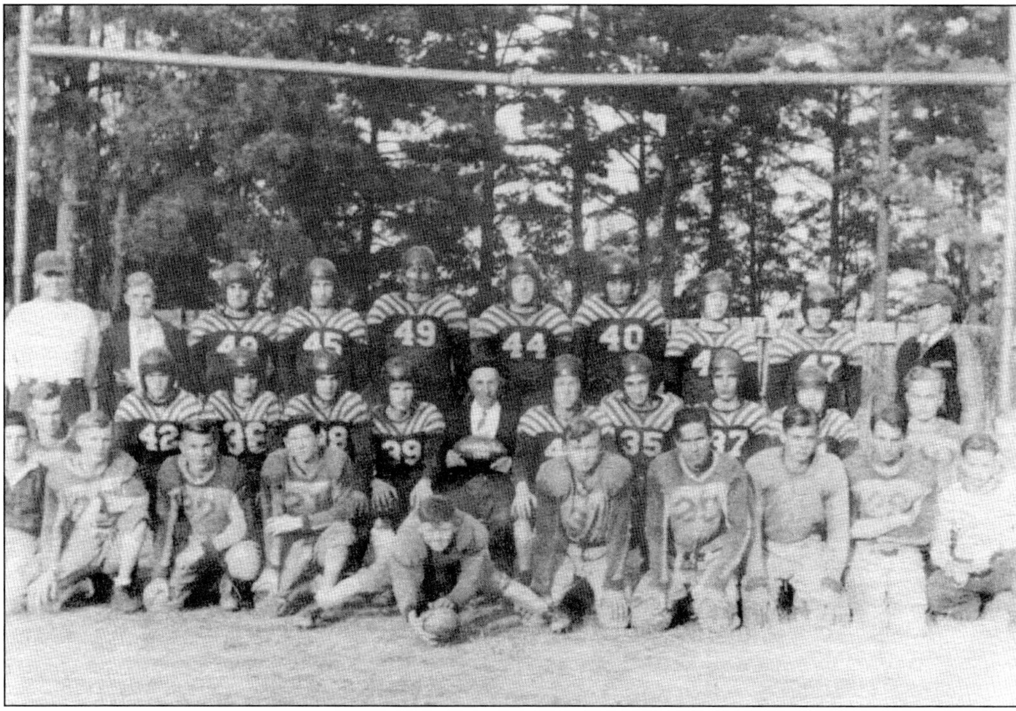

## FOOTBALL — 1941

A. S. Holt, Jr. .................... Coach
L. C. Ward .................... Coach
Guilford Huitt, Jr. .................... Manager

### SQUAD

| | |
|---|---|
| Gene Painter, Mgr. | Mr. Costner, Sponsor |
| Arthur Davis | Wayne Huffstetler |
| Boyd Arndt | Marion Fletcher |
| Paul Harkey | Bill Stowe |
| Ross McConnell | Paul Springs |
| Pete Johnson | Gwyne Baker |
| Lee Campbell | Boyce Wells |
| Hugh Mullis | Melvin Smith |
| Jimmy Dellinger | C. B. Hayes |
| Bill Hunsuck, Mgr. | Coyte Wilson |
| Ralph Williams | Howard Horton |
| Joe Bailes | George Fincher |
| Fred Gantt | Billy Cashion |
| Harry Gantt | Craig Lawing |
| James Cherry | Billy McCorkle |

### SCORES

| | | We | They |
|---|---|---|---|
| 9-25-1941 | Taylorsville | 13 | 0 |
| 10- 3-1941 | Cramerton | 21 | 0 |
| 10-10-1941 | Oakhurst | 19 | 6 |
| 10-17-1941 | Maiden | 33 | 0 |
| 10-23-1941 | Tech High | 6 | 0 |
| 10-31-1941 | Abbey Ramblers | 27 | 0 |
| 11- 7-1941 | Monroe | 13 | 7 |
| 11-14-1941 | Belmont | 35 | 0 |
| TOTAL | | 167 | 13 |

This team was one of the three teams in the state that was neither defeated nor tied during the 1941 season. We are quite proud of this record.

**UNDEFEATED MOUNT HOLLY HAWKS OF 1941.** Leather helmets and no faceguards were the norm in those days. There apparently was no state championship playoff system at the time. Note that only three weeks after the season ended, these boys' lives were changed forever by an attack on a little-known naval base called Pearl Harbor. (Both, courtesy of C. Alexander.)

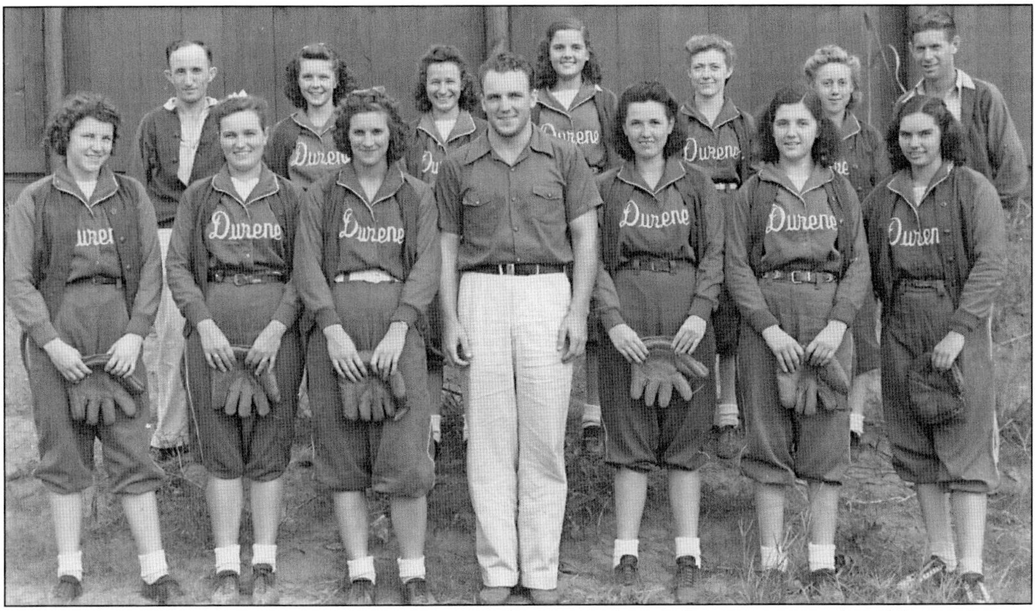


**State Champion Durene Softball, 1941.** The team played their games at the old Hutchison-Lowe Ballpark off Rankin Street. In this photograph are, from left to right, (first row) Mae Haney, Inez "Shine" Joye, Lucille Black, athletic director Charles Lowe, Daisy Sigmon, Mildred Satterfield, and Ruby Heafner; (second row) coach Weber Wilkerson, Gladys Ouzts, Vivian "Skeeter" Laye Broome, Dot Satterfield, Faye Harkey, Dennie McConnell, and manager Ed Horton. (Courtesy of Carlton and Cecelia Broome.)

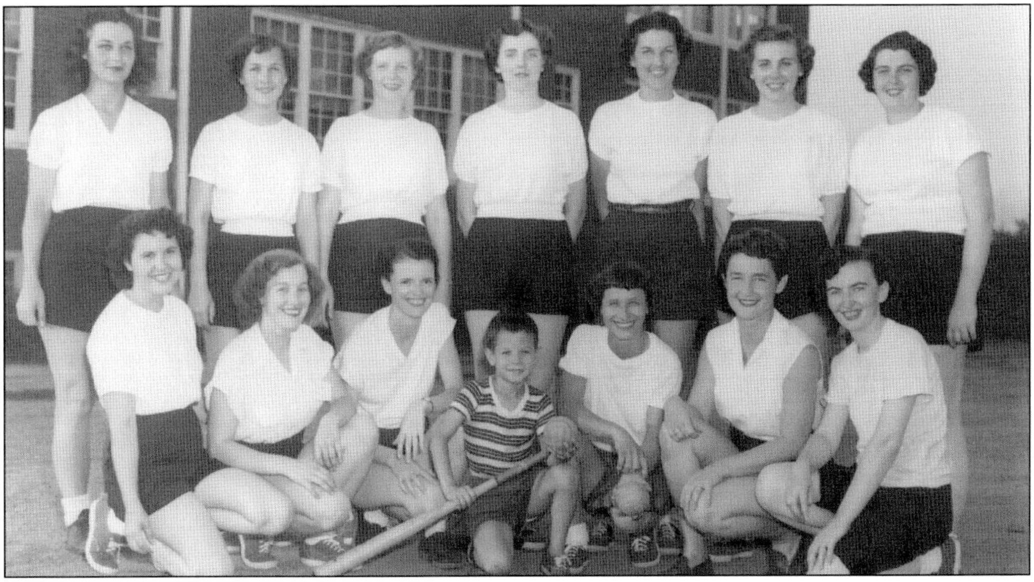

**Mount Holly Jaycette Softball Team.** Two of the players on this team, Vivian "Skeeter" Broome and Bertha Dunn, have been inducted into the Mount Holly Sports Hall of Fame. Included in this photograph are, from left to right, (first row) Joyce McManus, Johnsie Grier, Gini Henkle, Carlton Broome, Vivian "Skeeter" Broome, Ann (Harpy) Dixon, and Dot Arndt; (second row) Bertha Dunn, Joann (Perk) Clippard, Doris Helton, Patsy Broome, Marie Cochran, Rachel Jones, and June Garrett. (Courtesy of Carlton and Cecelia Broome.)

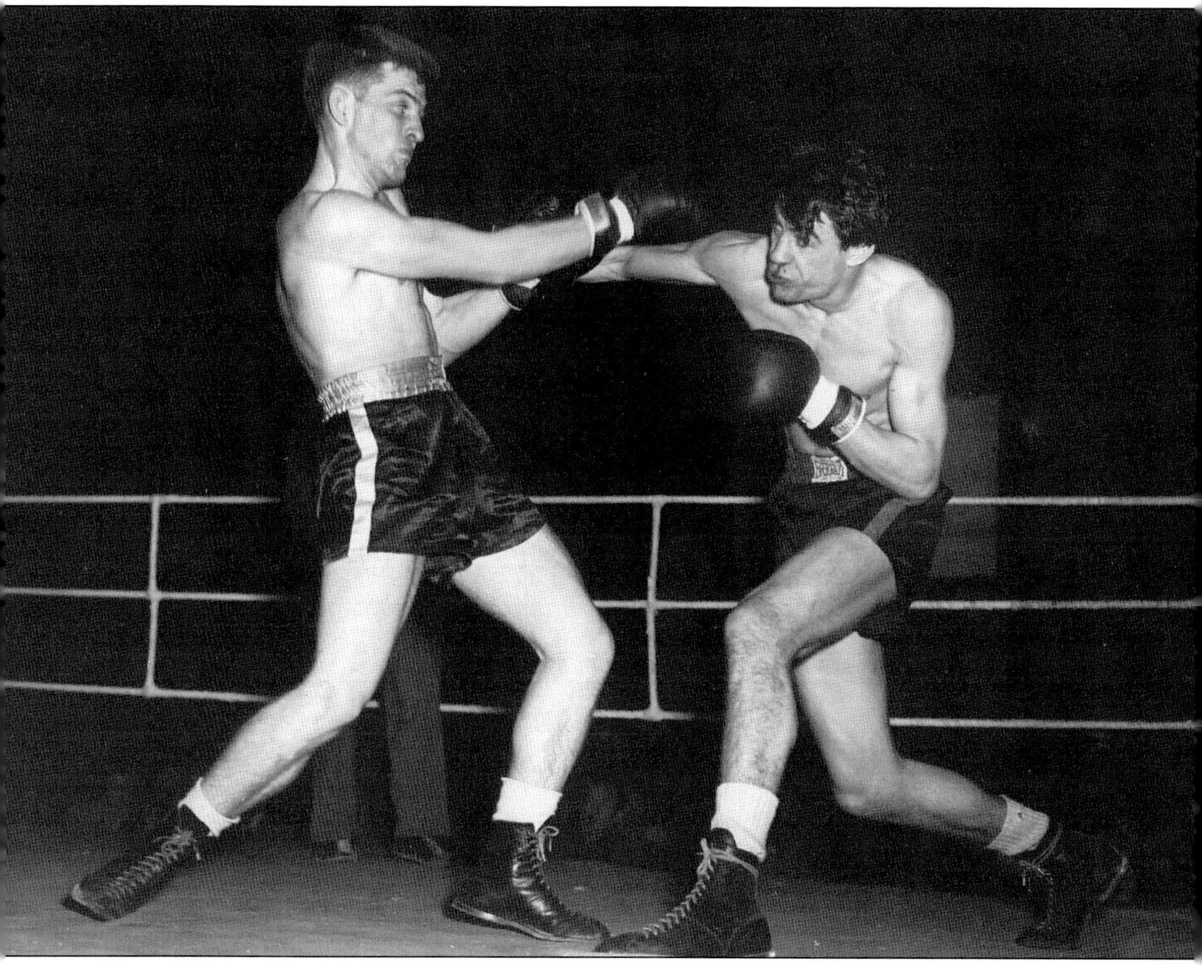

**Mount Holly Golden Gloves.** Pictured are Don Fortner (left) and Murray Beasley as they slug it out in an April 1949 match. Most of the boxing practices and matches were held at the Jaycee building on West Charlotte Avenue. From 1948 to 1974, Thomas L. McManus coached the Mount Holly team to over 2,400 individual wins and over 50 team championships. Coach McManus, along with his brothers Jim and Samuel "Dink," are inductees of the Mount Holly Sports Hall of Fame, joining fellow boxers Ray Campbell and the Davis brothers, Arthur, Bearl, Max, and Wilbern. (Courtesy of Millican Pictorial History Museum.)

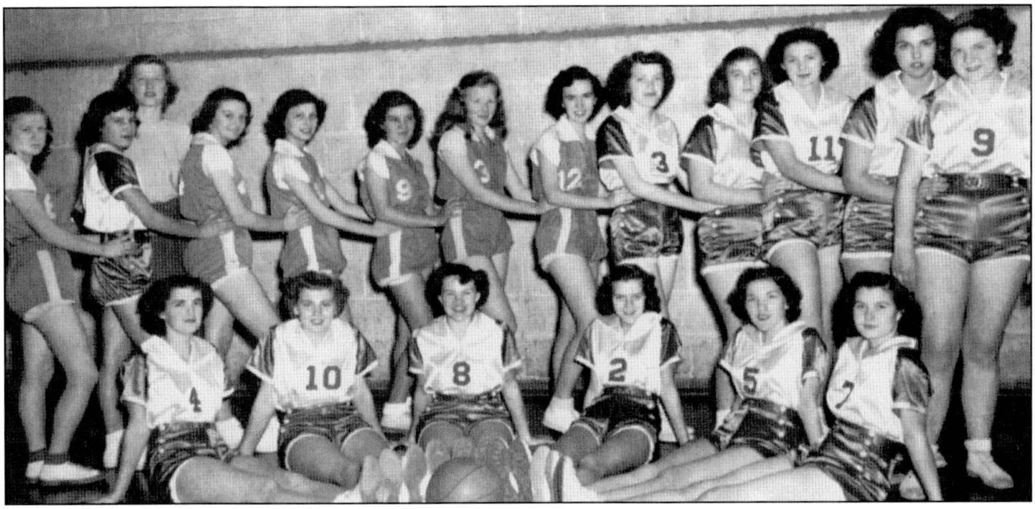

**BASKETBALL TEAM, C. 1950S.** Note the flashy satin uniforms on the varsity players of the Mount Holly High School Hawkettes. Before the 1970s, women's basketball had six players on the floor—two on offense, two on defense, and two "rovers" on both sides of the court. (Courtesy of Millican Pictorial History Museum.)

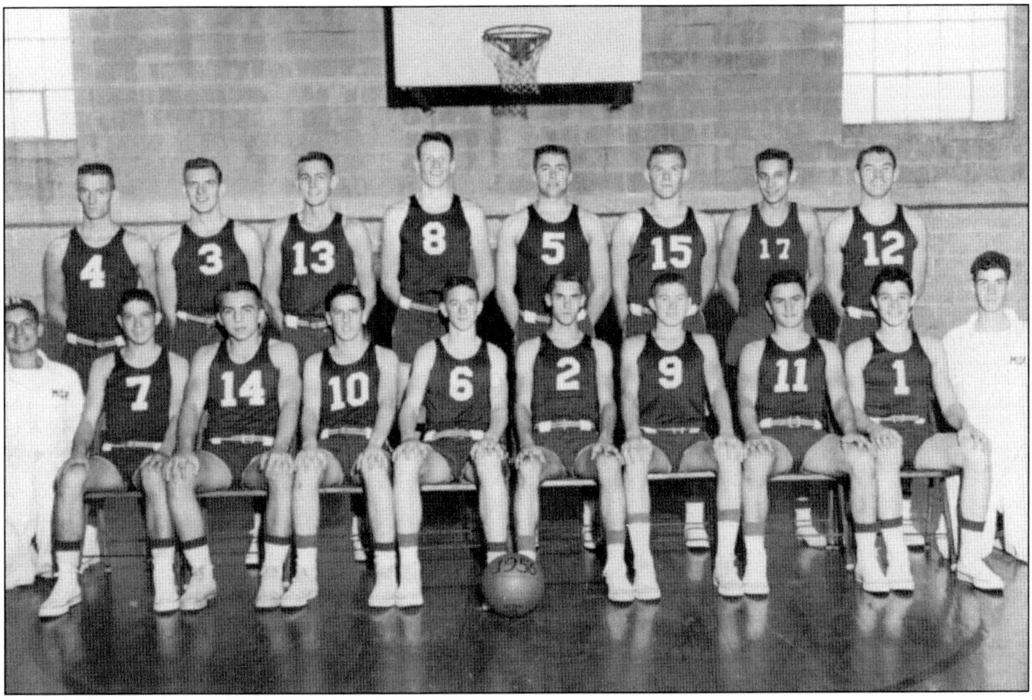

**BOYS' BASKETBALL TEAM, 1956.** Note the belts on the skimpy shorts. Many of the boys are wearing the universal basketball shoe of the 1930s through 1960s, Converse All-Star Chuck Taylors. (Courtesy of Millican Pictorial History Museum.)

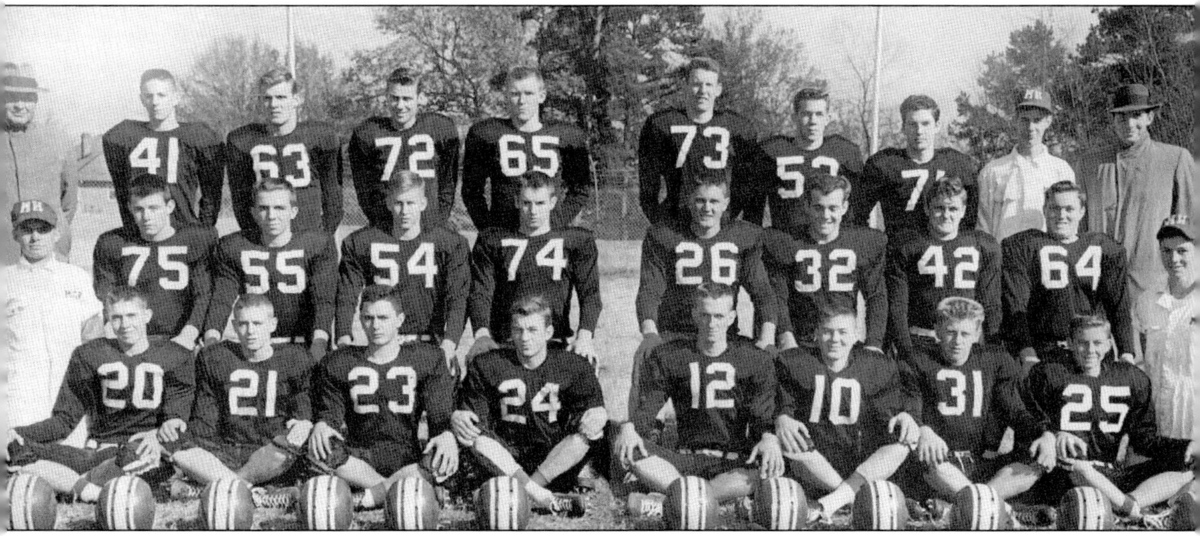

**Hawks Football, 1956.** This team was unscored on in conference play and undefeated in the regular season. Its only loss was to Granite Falls in the state playoffs, 7-13. Three seniors, Robert Jenkins, Perry Toomey, and Tommy Wilson, along with sophomore James Helton, went on to play scholarship college football. The team members are, from left to right, (first row) Charles Rick, Lane McCotter, Charles Kale, Max Davis, Tommy Wilson, Larry Jenkins, Sonny Helton, and Alfred Latham; (second row) unidentified, James Helton, Pat Toomey, LeeRoy Johnston, Robert Jenkins, Harold Norwood, Perry Toomey, James Lavender, Roger Hayes, and unidentified; (third row) head coach V.M. Morrison, Ken Medders, Russell Cannon, Don Grice, Floyd Coffin, Bob Jessen, Ned Edwards, David Ballard, unidentified, and assistant coach B.T. Wright. (Courtesy of Millican Pictorial History Museum.)

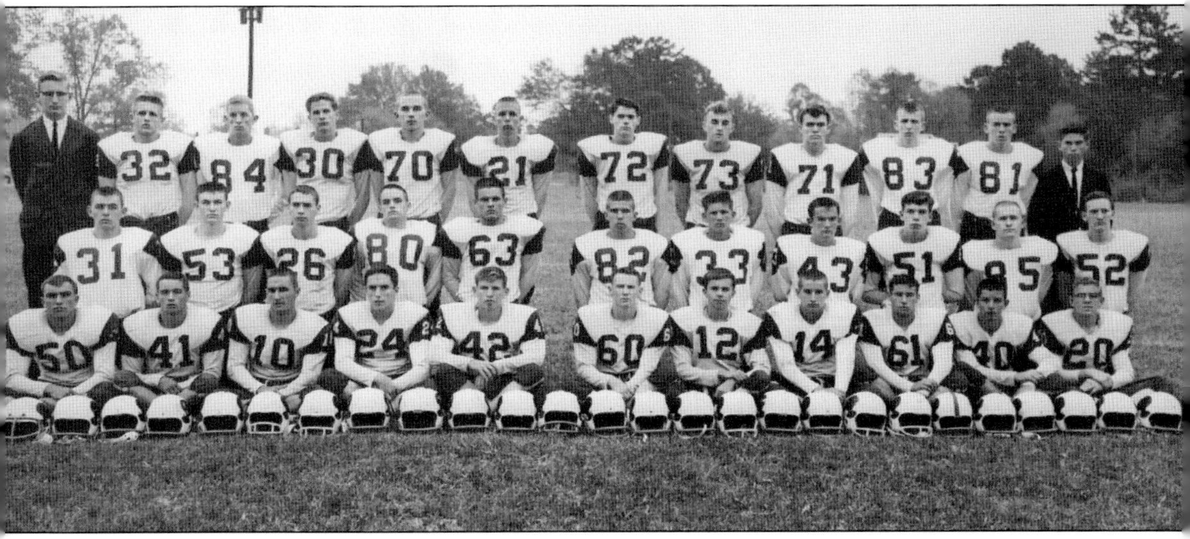

**1963 State Champions.** The day of Pres. John F. Kennedy's assassination, November 22, 1963, was also the date of the championship game, played at Mount Holly. There was strong sentiment to postpone the game, but the traveling team was already en route, so the schools decided to proceed. Led by head coach Delmer Wiles and assistant coaches Joe Spears and Don Killian, the Hawk football team was undefeated and untied in 11 games. This North Carolina Piedmont 2A championship team, along with its coaches, is now enshrined in the Mount Holly Sports Hall of Fame. These Mount Holly Hawk team members are, from left to right, (first row) Stanley Hawn, Bruce Bolick, Gene Thompson, Steve McCotter, Dwayne Moore, Johnny Holloway, Rickey Martin, Ernie Kelly, Johnny Carpenter, Roger Lawing, and Roger Bartee; (second row) Shan Williams, Larry Hartsell, Tommy McConnell, Ken Jones, John Payne, Buddy Guin, Harold Moore, Mike Shelby, Danny Huitt, Lynn Sifford, and Buddy Rhyne; (third row) Michael Kimray, Jimmy Wilson, Johnny McIntosh, Phil White, Jimmy Love, David Williams, Tommy Hollis, Jimmy Guin, Tommy Thompson, Grady Hoyle, Boyd Mayhew, and Dickie Price. (Courtesy of Mary Elizabeth Wiles.)

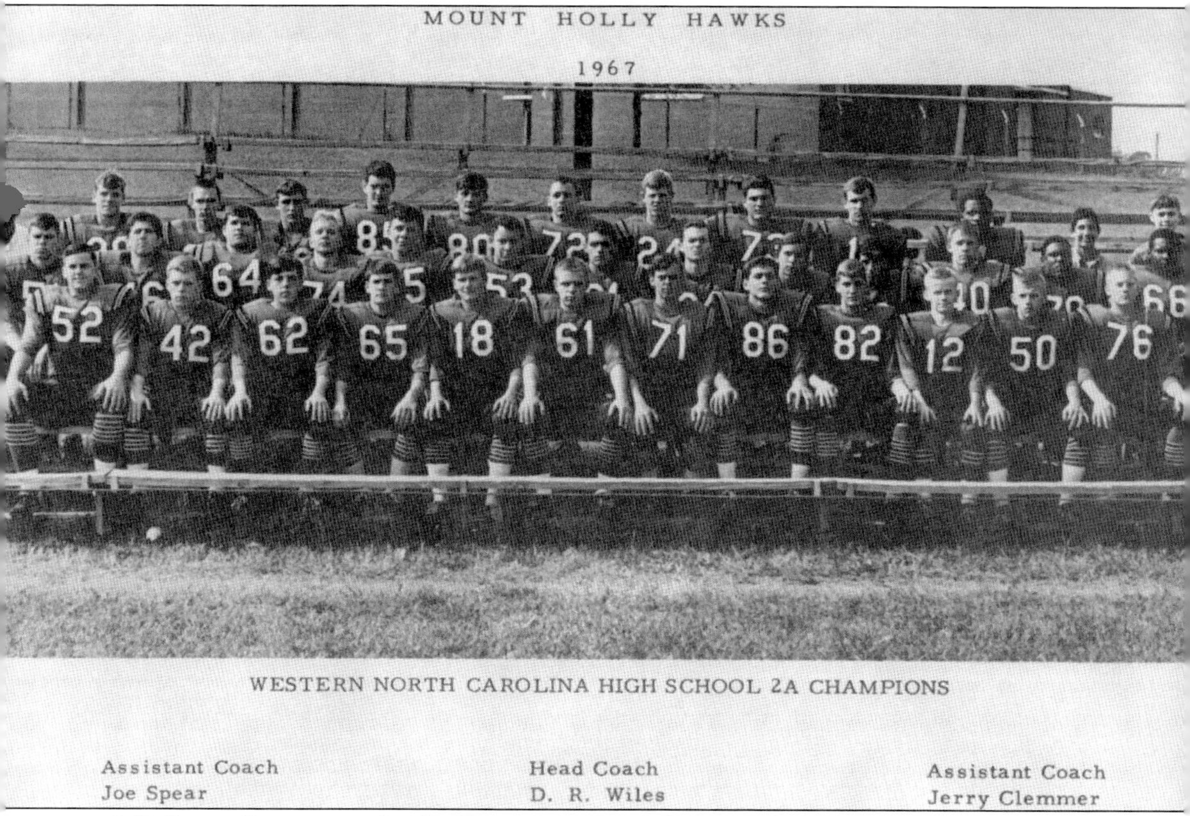


**1967 State Champions.** In the Western 2A state championship game played at Cherryville, Eddie Womack threw a 10-yard touchdown pass to Mike Manes with seven seconds to go, and the Mount Holly Hawks defeated Glen Alpine 26-20. In this team photograph are, from left to right, (first row) Maurice Sanderson, Eddie Womack, Jerry Wilson, Gary McManus, Charles Craig, David Cox, Richard Gibson, Larry Wilson, Gary Neely, Tommy Herms, John Crist, and Ervin Poteat; (second row) Bobby Stowe, Jerry Abernathy, Don Stewart, James Searcy, Tommy Cox, Eddie Cox, Noah Huffstetler, Gehrig Wiles, Terry Henderson, David Rhyne, George Devereux, James Gardin, and John Farrar; (third row) manager Ronnie McCorkle, Alex Rhyne, Tommy Cauthen, Tim Frazer, Mike Manes, Dan Hope, Hugh Frazer, Eddie Wilson, Gary Wilson, Dan White, Sherwood Henderson, manager Jerry Pittman, and manager David Adkins. The Hawks were coached by head coach Delmer Wiles and assistant coaches Joe Spears and Jerry Clemmer. (Courtesy of George Edward Wilson.)

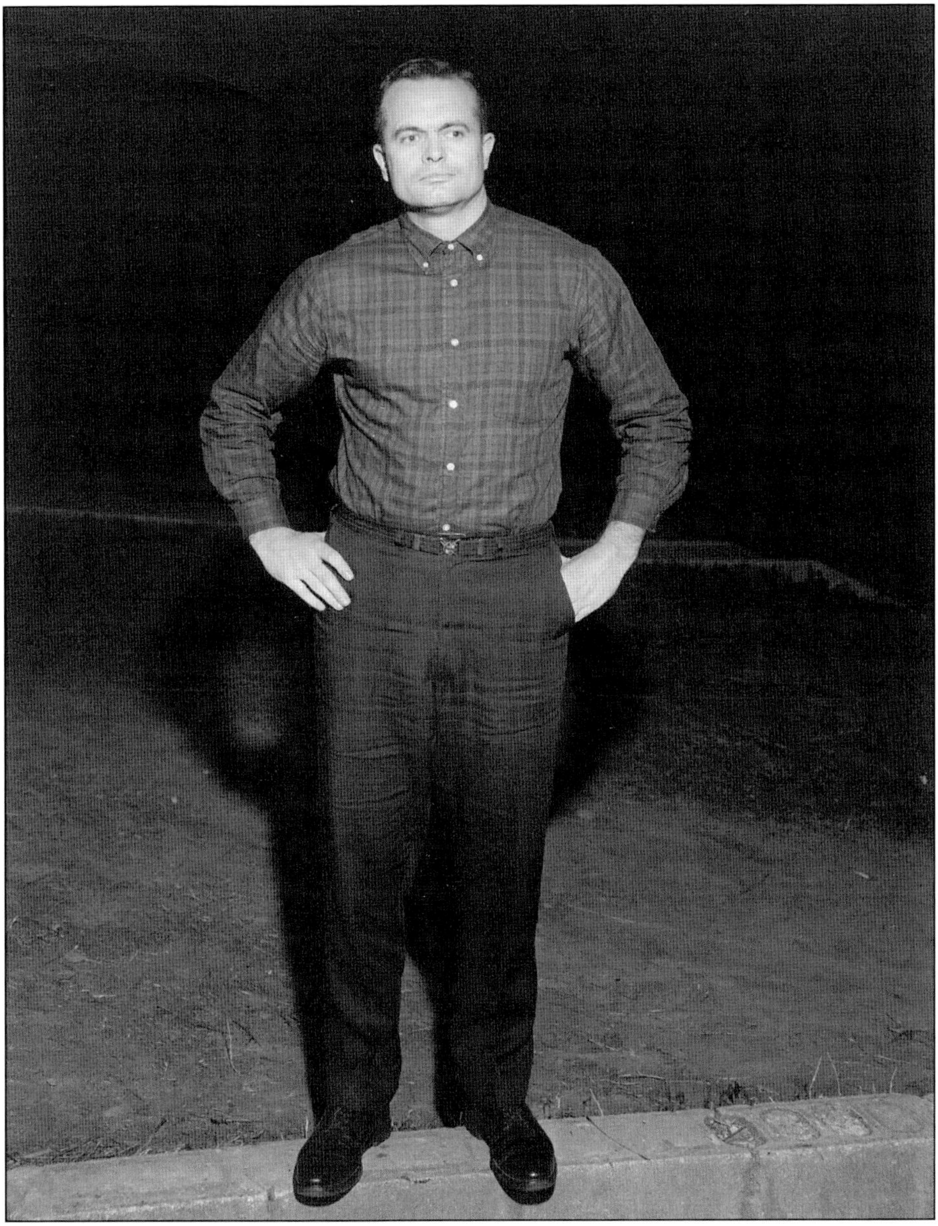

**FATHER, COACH, MARINE.** Delmer Ray Wiles (1925–2008) was the head baseball and football coach and physical education teacher at Mount Holly High School from 1960 until the school closed in 1972. He served in the Marines in the Pacific during World War II. On a troop ship sailing toward Japan, he vowed that if he made it home, he would become a teacher and coach. The Kannapolis native kept his vow and established a legacy of excellence and community pride in Mount Holly. His ninth-grade physical education course is legendary. Many Mount Holly men who took this mandatory course proudly state that they were in the best shape of their lives during their freshman year of high school. His baseball coaching record at Mount Holly was 104-48, with seven conference titles. His football record for the Hawks was 86-30-5, with seven conference titles and two state championships. Coach Wiles was inducted into the Gaston County Sports Hall of Fame in 2005. (Courtesy of Mary Elizabeth Wiles.)

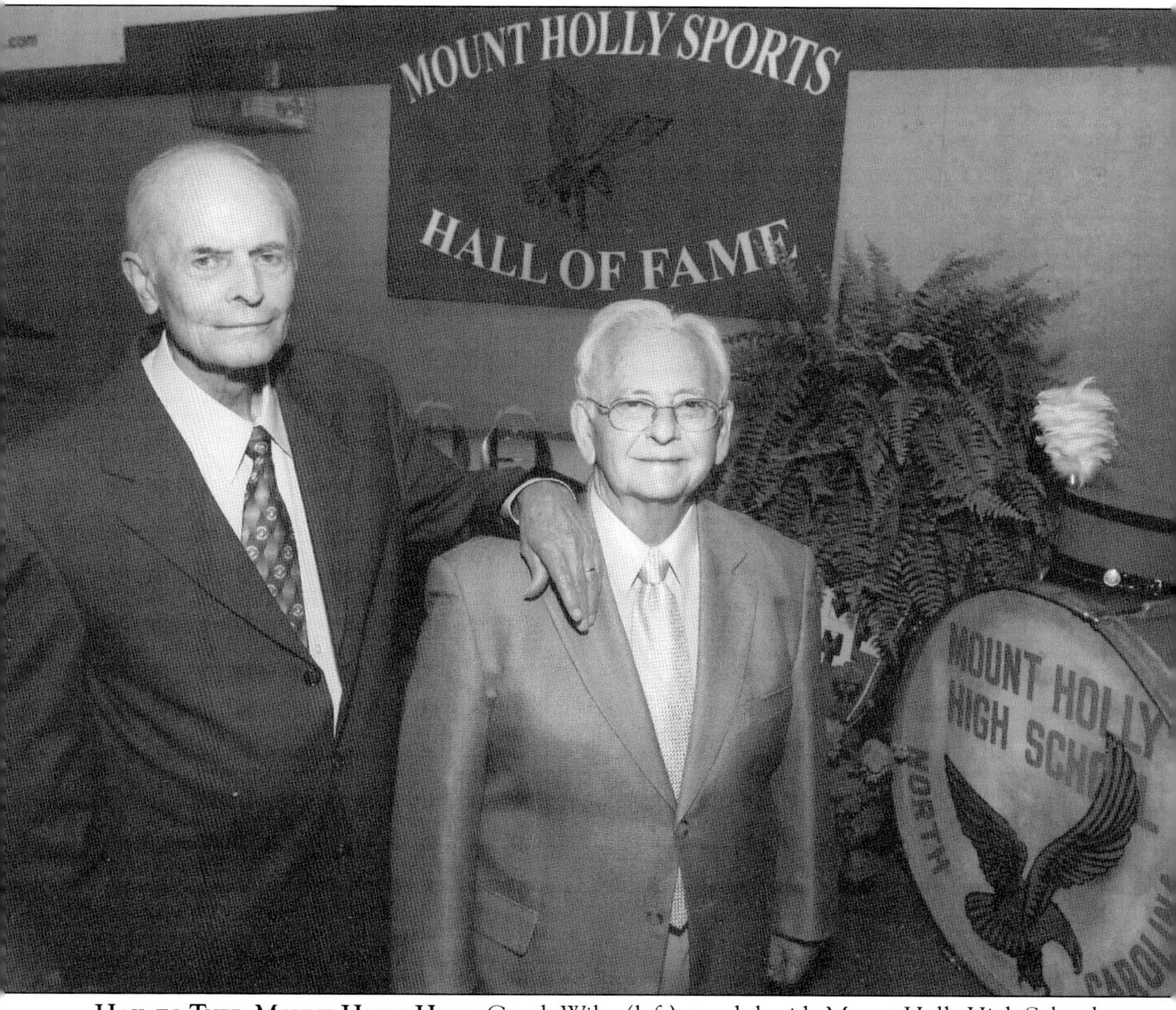


**HAIL TO THEE, MOUNT HOLLY HIGH.** Coach Wiles (left) stands beside Mount Holly High School music director Robert Black in 2007. They were the first inductees enshrined in the Mount Holly Sports Hall of Fame. Wiles and Black grew up in Kannapolis as the sons of textile workers and went to school together. Black came to Mount Holly in 1950. He taught school and directed the First Methodist Church choir for over four decades. His Hawk bands were the pride of the town. Wiles had a shorter tenure at Mount Holly High School but produced a winning record unsurpassed in the history of Mount Holly school athletics. During their time together at the home of the Hawks, these two men, along with their fellow teachers, made Hawthorne Street and Costner Field the center of the universe for Mount Holly residents. Mount Holly High School merged with Stanley High School in 1972, forming East Gaston High. One era closed as another began. (Courtesy of the *Gaston Gazette*.)

# Bibliography

Buchanan, John. *The Road to Guilford Courthouse, the American Revolution in the Carolinas.* Hoboken, NJ: John Wiley & Sons, Inc., 1997.

Cope, Robert and Manly Wade Wellman. *The County of Gaston.* Gaston County, NC: Gaston County Historical Society, 1961

Hall, Jacquelyn Dowd, James Leloudis, Robert Korstad, et. al. *Like A Family: The Making of a Southern Cotton Mill World.* Chapel Hill: University of North Carolina Press, 1987.

Hill, Michael, ed. *Guide to North Carolina Highway Markers.* 10th ed. Raleigh: Office of Archives and History, 2007.

Johnson, Rev. R.Z. *Goshen Presbyterian Church.* Shelby, NC: printed by C.P. Roberts, 1889.

Kratt, Mary, and Mary Manning Boyer. *Remembering Charlotte, Postcards from a New City.* Chapel Hill: University of North Carolina Press, 2000.

Love, James Lee. *R.C.G. Love, A Builder of the New South.* Chapel Hill: University of North Carolina Press, 1949.

———. *Recollections.* Washington, DC: Library of Congress, 1920–1921.

Puett, Minnie Stowe. *History of Gaston County.* Charlotte: Laney-Smith, Inc., 1939.

Ragan, Robert. *The Textile Heritage.* Charlotte: Loftin & Company Printers, 2001.

Separk, Joseph H. *Gastonia and Gaston County, Past, Present and Future.* Kingsport, TN: Kingsport Press, 1836.

Sherrill, William L. *Annals of Lincoln County.* Charlotte: Observer Printing House, 1937.

Withers Brengle, Kim. *The Architectural Heritage of Gaston County North Carolina.* Gastonia, NC: printed by Commercial Printers, Inc., 1982.

Consistent with our mission to preserve history on a local level, this book was printed in South Carolina on American-made paper and manufactured entirely in the United States. Products carrying the accredited Forest Stewardship Council (FSC) label are printed on 100 percent FSC-certified paper.